PRACTICE MAKES PERFECT®

Spanish
Reading and
Comprehension

Myrna Bell Rochester, PhD,
with Deana Smalley, PhD

McGraw Hill Education

New York   Chicago   San Francisco   Athens   London   Madrid
Mexico City   Milan   New Delhi   Singapore   Sydney   Toronto

1 2 3 4 5 6 7 8 9 10   RHR/RHR   1 0 9 8 7 6 5 4

ISBN   978-0-07-179888-4
MHID   0-07-179888-9

e-ISBN   978-0-07-179889-1
e-MHID   0-07-179889-7

Library of Congress Control Number 2013947034

McGraw-Hill Education, the McGraw-Hill Education logo, Practice Makes Perfect, and
related trade dress are trademarks or registered trademarks of McGraw-Hill Education
and/or its affiliates in the United States and other countries and may not be used
without written permission. All other trademarks are the property of their respective
owners. McGraw-Hill Education is not associated with any product or vendor mentioned
in this book.

McGraw-Hill Education products are available at special quantity discounts to use
as premiums and sales promotions or for use in corporate training programs. To contact
a representative, please visit the Contact Us pages at www.mhprofessional.com.

Flashcard App
Sets of flashcards that supplement this book can be found in the McGraw-Hill Education
Language Lab app. Go to mhlanguagelab.com for details on how to access this free
app, which is available for Apple and Android tablet and mobile devices, as well as for
computer via web browser.

This book is printed on acid-free paper.

Contents

VI   FRAGMENTOS LITERARIOS

VII   BELLAS ARTES Y CINE

ARQUEOLOGÍA Y ANTROPOLOGÍA

Preface

Have you studied Spanish for a year or two, or perhaps longer? Was it recently, or a while back? You've no doubt worked from textbooks that contained "controlled" reading materials. Now you find yourself *almost* able to read a Spanish article, essay, poem, short story, or novel, and you are motivated to do it. *Practice Makes Perfect: Spanish Reading and Comprehension*—either in a class or on your own—will provide you with the skills you need to take you to the next level: independent reading in Spanish.

Reading skills typically exceed listening, speaking, and writing skills. Reading provides its own satisfactions and discoveries: it enhances cultural awareness, while building vocabulary and focusing attention on structure and writing style.

Today the Spanish-speaking world offers an endless variety of reading, both in print and online. In addition, a number of U.S. media outlets are bilingual. The ease with which learners can access reading in their target languages is unprecedented.

The Internet, in particular, provides unlimited access to Spanish-language publications, classic literature, self-help features, blogs, forums, and government material. Many big-city newspapers in the United States now publish a Spanish edition, and Latin American and Spanish news outlets tend to have free online access. Public libraries and book distributors stock numerous Spanish titles. Your new literacy will open doors; you'll be able to explore alternative angles on current events from the inside.

In compiling the readings and excerpts for this book, we were overwhelmed with possibilities. We settled on eight thematic units to cover a range that allows practice in a variety of topics and in several registers: everyday living, news items, popular science, first-person memoirs and interviews, storytelling and fiction, poetry and song, and discussion of movies and the arts.

Practice Makes Perfect: Spanish Reading and Comprehension is useful for self-study, in tutoring, and in the classroom. Whatever approach is used, this book will help you reach your goal of independent reading in Spanish.

Myrna Bell Rochester

Acknowledgments

The authors wish to extend warm thanks to Karen S. Young and Christopher Brown of McGraw-Hill Education for the original concept of *Practice Makes Perfect: Spanish Reading and Comprehension* and for their clear-sighted attention in ushering it to completion. We also thank our production editors, who graciously and meticulously worked with us, from the big picture to the tiniest detail; their strong professional support is much appreciated. A special note from Myrna to Deana: your friendship, insight, and direction through every stage of this project have been precious.

Introduction

Each chapter of *Practice Makes Perfect: Spanish Reading and Comprehension* is in six parts:

- Each reading selection is preceded by **¿Estamos listos?** (*Are we ready?*), a set of pre-reading questions and topics that foreshadow the reading that follows. Many of the pre-reading questions also include thematic, functional vocabulary, which may or may not be new to you. **¿Estamos listos?** can be considered suggestions for group discussion or simply a way to familiarize yourself with issues related to the content. The questions can be used on your own or as a springboard for conversation in small groups, get-togethers, or in class.

- **¡Leamos!** (*Let's read!*) heads an authentic reading of between 300 and 900 words—either excerpted or complete. Selections include passages from novels, stories, memoirs, interviews, poems, songs, blogs, and news reports from a variety of Spanish-speaking regions.

- Words and phrases in bold that appear in the introductory material and the reading are listed with their English equivalents in the **Vocabulario** following the text. Try to read as naturally as possible, using the vocabulary for quick reference as needed and for later review. In the **Vocabulario**, English equivalents correspond to usage in that reading.

  Vocabulary items are listed in the order and form (verb conjugation, gender, number) that they appear in the reading. For nouns that are not "regular" (that is, for nouns *not* ending in -**a**, for feminine nouns, or -**o**, for masculine nouns), we provide a definite article (**el, la, los, las**). In general, verb infinitives are provided in square brackets following the form in which the verb appears in the reading. Irregular adjectives are followed by their basic form in square brackets.

- Comprehension activities are provided in the form of **Ejercicios** for each reading: matching exercises, multiple-choice questions, true/false statements (where you are asked to correct the false statements). The vocabulary exercises for each reading include a variety of activities covering synonyms, antonyms, substitutions, and whole-sentence fill-ins, all in Spanish. Try to do them immediately following your reading. As you do these activities, consult the **Vocabulario** and, when necessary, a bilingual (or better yet, an all-Spanish) dictionary or web resource.

  Reflexiones are exercises that offer general questions and topics arising from the reading. It is quite possible that you won't be able to articulate answers in Spanish that are as sophisticated as you might wish. However, we believe that such questions are worth consideration, as they enrich your reading experience. **Reflexiones** topics are meant to be open-ended. For self-study, they are a way into the issues or problems raised. In a class, they can be used to promote conversation and discussion. If your class includes writing practice, they may suggest themes and topics.

All single-answer responses are provided in the Answer key.

- **¡No se olvide!** (*Don't forget!*) provides targeted grammar review specific to each reading. Grammar topics may appear several times in a given reading. For independent reading, for work on speaking and writing skills, or for vocabulary and grammar usage not called out here, you will also need access to a first-year college Spanish grammar text, comprehensive verb charts, and a bilingual dictionary, either print or online. For a print dictionary, we recommend McGraw-Hill Education's *VOX Compact Spanish and English Dictionary*. At the time of this printing, we find the free language websites www.wordreference .com and www.linguee.com particularly useful. You'll likely find it convenient to use a combination of books and online resources.

- In **¡Vaya más lejos!** (*Go further!*), you are often invited to search for photos, videos, music, maps, additional information, or materials online to enrich your reading experience. Suggested search terms are in bold. When you use your search engine to find outside reading, visuals, music, spoken-word texts, videos, film, and other enrichment, remember to try a Spanish language one such as: www.google.es, http://es.yahoo.com/, or http://www.bing.com/?cc=es to access Spanish language sites. However, if you use Spanish keywords or phrases, English-language search engines regularly offer entries in Spanish.

This book has a companion practice flashcard app that features key vocabulary from the readings available for use online or with a mobile device or tablet. See the copyright page for details on how to access the practice app.

We hope we've supplied you with many of the tools you need to enjoy this book and your future reading in Spanish. *¡Buena lectura!*

Abbreviations

ADJ.	adjective	M.	masculine
CENT. AM.	Central America	MEX.	Mexico
F.	feminine	N.	noun
FAM.	familiar	PEJ.	pejorative
FIG.	figuratively	PL.	plural
FORM.	formal	P.R.	Puerto Rico
IMP.	imperative	PRON.	pronoun
INF.	infinitive	SING.	singular
LAT. AM.	Latin America	SP.	Spain
LIT.	literally	SUBJ.	subjunctive

FÁBULAS Y LEYENDAS

La Yusca, leyenda del Cedral

Homero Adame (México)

Todas las culturas tienen sus leyendas de **brujas**, de **hadas**, de **fantasmas**. Esta historia se cuenta en el Cedral, en el estado mexicano de San Luis Potosí.

¿Estamos listos?

1. A todos nos fascinan las historias fantásticas, que se cuentan y vuelven a contarse con cada nueva generación.

   Tenemos por ejemplo historias de... fantasmas [M.], hadas (*fairies*), brujas (*witches*), monstruos, zombis [M.], vampiros, hombres lobos, superhéroes...

2. ¿Cómo se cuentan estas historias?

   Se cuentan... oralmente, en familia o entre amigos, en libros, en cómics, en películas, en poesías y canciones, en obras de teatro, a través del baile (con máscaras), con dibujos y cuadros...

3. ¿Cuáles son los poderes típicos de los seres sobrenaturales?

   Salen de noche, pueden volar, se transforman en animales, pueden transformar a los demás...

4. ¿Cuál es su cuento de fantasmas favorito? ¿De qué tradición viene?

5. En nuestra cultura, ¿qué época del año se asocia con las brujas?

6. ¿Qué sabe usted sobre el Día de los Muertos? ¿Dónde se celebra tradicionalmente? ¿Ya lo ha celebrado? Si es así, ¿dónde lo ha celebrado?

¡Leamos!

Hace muchos años vivió en el Cedral una señora que le llamaban "la Yusca". Ella no tenía ojos. Era una mujer muy pobre que **vestía** ropa muy **sucia** y vieja. Aceptaba lo que cualquiera **le diera** en la calle, aunque no pedía nada, **no mendigaba**. Una extraña cualidad de ella es que siempre estaba en los **velorios** y, por alguna razón inexplicable, era la primera en llegar.

Decían que "la Yusca" de joven había sido bruja (todavía tenía ojos entonces) y que en las noches antes de **irse volando** o convertirse en un animal, **se quitaba** los ojos y los **ocultaba** entre unos **trastes** a un lado de los **tenamaxtles**; luego **se transfiguraba** en animal y se iba a hacer sus **brujerías**.

Una noche **desafortunada**, su marido regresó a casa, **se acercó** al **horno** para **calentar** café y, sin **darse cuenta** (**desconocía** las "**andanzas**" de su mujer), movió las cosas que estaban cerca del horno y los ojos cayeron al fuego. Por eso "la Yusca" **se quedó** sin ojos desde entonces y **comoquiera**, así **ciega**, sabía llegar adonde hubiera un velorio.

Lo curioso de "la Yusca" es que cuando los **lugareños** la veían que iba caminando muy **de prisa** (como estaba toda **encorvada** y viejita normalmente caminaba muy **al pasito**), sabían que se dirigía a donde estaba ya un cuerpo **tendido**. **Nunca le fallaba**. Nadie supo jamás cómo **se enteraba** dónde había un **difunto**, ni cómo podía ir sola y ciega hasta el velorio. En muchas ocasiones, **incluso** cuando llegaba a la casa, la persona aún no moría, pero ya estaba en su lecho de muerte. Es como si ella **presagiara** que tal persona iba a morir. Muchos creen que tal vez ella tenía algún acuerdo con la Muerte y era como su **mensajera**.

Homero Adame, from *Mitos y leyendas del Altiplano,* http://adameleyendas.wordpress.com. Used with the permission of Homero Adame. Many thanks to Homero Adame.

VOCABULARIO

brujas	*witches*	horno	*(wood) stove, oven*
hadas	*fairies*	calentar	*to heat (up)*
(los) fantasmas	*ghosts*	darse cuenta	*realizing*
vestía [vestir]	*wore*	desconocía	*he was unaware of*
sucia	*dirty*	[desconocer]	
le diera [dar]	*gave her*	andanzas	*adventures*
[IMPERFECT SUBJ.]		se quedó [quedarse]	*remained*
no mendigaba	*she didn't beg*	comoquiera	*however*
[mendigar]		ciega	*blind*
velorios	*(funeral) wakes, vigils*	lugareños	*local folk*
irse volando	*to take off (in flight)*	de prisa	*quickly, in a hurry*
se quitaba [quitarse]	*she took out, she took off*	encorvada	*bent over*
ocultaba [ocultar]	*she used to hide*	al pasito	*slowly, with tiny steps*
(los) trastes	*pots and pans*	tendido	*laid out*
(los) tenamaxtles	*clay griddles*	nunca le fallaba [fallar]	*she never missed*
se transfiguraba	*she transformed herself*	se enteraba [enterarse]	*she found out*
[transfigurarse]		difunto	*deceased person*
brujerías	*witchcraft, sorcery*	incluso	*even*
desafortunada	*unlucky*	presagiara [presagiar]	*she foretold*
se acercó	*he went over to*	[IMPERFECT SUBJ.]	
[acercarse a]		mensajera	*messenger*

¿De qué se trata? *Arrange the events in the order in which they occurred in the lives of La Yusca and her husband.*

1. _____   a. Los ojos cayeron al fuego.

2. _____   b. Después aprendió a presentir que tal persona iba a morir.

3. _____   c. Por eso "la Yusca" se quedó sin ojos desde entonces.

4. _____   d. Esa noche, su marido regresó a casa.

5. _____   e. Movió las cosas que estaban cerca del horno.

6. _____   f. "La Yusca" de joven se hizo bruja.

7. _____   g. Una noche, antes de salir, ella se quitó sus ojos y los dejó al lado del horno.

8. _____   h. Él se acercó al horno para calentar café.

Opciones *Choose the phrase or phrases that correctly complete each sentence. Include all correct responses.*

1. La Yusca vivió

   a. hace muchos años.   b. con su marido.   c. en el Cedral.

2. Ella vestía normalmente

   a. ropa de ama de casa.   b. ropa sucia y vieja.   c. ropa elegante.

3. No mendigaba,

   a. sino que trabajaba.   b. sino que rehusaba   c. pero aceptaba dinero.
                                ayuda.

4. Era ciega, pero

   a. calentaba el café.   b. cocinaba.   c. llegaba a los velorios.

5. Perdió sus ojos por

   a. una guerra.   b. una bruja.   c. un accidente.

6. Caminaba de prisa cuando

   a. iba al mercado.   b. iba a un velorio.   c. mendigaba.

7. Los vecinos creían que

   a. era mensajera de lo   b. era fea.   c. se transfiguraba en animal.
      sobrenatural.

EJERCICIO
1·3

¿Cierto o falso? *Indicate whether each statement is true or false, using* **C** *for* **cierto** *(true) or* **F** *for* **falso** *(false). If a statement is false, provide a corrected statement in Spanish.*

1. C F   De joven la Yusca había sido bruja.

_____

2. C F   Su marido también era brujo.

_____

3. C F   Ella llegaba la primera a todos los velorios.

_____

4. C F   La Yusca caminaba siempre despacio.

_____

5. C F   La acusaron de matar a algunos vecinos.

_____

6. C F   Decían que la Yusca podía prevenir la Muerte.

_____

EJERCICIO
1·4

Reflexiones *Consider the following themes and questions, and discuss them in Spanish.*

1. De niño/a, ¿a usted le gustaba la fantasía? ¿Cuáles eran sus historias y cuentos favoritos? ¿Los lee todavía?

_____

_____

_____

2. La leyenda de la Yusca, ¿le recuerda un cuento que ya conoce? ¿Cuál?

_____

_____

_____

3. ¿Ve usted diferencias entre las leyendas comunes (que conoce bien) y una leyenda como la de la Yusca?

_____

_____

_____

4. ¿Qué necesidades satisfacen las leyendas fantásticas? ¿La sed de lo desconocido? ¿de lo sobrenatural? ¿Por qué necesitamos esas ideas?

_____

_____

_____

Mi vocabulario *Select the word that does not belong in each group.*

1. a. miserable   b. desafortunado   c. dichoso   d. infeliz

2. a. estufa   b. cocina   c. coche   d. horno

3. a. envidia   b. mensajera   c. enviada   d. emisaria

4. a. ocupar   b. disimular   c. ocultar   d. esconder

5. a. vasto   b. vasija   c. ollas   d. trastes

6. a. aventuras   b. andanzas   c. marchas   d. anécdotas

7. a. prevenir   b. predecir   c. anunciar   d. presagiar

8. a. bruja   b. enamorada   c. hechicera   d. maga

Contrarios *Match each word or phrase with its opposite.*

1. _____ sucio   a. al pasito

2. _____ irse   b. limpio

3. _____ de prisa   c. encorvado

4. _____ dichoso   d. lugareños

5. _____ calentar   e. quedarse

6. _____ olvidarse   f. enterarse

7. _____ recto   g. desafortunado

8. _____ extranjeros   h. enfriar

Equivalentes *Complete each sentence by substituting words or phrases from the following list for the words or phrases in small type.*

- aventuras
- desplazó
- erraba
- estaba ciega
- ignoraba
- muerto
- permaneció
- saber
- sabía
- se transformaba
- solicitaba
- su magia

1. Ella _____.
   <small>no tenía ojos</small>

2. No pedía nada, no _____.
   <small>mendigaba</small>

3. Luego _____ en animal y se iba a hacer
   <small>se transfiguraba</small>

   _____.
   <small>sus brujerías</small>

4. Sin _____ (_____ las
   <small>darse cuenta</small>   <small>desconocía</small>

   _____ de su mujer), _____ las cosas que
   <small>"andanzas"</small>   <small>movió</small>

   estaban cerca del horno.

5. La Yusca _____ sin ojos desde entonces.
   <small>se quedó</small>

6. Nunca _____. Nadie supo jamás cómo _____
   <small>le fallaba</small>   <small>se enteraba</small>

   dónde había un _____.
   <small>difunto</small>

¡No se olvide! El imperfecto

You may have noticed that, except in the third paragraph, nearly all the verbs in the legend of **La Yusca** are in the Spanish imperfect tense. Why is that?

The Spanish imperfect tense is used in past narration to describe the following:

- ◆ A setting, a background, a place, or the weather at a past moment
- ◆ The characteristics of people, animals, or objects in the past
- ◆ Continuous or habitual actions in the past
- ◆ An action or actions going on (actions that were in progress) in the past, interrupted by an action in the preterit tense

¡Ojo!

Individual or countable actions or those that end at a certain point in the past are expressed in the Spanish preterit tense. (See Chapter 2.) Most narratives in Spanish are told with a combination of past tenses.

Forms of the imperfect tense are very regular. Drop the infinitive ending (-**ar**, -**er**, -**ir**), and add verb endings as follows:

-ar VERBS **hablar** *to speak, to talk*

(yo) habl**aba**	*I was speaking, I spoke, I used to speak*
(tú) habl**abas**	*you* [FAM.] *were speaking, you spoke, you used to speak*
(él, ella, usted) habl**aba**	*he/she was / you were speaking, he/she/you spoke, he/she/you used to speak*
(nosotros/as) habl**ábamos**	*we were speaking, we spoke, we used to speak*
(vosotros/as) habl**abais**	*you* [FAM. PL.] [SP.] *were speaking, you spoke, you used to speak*
(ellos, ellas, Uds.) habl**aban**	*they/you were speaking, they/you spoke, they/you used to speak*

-er AND **-ir** VERBS

	conocer *to know*	decir *to say*
yo	conoc**ía**	dec**ía**
tú	conoc**ías**	dec**ías**
él, ella, usted	conoc**ía**	dec**ía**
nosotros/as	conoc**íamos**	dec**íamos**
vosotros/as	conoc**íais**	dec**íais**
ellos, ellas, Uds.	conoc**ían**	dec**ían**

Only three Spanish verbs are considered irregular in the imperfect tense: **ir** *to go*, **ser** *to be*, and **ver** *to see*. Both **ir** and **ser** have irregular stems; the stem of **ver** includes the letter **e**.

	ir	ser	ver
yo	iba	era	veía
tú	ibas	eras	veías
él, ella, usted	iba	era	veía
nosotros/as	íbamos	éramos	veíamos
vosotros/as	ibais	erais	veíais
ellos, ellas, Uds.	iban	eran	veían

EJERCICIO

1·8

List each verb in the imperfect tense in the following phrases and sentences, and explain why the imperfect is used in each case, using the reasons given in **¡No se olvide!**

1. Ella no tenía ojos. Era una mujer muy pobre.

_____ _____

_____ _____

2. No pedía nada, no mendigaba.

_____ _____

_____ _____

3. Siempre estaba en los velorios y... era la primera en llegar.

_____   _____

_____   _____

4. Una noche... su marido regresó a casa,... (desconocía las "andanzas" de su mujer), movió las cosas que estaban cerca del horno y los ojos cayeron al fuego.

_____   _____

_____   _____

5. como estaba toda encorvada y viejita normalmente caminaba muy al pasito

_____   _____

_____   _____

6. Cuando (ella) llegaba a la casa, la persona aún no moría, pero ya estaba en su lecho de muerte.

_____   _____

_____   _____

_____   _____

¡Vaya más lejos!

◆ Busque **Cedral, San Luis Potosí, México**, para ver fotos de esa región mexicana.

◆ Busque **leyendas** para leer otras leyendas tradicionales en español.

◆ Busque sitios web sobre el **Día de los Muertos**.

La leyenda del Sajama
(Bolivia)

Las **cumbres** de los Andes han tenido siempre un lugar importante dentro de las leyendas del **Altiplano**. Una de las leyendas más conocidas es la del **Sajama**.

¿Estamos listos?

1. ¿Le gustan las montañas y las regiones montañosas?

2. ¿Qué cordilleras (cadenas de montañas) conoce usted?
   Conozco... las montañas Rocosas, las Cascadas, la Sierra Nevada, los Alpes, los Andes, el Himalaya...

3. ¿Dónde se sitúan esas cordilleras?
   Se sitúan... en Canadá, en Colorado, en Nuevo México, en Wyoming, en Utah, en Montana, en California, en Nevada, en Washington; en Suiza, en Francia, en Austria; en Argentina, en Bolivia, en Chile, en Colombia, en Ecuador, en Perú, en Venezuela; en Bután, en India, en Nepal, en China, en Pakistán...

4. ¿Qué hace usted en las montañas, solo/a o con sus amigos?
   Me gusta(n) / Me gusta hacer... caminatas, senderismo (*hiking*), camping, esquí, alpinismo, raqueta (*snowshoeing*), snowboard, natación, fotografía; observar los aves, ir de caza (*hunting*), ir a pescar, salir en moto de nieve (*snowmobile*)...

5. Mencione unos volcanes bien conocidos. ¿Están activos o extintos?
   Hay... el monte Fuji, el Vesubio, el monte Saint Helen, el monte Etna, el Krakatoa, el Mauna Loa, el Eyjafjallajokull, el Thera (Santorini), el Sajama...

6. ¿Dónde se sitúan esos volcanes? Asocie los volcanes con su localización.
   Se sitúan... en Bolivia, en Grecia, en Islandia, en Sicilia, en Italia; en Japón, en Indonesia; en Washington, en Hawái...

7. ¿Ya ha visitado un volcán? ¿Ya vio una erupción volcánica o los efectos de una erupción? ¿Adónde fue para verlos?

¡Leamos!

"Dios está lejos y tenemos que negociar con sus intermediarios, las montañas."

El **Nevado** Sajama (**aimara**: *chak xaña*, 'oeste') es un **estratovolcán** en Bolivia, **ubicado** en el Parque Nacional Sajama al oeste del país en el departamento de Oruro. Forma parte de la **Cordillera Occidental** y es el pico más alto del país. Tiene más de 6500 metros de **altura** y se encuentra en el corazón del parque (el primero que se creó en Bolivia, en 1941). No se tiene con certeza la fecha de su **última** erupción, **sin embargo**, se le considera un volcán extinto. Las **laderas** del nevado se encuentran habitadas por la **queñua** (*Polylepis tarapacana*), formando un **bosque** abierto y **achaparrado**, el cual es considerado como uno de los bosques más altos del mundo.

◆ ◆ ◆

Hace mucho tiempo **tuvo lugar** una guerra **despiadada** entre las montañas. El **Huayana Potosí**, el **Condoriri**, el **Ancohuma** e **inclusive** el **Illampu perseguían** el mismo sueño: ¡ser el más grande de todos!

"**Pacha**", el **creador**, cansado de estas disputas, ordenó el fin de las hostilidades. En el momento de la **tregua**, el **Illimani** era el gran **vencedor**. Pero un vecino ambicioso **discutió** su victoria. Perturbado durante su **sueño**, "Pacha" decidió **castigar** al insolente cortándole la cabeza.

"Pacha" **hizo girar** su terrible **honda**... las montañas, impresionadas, se hicieron pequeñitas, el viento del **arma cósmica quemaba** las **heridas** recién **cicatrizadas** que **se habían infligido** las unas a las otras. Escucharon entonces el **silbido** del **proyectil** y el terrible **estruendo** del impacto. Cuando el **polvo** desapareció, **faltaba** toda la parte superior del **imprudente**. Su cabeza reposaba lejos en el Altiplano, los hombres lo llaman ahora Sajama, que significa en aymara "el que está lejos". **En cuanto al** otro, del cual se puede admirar la cumbre que tiene forma, no de una **cima** sino de una **basta planicie** nevada, se le llama **Mururata**, "el decapitado".

From *Terra Andina*, http://www.bolivia-turismo.com.

VOCABULARIO			
(las) cumbres	*summits, peaks*	altura	*height*
Altiplano	*Altiplano, high plateau of the Andes*	última	*last, most recent*
		sin embargo	*nevertheless*
(el) Sajama	*highest peak in Bolivia (~21,500 ft.)*	laderas	*slopes, mountainsides*
		queñua	*Andean shrub or small tree*
nevado	*snow-capped (mountain)*	(el) bosque	*forest, wood(s)*
(el) aimara (aymara)	*Andes/Altiplano language (Bolivia, Peru, Chile)*	achaparrado	*low, stunted*
		tuvo [tener] lugar	*(there) took place*
(el) estratovolcán	*stratovolcano, composite volcano (conical and layered)*	despiadada	*cruel, savage*
		(el) Huayana Potosí	*closest high mountain to La Paz, Bolivia (~20,000 ft.)*
ubicado	*located*		
cordillera (occidental)	*(western) mountain range*	(el) Condoriri	*Condor, mountain north of La Paz (~18,500 ft.)*

(el) Ancohuma	White Water, third highest peak in Bolivia (~21,000 ft.)	honda	slingshot
		arma cósmica	cosmic weapon
inclusive	including	quemaba [quemar]	burn, scorch
(el) Illampu	fourth highest mountain in Bolivia (~21,000 ft.)	heridas	wounds, injuries
		cicatrizadas	healed
perseguían [perseguir]	were pursuing, were seeking	se habían infligido [infligirse]	they had inflicted (on each other)
		silbido	whistling
Pacha	Cosmos, World (Aymara or Quechua languages)	(el) proyectil	projectile
		estruendo	bang, crash
(el) creador	creator	polvo	dust
tregua	truce, ceasefire	faltaba [faltar]	(there) was missing
(el) Illimani	highest mountain in the Cordillera Real (over 21,000 ft.)	imprudente	irresponsible (one), reckless (one)
		en cuanto al	as far as... is concerned
(el) vencedor	winner, victor	cima	mountain peak
discutió [discutir]	objected to, took issue with	basta	rough, uneven
sueño	sleep	(la) planicie	mesa, plateau
castigar	to punish	Mururata	flat-topped mountain east of La Paz
hizo [hacer] girar	spun, whirled		

EJERCICIO

2·1

¿De qué se trata? *Arrange the events in order to tell the legend of Sajama.*

1. _____   a. Una montaña vecina se opuso a la victoria del Illimani.

2. _____   b. El Illimani fue el gran vencedor.

3. _____   c. Durante una guerra se habían infligido muchas heridas las unas a las otras.

4. _____   d. La cumbre sin cabeza se llama ahora Mururata.

5. _____   e. Cada montaña de la Cordillera quería ser la más grande de todas.

6. _____   f. La honda del creador le cortó la cabeza a la montaña insolente.

7. _____   g. Pacha, perturbado, quería dormir; decidió castigar al imprudente.

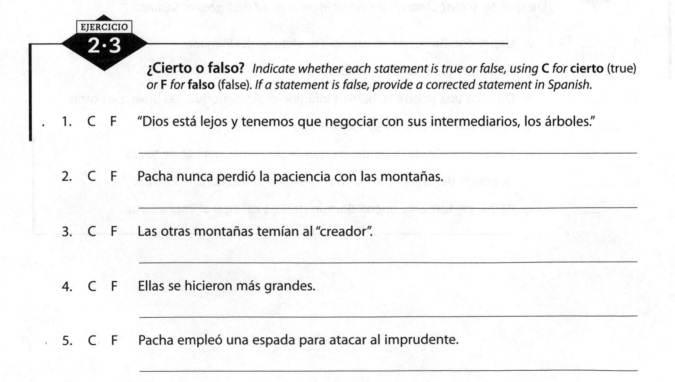

Opciones *Choose the phrase or phrases that correctly complete each sentence. Include all correct responses.*

1. El Sajama es

   a. un estratovolcán.   b. el creador.   c. un bosque abierto.

2. El Sajama es también

   a. activo.   b. extinto.   c. nevado.

3. El pico más alto de Bolivia es

   a. el Illimani.   b. el Sajama.   c. el Condoriri.

4. La queñua es

   a. una lengua.   b. un alimento.   c. un árbol achaparrado.

5. Pacha es

   a. el cosmos.   b. el creador.   c. el mundo.

6. En 1941, se creó el primer

   a. departamento de Bolivia.   b. estratovolcán.   c. parque nacional boliviano.

¿Cierto o falso? *Indicate whether each statement is true or false, using* **C** *for* **cierto** *(true) or* **F** *for* **falso** *(false). If a statement is false, provide a corrected statement in Spanish.*

1. C   F   "Dios está lejos y tenemos que negociar con sus intermediarios, los árboles."

   _____

2. C   F   Pacha nunca perdió la paciencia con las montañas.

   _____

3. C   F   Las otras montañas temían al "creador".

   _____

4. C   F   Ellas se hicieron más grandes.

   _____

5. C   F   Pacha empleó una espada para atacar al imprudente.

   _____

6. C F El Sajama se componía de la "cabeza" de la montaña insolente.

_____

7. C F El imprudente quedó el más alto de todos.

_____

Reflexiones *Consider the following themes and questions, and discuss them in Spanish.*

1. ¿Le interesan la mitología y las leyendas tradicionales?

_____

_____

_____

_____

2. ¿Conoce usted otras leyendas que tienen lugar en las montañas? Por ejemplo, la del "rey bajo la montaña" o del "héroe que duerme en las montañas" (hasta que salga para salvar a su pueblo).

_____

_____

_____

_____

3. ¿Conoce otra leyenda (por ejemplo, de origen africano o nativo-americano)? ¿Puede relatarla?

_____

_____

_____

_____

4. ¿Puede explicar la personificación de las cosas inanimadas y de los animales en las leyendas de este tipo? ¿Por qué y cómo pueden hablar y actuar?

_____

_____

_____

Mi vocabulario *Select the word that does not belong in each group.*

1. a. cadena   b. sierra   c. cordero   d. cordillera

2. a. parque   b. desierto   c. bosque   d. selva

3. a. colocado   b. ubicado   c. situado   d. desplazado

4. a. hostilidad   b. tregua   c. pausa   d. armisticio

5. a. cumbre   b. planicie   c. cima   d. altura

6. a. disciplinar   b. castigar   c. perdonar   d. punir

7. a. cicatrización   b. herida   c. contusión   d. lesión

8. a. inclinación   b. rampa   c. ladera   d. llano

Contrarios *Match each word with its opposite.*

1. _____ estruendo   a. quemar

2. _____ apagar   b. última

3. _____ depresión   c. valles

4. _____ inclusive   d. alto

5. _____ batalla   e. silencio

6. _____ primera   f. altura

7. _____ cumbres   g. exclusive

8. _____ achaparrado   h. tregua

Equivalentes *Complete each sentence by substituting words or phrases from the following list for the words or phrases in small type.*

alturas	ganador	bárbara	se opuso a
causado	papel	cesación de hostilidades	hubo
curadas	picaba	ya no estaba	temerario

1. Las _____ de los Andes han tenido siempre un
   <small>cumbres</small>

   _____ importante dentro de las leyendas.
   <small>lugar</small>

2. Hace mucho tiempo _____ una guerra
   <small>tuvo lugar</small>

   _____.
   <small>despiadada</small>

3. En el momento de la _____, el Illimani era el gran
   <small>tregua</small>

   _____.
   <small>vencedor</small>

4. Un vecino ambicioso _____ su victoria.
   <small>discutió</small>

5. El viento del arma cósmica _____ las heridas recién
   <small>quemaba</small>

   _____ que se habían _____.
   <small>cicatrizadas</small>   <small>infligido</small>

6. Cuando el polvo desapareció, _____ toda la parte superior del
   <small>faltaba</small>

   _____.
   <small>imprudente</small>

¡No se olvide! El pretérito

The preterit, or simple past tense, is the most common way to express completed action in the past (whether a single action or a series of actions), a completed state, or a condition completed in the past. Because narration in Spanish makes use of several past tenses, the preterit is often combined with the imperfect, the pluperfect, the past subjunctive, or the conditional.

With the exception of verbs that have a stem change, Spanish verbs are regular in the preterit. Add the preterit endings to the infinitive stem of **-ar**, **-er**, and **-ir** verbs, as follows.

For **-ar** verbs, the endings are **-é, -aste, -ó, -amos, -asteis, -aron**.

-ar VERBS **hablar** *to speak, talk*	
(yo) habl**é**	*I spoke*
(tú) habl**aste**	*you* [FAM.] *spoke*
(él, ella, usted) habl**ó**	*he/she/you spoke*
(nosotros/as) habl**amos**	*we spoke*
(vosotros/as) habl**asteis**	*you* [FAM. PL.] [SP.] *spoke*
(ellos, ellas, Uds.) habl**aron**	*they/you spoke*

For -er and -ir verbs, the endings are -í, -iste, -ió, -imos, -isteis, -ieron.

-er AND -ir VERBS

	comer *to eat*	**asistir** *to attend*
yo	com**í**	asist**í**
tú	com**iste**	asist**iste**
él, ella, usted	com**ió**	asist**ió**
nosotros/as	com**imos**	asist**imos**
vosotros/as	com**isteis**	asist**isteis**
ellos, ellas, Uds.	com**ieron**	asist**ieron**

All the irregular verbs in the preterit have a change in the stem: **estar** (**estuv-**), **poder** (**pud-**), **querer** (**quis-**), **tener** (**tuv-**), **saber** (**sup-**), **venir** (**vin-**). In addition, irregular verbs have a slightly different set of preterit endings: **-e, -iste, -o, -imos, -isteis, -ieron.** (Note that the first- and third-person singular endings do not carry an accent mark.)

Consult verb charts for a complete list of irregular verbs in the preterit. They will be relatively easy to recognize for reading; however, for speaking and writing, you will need to memorize them.

Here are the conjugations of the irregular verbs **dar**, **ir**, and **ser**. The conjugations of **ir** and **ser** are identical. Meaning is usually clear from the context.

dar *to give*	**ir** *to go*	**ser** *to be*
di	fui	fui
diste	fuiste	fuiste
dio	fue	fue
dimos	fuimos	fuimos
disteis	fuisteis	fuisteis
dieron	fueron	fueron

EJERCICIO 2·8

Give (a) the preterit tense verb in each of the following phrases or sentences, and provide its (b) meaning and (c) infinitive.

1. el primero que se creó en Bolivia

   a. _____   b. _____   c. _____

2. Hace mucho tiempo tuvo lugar una guerra.

   a. _____   b. _____   c. _____

3. "Pacha"... ordenó el fin de las hostilidades.

   a. _____   b. _____   c. _____

4. Pero un vecino ambicioso discutió la victoria.

   a. _____   b. _____   c. _____

5. "Pacha" decidió castigar al insolente.

   a. _____   b. _____   c. _____

6. "Pacha" hizo girar su terrible honda.

a. _____   b. _____   c. _____

7. Las montañas, impresionadas, se hicieron pequeñitas.

a. _____   b. _____   c. _____

8. Escucharon entonces el silbido del proyectil.

a. _____   b. _____   c. _____

9. Cuando el polvo desapareció, faltaba toda la parte superior del imprudente.

a. _____   b. _____   c. _____

¡Vaya más lejos!

- ¿Dónde está **Bolivia**? Búsquelo en línea o en un atlas.
- ¿Cuáles son los otros países del **Altiplano**? ¿Cómo están conectados?
- Busque fotos de la **Cordillera Occidental**.
- Busque otros **parques nacionales** de América Latina. ¿Dónde se encuentran? ¿Cuáles son sus características más notables?
- Busque información sobre la orquesta chilena **Inti-Illimani**. Escuche su música.

El nacimiento del arco iris
(Argentina)

Cada cultura explica este fenómeno natural espectacular—el **arco iris**—a su manera. Esta leyenda viene de Argentina.

¿Estamos listos?

1. ¿Qué nos dicen las leyendas? ¿Son propias de una cultura o son generales? ¿Son diferentes de los cuentos de hadas (*fairies*)?

   Las leyendas tratan de explicar... el origen de experiencias compartidas o universales, los fenómenos naturales (antes de la llegada de los humanos), el comportamiento y la moralidad de los animales, las fuerzas naturales (el viento, el sol, la luna, el calor, el frío, el fuego, los cuerpos celestes)...

2. ¿Cuáles son los colores tradicionales del arco iris? ¿En qué orden se colocan esos colores?

   Son... rojo, naranja, amarillo, verde, azul, índigo (o añil) y violeta.

3. ¿Conoce leyendas sobre el arco iris o/y su creación?

   Sí, conozco una leyenda... irlandesa (el leprechaun/duende y el tesoro de la olla de oro), hawaiana (Kahala, la doncella del arco iris, que necesita desesperadamente reunir su cuerpo con su espíritu), australiana (Ngalyod, la serpiente arco iris, creador de la estación de las lluvias), iroquesa (los animales suben el puente del arco iris hasta el cielo donde se transforman en constelaciones), filipina (un agricultor se casa con un hada caída del cielo; después de su ascensión al cielo con su hijo, los dioses crean un arco iris para su esposo terrenal (*earthly*)—un puente entre la tierra y el cielo), africana (la madre Lluvia—que lleva un cinturón en forma de arco iris—ha perdido a su hijo; desciende del cielo en forma de tormenta para matar al Lobo malo)...

¡Leamos!

Hace mucho, mucho tiempo, en la **espesa selva** verde **esmeralda**, habitaban unos pequeños animalitos que provocaban la admiración de todos aquellos que **tenían la suerte** de poder verlos. Eran siete magníficas **mariposas**, todas diferentes, pero cada una con sus alas pintadas de un color brillante y único. Su belleza era tal, que las flores de la selva se sentían **opacadas** cada vez que las mariposas **revoloteaban en su alrededor**.

Eran inseparables, y cuando **recorrían** la selva parecían una nube de colores, **deslumbrante** y **movediza**. Pero un día, una de ellas **se hirió** con una **aguda espina** y ya no pudo volar con sus amigas. El resto de las mariposas la **rodeó**, y pronto comprendieron que la profunda **herida** era **mortal**. Volaron hasta el cielo para estar cerca de los **dioses** y, **sin dudarlo**, ofrecieron realizar cualquier sacrificio **con tal de que** la muerte de su amiga no las separara. Una voz grave y profunda **quebró** el silencio de los cielos y les preguntó si estaban **dispuestas** a dar sus propias vidas con tal de **permanecer** juntas, a lo que todas contestaron afirmativamente. En ese mismo instante fuertes vientos cruzaron los cielos, las nubes **se volvieron** negras y la lluvia y los **rayos** formaron una **tormenta** como nunca se había conocido. Un **remolino envolvió** a las siete mariposas y las elevó **más allá** de las nubes. Cuando todo se calmó y el sol **se disponía** a comenzar su trabajo para **secar** la tierra, una **imponente** curva luminosa cruzó el cielo, un arco que estaba pintado con los colores de las siete mariposas, y que brillaba gracias a las **almas** de estas siete amigas que **no temieron a** la muerte con tal de permanecer juntas.

From *Poemas y relatos: Portal de literatura*, http://www.poemasyrelatos.com.

VOCABULARIO

arco iris	*rainbow*	mortal	*fatal*
espesa	*thick, dense*	(los) dioses	*gods*
selva	*jungle*	sin dudarlo	*unhesitatingly*
esmeralda	*emerald (green)*	con tal de que	*so that, provided that*
tenían [tener] la suerte	*were lucky enough*	quebró [quebrar]	*broke*
		dispuestas	*ready, prepared*
mariposas	*butterflies*	permanecer	*to remain*
opacadas	*eclipsed, outshone*	se volvieron [volverse]	*changed into*
revoloteaban [revolotear]	*flitted, fluttered*	rayos	*bolts of lightning*
		tormenta	*storm*
en su alrededor	*around them*	remolino	*gust, whirlwind*
recorrían [recorrer]	*crisscrossed*	envolvió [envolver]	*enveloped*
deslumbrante	*brilliant, glowing*	más allá	*beyond*
movediza	*shifting, changeable*	se disponía [disponerse]	*was getting ready*
se hirió [herirse]	*injured herself*		
aguda	*sharp*	secar	*to dry*
espina	*thorn*	imponente	*impressive, imposing*
rodeó [rodear]	*surrounded*	almas	*souls, spirits*
herida	*wound, injury*	no temieron [temer] a	*didn't fear*

¿De qué se trata? *Match the beginning of each sentence with the phrase that correctly completes it to tell the story of the birth of the rainbow.*

1. __D__ Habitaban unos pequeños animalitos

2. __F__ Las siete magníficas mariposas

3. __A__ Las flores se sentían opacadas

4. __B__ Un día, una de ellas se hirió

5. __C__ Las otras ofrecieron e

6. __e__ Después de la tormenta c

a. cuando las mariposas se acercaban.

b. y no pudo volar con sus amigas.

c. una curva luminosa y pintada cruzó el cielo.

d. en la espesa selva verde.

e. dar sus propias vidas para quedar junto a su amiga.

f. tenían sus alas pintadas de un color brillante y único.

Opciones *Choose the phrase or phrases that correctly complete each sentence. Include all correct responses.*

1. Las siete mariposas provocaban la admiración porque eran

   a. bellas.   b. deslumbrantes.   c. opacadas.

2. Cada una tenía las alas pintadas de

   a. un color único.   b. colores diferentes.   c. colores movedizos.

3. La amiga herida

   a. se curó rápidamente.   b. se moría.   c. desapareció.

4. Las mariposas volaron primero

   a. cerca de las flores.   b. hasta el cielo.   c. para estar cerca de los dioses.

5. La tormenta incluía

   a. lluvia.   b. rayos.   c. un fuerte remolino.

6. Cuando la tormenta se calmó

   a. el sol salió.   b. las mariposas volvieron.   c. apareció un arco luminoso.

¿Cierto o falso? *Indicate whether each statement is true or false, using* **C** *for* **cierto** (true) *or* **F** *for* **falso** (false). *If a statement is false, provide a corrected statement in Spanish.*

1. C   F   Las mariposas nunca se acercaban a las flores.

_____

2. C   F   Al lado de las mariposas, las flores se sentían muy bellas.

_____

3. C   F   Las mariposas eran celosas unas de las otras.

_____

4. C   F   Un día, una espina aguda dañó a una de las mariposas.

_____

5. C   F   La mariposa herida les dijo a las otras que la dejaran.

_____

6. C   F   Durante la tormenta, un remolino las elevó más allá de las nubes.

_____

7. C   F   Así el arco iris representa las almas unidas de las siete amigas.

_____

Reflexiones *Consider the following themes and questions, and discuss them in Spanish.*

1. Explique "una voz grave... quebró el silencio". ¿Quién habló? En su opinión, ¿las leyendas siempre necesitan una fuerza o unos seres superiores?

_____

_____

_____

_____

2. ¿Conoce otras leyendas sobre la creación de fenómenos naturales? ¿Cuáles recuerda de su infancia?

_____

_____

_____

_____

3. Imagine una nueva leyenda para explicar un fenómeno natural. Dé un título posible.

_____

_____

_____

_____

Complete the following paragraph—a scientific explanation of how we perceive the colors of the rainbow—using the appropriate words or expressions from the following list.

arco iris	longitud de onda	secundarios	biológico
ojo	seis	colores	primarios
sensible	combinación	receptores de color	tres
conos			

En realidad, los (1) _____ son un concepto (2) _____ ,

no un concepto físico. Hay tres tipos de (3) _____ en el

(4) _____ humano. Estos son los (5) _____, y se les

puede asociar a ellos los colores (6) _____—azul, rojo y verde. (Los artistas

visuales, que se ocupan de pigmentos (no de luz), colocan el amarillo en la tercera posición,

en vez del verde.) Cada uno de los receptores es más (7) _____ a la

(8) _____ de uno de estos colores. Por eso, se puede decir que el

(9) _____ tiene únicamente (10) _____ colores.

Si se introducen los colores (11) _____ que resultan de la

(12) _____ de pares de colores primarios, podemos distinguir

(13) _____ colores. No se ha distinguido el añil—el séptimo color del

arco iris enumerado por muchas personas.

Match the beginning of each sentence with the phrase that correctly completes it to review the scientific explanation for the perception of the colors of the rainbow.

1. _____ El arco iris tiene

2. _____ El ojo

3. _____ Los receptores del ojo se llaman

4. _____ Los colores primarios son

5. _____ Los colores secundarios resultan de

a. los conos.

b. la combinación de ciertos colores primarios.

c. azul, rojo y verde.

d. recibe la luz visible.

e. solamente tres colores.

Mi vocabulario *Select the word that does not belong in each group.*

1. a. herido   b. dispuesto   c. listo   d. preparado

2. a. denso   b. tupido   c. espeso   d. turbio

3. a. menudo   b. imponente   c. grandioso   d. impresionante

4. a. durar   b. quedarse   c. dejar   d. permanecer

5. a. huracán   b. tormenta   c. temporada   d. tempestad

6. a. romper   b. interrumpir   c. quebrar   d. quemar

7. a. relámpagos   b. rayos   c. chismes   d. chispas

8. a. movedizo   b. inconstante   c. moreno   d. variable

Contrarios *Match each word or phrase with its opposite.*

1. _____ cuerpo   a. quedarse inmóvil

2. _____ revolotear   b. allá

3. _____ confrontar   c. alma

4. _____ nacimiento   d. deslumbrante

5. _____ secar   e. curarse

6. _____ herirse   f. agudo

7. _____ opaco   g. temer

8. _____ aquí   h. mojar

9. _____ embotado   i. muerte

Equivalentes *Complete each sentence by substituting words or phrases from the following list for the words or phrases in small type.*

borrasca	fatal	poderosos	cerca de ellas
en seguida	se pusieron	cercó	lesión
recorrieron	eclipsadas	lindeza	relámpagos
jamás vista	mariposeaban		

1. Su _____ era tal, que las flores de la selva se sentían
   belleza

   _____ cada vez que las mariposas _____
   opacadas   revoloteaban

   _____.
   en su alrededor

2. El resto de las mariposas la _____, y _____
   rodeó   pronto

   comprendieron que la profunda _____ era _____.
   herida   mortal

3. En ese mismo instante _____ vientos _____
   fuertes   cruzaron

   los cielos, las nubes _____ negras y la lluvia y los
   se volvieron

   _____ formaron una _____
   rayos   tormenta

   _____.
   como nunca se había conocido

¡No se olvide! ¿El pretérito o el imperfecto?

When expressing an action, state, or condition in the past, Spanish speakers and writers must choose between the preterit and the imperfect tenses; both can appear in the same sentence. Each tense conveys a different way of viewing the past. (See Chapters 1 and 2 for a review of the forms of the imperfect and the preterit.)

Use of the preterit indicates that a past action or series of past actions have already been completed. The speaker or writer knows when these actions started and ended.

Llovió ayer.	*It rained yesterday.*
Llegaron, trabajaron; después **partieron**.	*They arrived, they worked; then they left.*

Use of the imperfect indicates that the action, condition, or state is ongoing in the past. The beginning and end of the action are indeterminate. The imperfect tense paints a background setting (time, weather, situation); it also expresses habitual actions and provides description in the past ("what was going on").

Estaba todavía en la cama cuando **empezó** a llover.	*I was still in bed when it started to rain.*
De niños, **íbamos** a la playa todos los domingos en verano.	*As children, we used to go to the beach every Sunday in the summer.*
Un día de julio, no **pudimos** ir; la tía Julia no **se sentía** bien.	*One day in July, we couldn't go; Aunt Julia wasn't feeling well.*

In two of the previous examples, both past tenses appear in the same sentence. Can you explain why these forms are used?

EJERCICIO
3·10

*In the following excerpt from **El nacimiento del arco iris**, the verbs in bold are in the preterit or the imperfect tense. Complete the chart that follows with the correct infinitive, verb tense (preterit or imperfect), and reason for using that tense for each verb listed.*

(1) **Eran** inseparables, y cuando (2) **recorrían** la selva (3) **parecían** una nube de colores, deslumbrante y movediza. Pero un día, una de ellas (4) **se hirió** con una aguda espina y ya no (5) **pudo** volar con sus amigas. El resto de las mariposas la (6) **rodeó** y pronto (7) **comprendieron** que la profunda herida (8) **era** mortal. (9) **Volaron** hasta el cielo para estar cerca de los dioses y, sin dudarlo, (10) **ofrecieron** realizar cualquier sacrificio con tal de que la muerte de su amiga no las separara. Una voz grave y profunda (11) **quebró** el silencio de los cielos y les (12) **preguntó** si (13) **estaban** dispuestas a dar sus propias vidas con tal de permanecer juntas, a lo que todas (14) **contestaron** afirmativamente.

VERB	INFINITIVE	VERB TENSE	REASON
1. eran	_____	_____	_____
2. recorrían	_____	_____	_____
3. parecían	_____	_____	_____
4. se hirió	_____	_____	_____
5. pudo	_____	_____	_____
6. rodeó	_____	_____	_____

VERB	INFINITIVE	VERB TENSE	REASON
7. comprendieron			
8. era			
9. volaron			
10. ofrecieron			
11. quebró			
12. preguntó			
13. estaban			
14. contestaron			

EJERCICIO

3·11

Complete this excerpt from **El nacimiento del arco iris** *with the correct verb form (preterit or imperfect) of the appropriate infinitive, chosen from the following list. One of the infinitives is used twice.*

brillar	elevar	formar	calmarse
envolver	temer	cruzar	estar
volverse	disponerse		

En ese mismo instante fuertes vientos (1) _____ los cielos, las nubes

(2) _____ negras y la lluvia y los rayos (3) _____ una

tormenta como nunca se había conocido. Un remolino (4) _____ a las siete

mariposas y las (5) _____ más allá de las nubes. Cuando todo

(6) _____ y el sol (7) _____ a comenzar su trabajo para

secar la tierra, una imponente curva luminosa (8) _____ el cielo, un arco

que (9) _____ pintado con los colores de las siete mariposas, y que

(10) _____ gracias a las almas de estas siete amigas que no

(11) _____ a la muerte con tal de permanecer juntas.

¡Vaya más lejos!

- Busque en línea videos en español para niños que aprenden los **colores del arco iris**.
- Busque en línea otras **leyendas tradicionales** en español. ¿De dónde vienen?

BIENESTAR Y COMIDA

¿Qué comemos?
La alimentación y la salud
(Canadá)

Todos desean comer bien y saludablemente. Además, muchas personas desean o deben perder peso. Para realizar estos objetivos, es importante tener un conocimiento de la **alimentación** y la **salud**.

¿Estamos listos?

1. ¿Qué necesita usted hoy en el supermercado? Haga una lista de compras.

    Me falta(n)... pan, galletas (*cookies*), condimentos, frutas, verduras, leche, queso, yogurt, pescado, pollo, pavo (*turkey*), carne (de res), bebidas, postres (*desserts*), productos de limpieza (*cleaning*), papel de cocina, papel higiénico...

2. ¿Dónde prefiere hacer compras?

    Voy de preferencia a los/las... tiendas pequeñas, supermercados, mercados agrícolas (al aire libre), tiendas de gran formato...

3. ¿Cocina usted? ¿para usted mismo? ¿para su familia? Si no es así, ¿quién cocina en casa?

    Es mi... esposo/a, compañero/a (de hogar), novio/a, amigo/a, madre, padre, hermano/a, hijo/a...

4. ¿Cuántas veces por semana sale a comer? ¿Por qué?

    Salgo a comer porque... prefiero la cocina y el ambiente de los restaurantes, estoy cansado/a por la tarde, estoy demasiado ocupado/a, no tengo tiempo para ir de compras y cocinar, encuentro allí a mis amigos, viajo mucho...

5. En su opinión, ¿qué hábitos ayudan a controlar el peso?

    Por lo general,... comer menos durante el día; comer más verduras y frutas; comer menos grasas, dulces, azúcares y carbohidratos; no consumir bebidas azucaradas; hacer ejercicio de todo tipo...

¡Leamos!

Cómo comprar y presupuestar alimentos saludables

◆ **Planee** sus menús de acuerdo con las **ofertas** de la semana.

◆ Haga su lista de compras en la casa y **respétela** cuando esté en la tienda.

◆ Lea las **etiquetas** de los productos. Compre el alimento, no la **marca** o el **juego** que venga en un paquete atractivo.

◆ **Siempre que** vaya a usar **a corto plazo** el contenido de un paquete, de preferencia compre el **tamaño** grande y no el pequeño, si tiene espacio para guardarlo.

◆ Compre frutas frescas y verduras de la estación y, si no puede **conseguirlas**, utilice las **congeladas** o **enlatadas**.

◆ **Mantenga** a un mínimo sus compras impulsivas. Evite las visitas no planeadas y las no **programadas** a los supermercados.

◆ No vaya de compras cuando tenga hambre.

Cómo leer las etiquetas

Todos los productos **alimenticios** con más de un ingrediente (sopas, **galletas**, cereales, etc.) deban listarlos. **Sin embargo**, cuando **se envasa** jugo de naranja 100% puro, por ejemplo, sólo se describe el producto.

Los **fabricantes** listan las cantidades de los ingredientes comenzando con la mayor.

Los ingredientes se describen de varias maneras. Por ejemplo, si lo que se explica es el contenido en azúcares, se incluirán las **mieles** de **abeja**, de **malta**, **maíz** o **melazas**. También hay que buscar las palabras terminadas en **OSA**, que por lo general describen los componentes del azúcar. Los ejemplos incluyen, entre otras, la glucosa, dextrosa, fructosa, lactosa, maltosa, **sacarosa** y **levulosa**.

Vale la pena notar que todas estas formas de azúcar son alimentos **energéticos** que contienen 4 calorías (17 kilojulios) por cada gramo (0.035 onza).

Las personas que desean evitar la sal deben buscar la palabra SODIO en las etiquetas.

Sugerencias útiles para bajar de peso

◆ Puede sustituir la leche entera por leche descremada o semidescremada.

◆ Utilice yogurt en vez de mayonesa para las **salsas** y los **aderezos** de ensaladas.

◆ Escoja los quesos fabricados con leche descremada o semidescremada que, **por lo tanto**, tienen menor contenido calórico.

◆ Consuma pocos alimentos fritos o bañados con salsa.

◆ Refrigere los **caldos** y salsas. De esta manera, las **grasas** suben a la **superficie** y se quitan con facilidad.

◆ Contrariamente a la **creencia** popular, el **cocinar** con vino **no añade** calorías extra a sus **platillos**. Por lo general, en la cocina se utiliza vino seco. El alcohol se evapora **al hervir**, dejando sólo el vino de bajas calorías.

Mitos acerca de los alimentos

*"La **toronja** disuelve las grasas."*

Falso. Ningún alimento puede hacer esto, **aunque** sea ácido. En cualquier caso, ¿cómo un alimento que contiene glúcidos (azúcares) podría ayudar a perder peso? La única manera de perder peso es **disminuir** el consumo de calorías a una cantidad menor que sus requerimientos de energía y así el cuerpo se verá forzado a **quemar** sus reservas de grasa.

*"Una persona que desee bajar de peso debe eliminar de su dieta el pan, las **papas** y las pastas."*

Falso. Lo más frecuente es que el **abuso** de estos alimentos y sus **guarniciones—mantequilla**, margarina, mermeladas, crema, salsas y crema **agria** los convierta en altamente calóricos…. En cualquier caso, no olvide que el pan, las papas y las pastas son **fuentes** importantes de vitaminas y minerales.

*"Un **plátano** puede sustituir a un bistec."*

Falso. Una fruta constituida básicamente por glúcidos no puede sustituir a una fuente de proteínas y grasas.

*"Las gelatinas **endurecen** las **uñas**."*

Falso. La gelatina es una proteína que se digiere de la misma manera que las proteínas de otras fuentes. Por tanto, no **influye** directamente en algo tan específico como las uñas.

From *¿Qué comemos?* (Montreal / Saint-Laurent: Tormont Publications, 1993).

VOCABULARIO

(la) alimentación	*food, diet*	levulosa	*fructose*
(la) salud	*health*	energéticos [ADJ.]	*energy*
presupuestar	*to budget, estimate*	bajar de peso	*to lose weight*
planee [planear]	*plan*	salsas	*sauces, dips*
ofertas	*(store) specials*	aderezos	*salad dressings*
respétela [respetar]	*follow it, respect it*	por lo tanto	*thus, therefore*
etiquetas	*labels*	caldos	*broths, bouillons*
marca	*brand*	grasas	*fats*
juego	*toy, game*	(la) superficie	*surface*
siempre que	*whenever*	creencia	*belief*
a corto plazo	*within a short time*	(el) cocinar	*cooking*
tamaño	*size*	no añade [añadir]	*doesn't add*
conseguirlas	*obtain them*	platillo	*dish, course*
congeladas	*frozen (ones)*	al hervir	*when boiling*
enlatadas	*canned (ones)*	toronja	*grapefruit*
mantenga [mantener]	*keep, maintain*	aunque	*even though, even if*
programadas	*scheduled (ones)*	disminuir	*to reduce, diminish*
alimenticios [ADJ.]	*food*	quemar	*to burn*
galletas	*cookies*	papas	*potatoes*
sin embargo	*nevertheless*	abuso	*excessive use*
se envasa [envasarse]	*is packaged, is bottled*	(las) guarniciones	*garnishes,*
(los) fabricantes	*manufacturers*		*accompaniments*
(las) mieles	*sweeteners, syrups*	mantequilla	*butter*
abeja	*bee*	agria	*sour*
malta	*malt (extract)*	(las) fuentes	*sources*
(el) maíz	*corn*	plátano	*banana*
melazas	*molasses*	endurecen [endurecer]	*harden*
OSA	*-ose*	uñas	*fingernails*
sacarosa	*sucrose*	influye [influir] (en)	*influence, act on*

¿De qué se trata? *Read the statements below. Is the speaker following the suggestions given in the reading? Respond with* **sí** *(yes) or* **no** *(no).*

	SÍ	NO
1. "Voy al supermercado todos los días a las cinco de la tarde."	☐	☐
2. "Compro únicamente alimentos preparados y rápidos."	☐	☐
3. "No hago compras si no tengo hambre."	☐	☐
4. "Controlo mi peso, por eso no consumo platillos fritos."	☐	☐
5. "Si es posible, escojo productos lácteos descremados."	☐	☐
6. "Pero, para mí, las papas deben estar bañadas en mantequilla."	☐	☐
7. "Son importantes las vitaminas, los minerales, las proteínas, las grasas y también los glúcidos."	☐	☐
8. "Primero debo calcular la cantidad de calorías recomendada para mi estatura y estilo de vida."	☐	☐

Opciones *Choose the phrase or phrases that correctly complete each sentence. Include all correct responses.*

1. En el supermercado

   a. haga su lista.   b. siga su lista.   c. compre alimentos que estén en oferta.

2. En las etiquetas se encuentra(n)

   a. la descripción del producto.   b. el número de calorías.   c. los ingredientes.

3. Los azúcares incluyen las/los

   a. gramos.   b. mieles.   c. melazas.

4. Las frutas contienen principalmente

   a. proteínas.   b. glúcidos.   c. grasas.

5. Las guarniciones típicas para las papas son

   a. margarina.   b. gelatinas.   c. crema agria.

6. En la tienda de comestibles, las verduras fuera de estación frecuentemente son

   a. programadas.   b. congeladas.   c. enlatadas.

¿Cierto o falso? *Indicate whether each statement is true or false, using* **C** *for* **cierto** *(true) or* **F** *for* **falso** *(false). If a statement is false, provide a corrected statement in Spanish.*

1. C   F   En el supermercado, es mejor evitar las ofertas de la semana.

   _____

2. C   F   La palabra "sodio" indica la presencia de sal en los alimentos.

   _____

3. C   F   Un plátano puede sustituir a un bistec.

   _____

4. C   F   Para perder peso debe eliminar de su dieta el pan, las papas y las pastas.

   _____

5. C   F   La toronja no puede disolver las grasas.

   _____

6. C   F   Las gelatinas endurecen las uñas.

   _____

7. C   F   El cocinar con vino no añade calorías extra a los platillos.

   _____

Reflexiones *Consider the following themes and questions, and discuss them in Spanish.*

1. ¿En qué alimentos o tipos de alimentos "cree" usted?

   _____

   _____

   _____

   _____

2. ¿Usted es omnívoro/a? ¿vegetariano/a? ¿vegano/a? ¿Puede explicar por qué?

   _____

   _____

   _____

   _____

Read the following label information and respond in Spanish to the questions.

Ingredientes descritos en la etiqueta

Azúcar, pasta de cacao procesado con álcali, lecitina de soja, aceites (*oils*) vegetales (palma, shea y/o illipe).

Para prepararlo

Mezcla 1 tablilla en 4 tazas de leche sobre fuego medio. Revuelve constantemente con un batidor, o molinillo, hasta que la tablilla quede derretida y tu chocolate quede aromático y espumoso; puedes añadir azúcar antes de disfrutarlo.

Datos de nutrición

Tamaño por porción 1/4 tablilla (23g). Porciones por envase (*package*) aprox. 48.

Calorías 100 / Cal. de grasa 30

		Valor diario
Grasa total	3.5 g	5%
Grasa saturada	2 g	10%
Grasa trans	0 g	
Grasa poliinsaturada	0 g	
Grasa monoinsaturada	1 g	
Colesterol	0 g	0%
Sodio	0 g	0%
Carbohidrato total	18 g	6%
Azúcares	17 g	
Proteínas	<1 g	

No es una fuente significativa de fibra dietética, vitamina A, vitamina C, calcio y hierro (*iron*).

Los porcentajes de Valores Diarios están basados en una dieta de 2.000 calorías.

1. ¿Qué es este producto?

   _____

2. ¿Cuál es el primer ingrediente? ¿Y los otros?

   _____

   _____

3. ¿Cuántas calorías hay por porción? ¿Qué elementos nutritivos tiene este alimento? ¿Qué elementos no tiene?

   _____

   _____

   _____

   _____

   _____

   _____

4. Explique su preparación. ¿Qué ingrediente se mezcla normalmente con este producto? ¿A qué hora del día le gusta consumirlo?

_____

_____

_____

_____

_____

4·6

Mi vocabulario *Select the word that does not belong in each group.*

1. a. presupuestar   b. planear   c. planchar   d. determinar

2. a. limosna   b. naranja   c. limón   d. toronja

3. a. guisado   b. sopa   c. gazpacho   d. caldo

4. a. platillo   b. platino   c. comida   d. plato

5. a. frito   b. hervido   c. crudo   d. cocido

6. a. aderezo   b. guarnición   c. adobo   d. adobe

7. a. leche   b. queso   c. lecho   d. yogurt

8. a. azúcar   b. manzana   c. melazas   d. miel

EJERCICIO

4·7

Contrarios *Match each word or phrase with its opposite.*

1. _____ a la larga   a. bajar de peso

2. _____ salud   b. congelado

3. _____ añadir   c. a corto plazo

4. _____ dulce   d. fondo

5. _____ engordar   e. enfermedad

6. _____ superficie   f. quemar

7. _____ apagar   g. agrio

8. _____ derretido   h. disminuir

Equivalentes *Complete each phrase or sentence by substituting words or phrases from the following list for the words or phrases in small type.*

al contrario de	derrite	proyecte	el almacén
se emplea	se retiran	ascienden	es importante
según	darse cuenta	opinión	sígala

1. _____ sus menús _____ las ofertas de la semana.

Planee   de acuerdo con

2. _____ cuando esté en _____.

Respétela   la tienda

3. _____ _____ que todas estas formas de azúcar

Vale la pena   notar

   son alimentos energéticos.

4. De esta manera, las grasas _____ y _____ con

                            suben a la superficie   se quitan

   facilidad.

5. _____ la _____ popular

contrariamente a   creencia

6. Por lo general, en la cocina _____ vino seco.

                                  se utiliza

7. "La toronja _____ las grasas."

                  disuelve

¡No se olvide! El imperativo: **Ud./Uds.**

Commands, orders, instructions, and suggestions are expressed in Spanish with the imperative forms of the verb. The imperative is a mood, like the indicative, the subjunctive, and the conditional.

The imperative forms for **usted/ustedes** are the same as the forms of the present subjunctive. Their stem is the **yo** form of the present indicative (for both regular and irregular verbs).

- ◆ **-Ar** verbs end in **-e/-en**:

    (yo) habl**o**   >   Habl**e** (usted). Habl**en** (ustedes).

- ◆ **-Er** and **-ir** verbs end in **-a/-an**:

    (yo) com**o**   >   Com**a** (usted). Com**an** (ustedes).

The imperative of irregular verbs is formed in the same way.

   (yo) veng**o**   >   Veng**a** aquí. Veng**an** aquí.
   (yo) dig**o**   >   Dig**a** la verdad. Dig**an** la verdad.
   (yo) pid**o**   >   Pid**a** permiso. Pid**an** permiso.

In the negative, **usted/ustedes** imperatives are preceded by **no**.

No salga. | *Don't leave.*
No coman esto. | *Don't [PL.] eat this.*
No compre esos mariscos. | *Don't buy that seafood.*

Five Spanish verbs have imperatives with irregular stems (that is, the stem is not formed from the present indicative **yo** stem).

dar **dé** (usted) **den** (ustedes)
estar **esté** (usted) **estén** (ustedes)
saber **sepa** (usted) **sepan** (ustedes)
ser **sea** (usted) **sean** (ustedes)
ir **vaya** (usted) **vayan** (ustedes)

EJERCICIO
4·9

First (a) give the infinitive for each imperative form in the following suggestions from the reading. Then (b) use the same verb to create another suggestion or command, using either the affirmative or negative imperative.

1. Haga su lista de compras en la casa.

 a. _____

 b. _____

2. No vaya de compras cuando tenga hambre.

 a. _____

 b. _____

3. Mantenga a un mínimo sus compras impulsivas.

 a. _____

 b. _____

4. Lea las etiquetas de los productos.

 a. _____

 b. _____

5. Escoja los quesos fabricados con leche descremada.

 a. _____

 b. _____

6. Utilice yogurt en vez de mayonesa.

 a. _____

 b. _____

7. Consuma pocos alimentos fritos.

a. _____

b. _____

¡Vaya más lejos!

♦ Escoja otra etiqueta en español y analice sus ingredientes. Describa ese producto. En su opinión, ¿es bueno (o malo) para la salud? ¿Por qué?

♦ Busque en línea una receta del mundo hispanohablante. Prepárela, si es posible. Enumere y analice en lo posible sus ingredientes.

Para tener hijos sanos...
Sonia Ramírez (México)

Para tener hijos **sanos hace falta ser** una mamá sana y equilibrada. Los padres—es decir, madres así como padres—reciben consejos incesantes: de parte de sus padres y parientes, amigos y vecinos, sin mencionar la prensa e internet. Pero las siguientes sugerencias nos parecen particularmente útiles.

¿Estamos listos?

1. ¿Vive usted solo/a? ¿Vive con otras personas? ¿Con quién vive?

   Vivo con mi(s)... padre/papá, madre/mamá, hermano(s)/hermana(s), abuelo(s)/abuela(s), hijo(s)/hija(s), tío(s)/tía(s), primo(s)/prima(s), sobrino(s)/sobrina(s), nieto(s)/nieta(s), esposo/a, novio/a, amigo(s)/amiga(s), compañero(s)/compañera(s) de cuarto...

2. Si usted tiene hijos, ¿cuántos hijos tiene? ¿Cuántos años tienen sus hijos? ¿Con quién comparte usted las responsabilidades de familia?

   Comparto su cuidado con mi/el/la... esposo/a, novio/a, madre, padre, abuelo/a, niñero/a (*nanny*), casa cuna (*daycare*), escuela de párvulos (*preschool*), escuela primaria...

3. ¿Cuándo se siente usted estresado/a?

   Me siento estresado/a... en el trabajo, en clase (en la universidad, en la escuela), en familia, en el coche, en la carretera, en el transporte público, en las tiendas, cuando me acuesto, cuando me despierto...

4. Y usted, ¿duerme bien y lo suficiente? ¿Hace ejercicio? ¿Mantiene una dieta saludable? ¿Se divierte lo suficiente?

5. Discuta algunos factores o cambios que podrían llevar a alguien a un profundo estrés.

   Podría ser... la enfermedad, la pérdida de un ser querido, el parto (*birth of a child*), los problemas familiares (*family*), la pérdida del empleo, las deudas (*debts*), la búsqueda de empleo, el cambio (de casa, de escuela, de profesión, de nivel de vida)...

6. ¿Qué estrategias le son útiles cuando está estresado/a?

   Para mí, podría ser... descansar, dormir, comer bien, cocinar, divertirme, charlar (*chat*) con mis amigos, hacer ejercicio/caminatas/jogging/yoga/meditación, andar en bicicleta, escuchar/tocar música, hacer artes o artesanías, ver la televisión, ver una buena película, leer, navegar en internet, jugar videojuegos, usar redes sociales, ir de compras, viajar, hablar con mi terapeuta...

¡Leamos!

Algunas veces, las mamás se olvidan de su propia **salud** y necesidades, **anteponiendo** el **bienestar** de sus hijos. Pero lo que **no se ponen a** pensar es que los niños necesitan mamás sanas y felices, no mamás enfermas, **agotadas** y **estresadas**. ¿Pero cómo pueden las mujeres encontrar el balance para **cumplir tanto** con sus labores **a nivel** profesional **como** para resolver todos los **asuntos** de su **hogar**, sin ser negligentes con ellas mismas? Porque lo que muchas madres **alegan** es que en medio de tanta **revolución**, nunca tienen tiempo para ellas.

"Sí, es muy cierto. Vivimos en tiempos locos y ocupados", afirma Mary B. Seger, experta en estrategias de **crianza** [...] "Es esencial que las madres se tomen tiempo para ellas mismas. Ser **padre** es muy **estresante**. **Por supuesto**, amas a tus niños y harías todo por ellos, pero la vida **se te va en dar**. Existe un límite **en qué tanto** puede dar una mamá antes de **agotarse**. Es imperativo tomarse tiempo para **disfrutar** como adulta, para que entonces haya suficiente energía para ser padre, **recordando** siempre que eres el padre, no el amigo de tu hijo".

"Mira tu vida. Si te sientes **vacía** porque lo único que haces todo el día es dar, pregúntate a ti misma si es así como quieres que sean tus hijos cuando se conviertan en adultos. Recuerda que te observan e imitarán lo que hagas. También **podrás darte cuenta de que** cuando estás 'vacía', tus niños quieren más de ti. Ellos sienten que no obtienen nada de ti— porque no hay nada más que dar. Tómate **descanso** y **llena** tu vida. Sé **egoísta**, **supera culpa**. Las cosas en casa serán mucho más **sencillas**". [...]

"Llevar un estilo de vida **saludable** te ayuda a sentirte bien, a tener buena energía, y a disfrutar la vida. El balance—todo en moderación—conduce a un estilo de vida sano", nos dice Seger. [...] Tómate tiempo para ti y para tu esposo. Sé una madre que **provea a** los niños y a ti misma de alimentos saludables. **Apaga** el televisor y **realiza** actividades con tus hijos".

Y **de nuevo**, Seger **hace hincapié en que** el secreto para **lograr** el balance es el **autoanálisis** y el **imaginar** el futuro de nuestros hijos. "No puedes ser todo y hacer todo para tus hijos. Con el **paso** del tiempo, **tratar de** ser la **Mujer Maravilla** sólo **te dejará** sentimientos de vacío, depresión, y **desesperanza**. Sé firme contigo misma y tómate tiempo para comer bien, ejercitarte y divertirte. Serás mejor madre si lo haces así".

Sonia Ramírez, excerpt from *The Huffington Post: Voces*, http://voces.huffingtonpost.com. Used with the permission of Sonia Ramírez and *The Huffington Post: Voces*. Many thanks to Sonia Ramírez.

VOCABULARIO

sanos	*healthy*	tanto... como	*both . . . and*
hace [hacer] falta ser	*you need to be, you have to be*	a nivel	*at the level*
		asuntos	*matters, details*
(la) salud	*health*	(el) hogar	*household, home*
anteponiendo [anteponer]	*giving preference to*	alegan [alegar]	*declare, allege*
		(la) revolución	*tumult, uproar*
(el) bienestar	*well-being*	crianza	*child rearing*
no se ponen a [ponerse a]	*don't begin to*	(el) padre	*parent*
		estresante	*stressful*
agotadas	*exhausted*	por supuesto	*of course*
estresadas	*(over)stressed*	se te va [irse] en dar	*gets used up in giving*
cumplir	*to fulfill*	en qué tanto	*of (just) how much*

agotarse	*exhausting herself*	apaga [apagar]	*turn off*
disfrutar	*to enjoy (oneself)*	realiza [realizar]	*do, carry out*
recordando [recordar]	*remembering*	de nuevo	*once more, again*
vacía	*empty, vacant*	hace [hacer] hincapié	*emphasizes that*
podrás [poder] darte	*you will be able to realize*	en que	
cuenta de que	*that*	lograr	*achieve, obtain*
descanso	*rest, a break*	(el) autoanálisis	*self-knowledge*
llena [llenar]	*fill up, occupy*	(el) imaginar	*imagining*
egoísta	*selfish*	paso	*passage*
supera [superar] culpa	*get over, overcome guilt*	tratar de	*to try to*
sencillas	*simple*	Mujer Maravilla	*Wonder Woman*
saludable	*healthy, healthful*	te dejará [dejar]	*will leave you with*
provea a [proveer a]	*provides*	desesperanza	*despair*

EJERCICIO
5·1

¿De qué se trata? *Match the beginning of each sentence with the phrase that correctly completes it to review the advice given in the reading. Include all correct responses.*

1. _____ Las mamás se olvidan a menudo de

2. _____ No se ponen a pensar que

3. _____ Cómo pueden las mujeres

4. _____ Muchas madres alegan que

5. _____ Es esencial que las madres

6. _____ Cuando estás vacía

7. _____ Pregúntate si es así como

8. _____ Tómate

a. encontrar el balance saludable.

b. nunca tienen tiempo para ellas.

c. quieres que sean tus hijos adultos.

d. tus niños quieren más de ti.

e. su propia salud y necesidades.

f. tiempo para ti y para tu esposo.

g. se tomen tiempo para ellas mismas.

h. los niños necesitan mamás sanas.

Opciones *Choose the phrase or phrases that correctly complete each sentence. Include all correct responses.*

1. Ser padre es muy

   a. agotador.   b. estresante.   c. fácil.

2. Mary Seger es experta en estrategias

   a. de química.   b. de cocina.   c. de crianza.

3. Las mujeres deben resolver

   a. su egoísmo.   b. los asuntos del hogar.   c. sus labores profesionales.

4. Llevar un estilo de vida saludable ofrece

   a. programas de televisión.   b. más simplicidad.   c. buena energía.

5. Cuando les proveen buenos alimentos a sus hijos, las madres

   a. también se beneficiarán.   b. serán vacías.   c. ganarán peso.

6. Se recomienda tratar de apagar

   a. los videojuegos.   b. el televisor.   c. el refrigerador.

7. Para lograr el balance se necesita dedicarse

   a. al autoanálisis.   b. a la desesperanza.   c. al futuro de los hijos.

8. Tómate tiempo para

   a. divertirte.   b. comer bien.   c. ejercitarte.

¿Cierto o falso? *Indicate whether each statement is true or false, using* **C** *for* **cierto** *(true) or* **F** *for* **falso** *(false). If a statement is false, provide a corrected statement in Spanish.*

1. C   F   Las mamás recuerdan siempre su propia salud y necesidades.

   _____

2. C   F   Parece que no es difícil anteponer el bienestar de sus hijos.

   _____

3. C   F   No es normal tratar de cumplir con las labores profesionales así como con los asuntos del hogar.

   _____
   _____

4. C F La existencia de estas mujeres está llena de revolución y estrés.

_____

5. C F El peligro está en que su vida se les va en dar.

_____

6. C F Los padres deben ser sobre todo los amigos de sus hijos.

_____

7. C F Los niños nunca observan ni imitan a sus padres.

_____

8. C F Para ser buenos padres, las madres y también los padres tendrán que volverse más egoístas.

_____

_____

_____

EJERCICIO
5·4

Reflexiones *Consider the following themes and questions, and discuss them in Spanish.*

1. Tenga o no hijos, ¿en quién (o en qué) invierte la mayor parte de su energía?

_____

_____

_____

_____

2. En su opinión, ¿por qué los niños exigirán más de usted cuando está "vacío/a"?

_____

_____

_____

_____

3. ¿Conoce a algunas "Mujeres Maravillas"? Descríbalas. ¿Tienen éxito?

_____

_____

_____

_____

4. En su opinión, ¿cuáles son los motivos para tener hijos o para formar una familia?

_____

_____

_____

_____

5. En su opinión, ¿cuáles son los motivos de la gente que decide *no* formar una familia?

_____

_____

_____

_____

6. Si tiene hijos, ¿cómo quiere que sean cuando se conviertan en adultos?

_____

_____

_____

_____

EJERCICIO
5·5

Mi vocabulario *Select the word that does not belong in each group.*

1. a. vital	b. sano	c. robusto	d. flojo
2. a. anteponer	b. anticipar	c. aventajar	d. preferir
3. a. desdicha	b. felicidad	c. bienestar	d. confort
4. a. agotado	b. fatigado	c. agradecido	d. vacío
5. a. ejercitar	b. realizar	c. cumplir	d. satisfacer
6. a. tarea	b. asunto	c. trabajo	d. astucia
7. a. domicilio	b. casa	c. hoja	d. hogar
8. a. declarar	b. alegar	c. alegrar	d. explicar
9. a. revolución	b. rotación	c. agitación	d. tumulto
10. a. formación	b. educación	c. crianza	d. criada

Contrarios *Match each word with its opposite.*

1. _____ sencillo   a. fracasar

2. _____ disfrutar   b. enérgico

3. _____ egoísta   c. vacío

4. _____ lograr   d. complicado

5. _____ salud   e. altruista

6. _____ agotado   f. aburrirse

7. _____ lleno   g. encender

8. _____ apagar   h. enfermedad

9. _____ recordar   i. olvidarse

Equivalentes *Complete each sentence by substituting words or phrases from the following list for the words or phrases in small type.*

adivinan	empiezan	hay	se te agota
equilibrio	otra vez	apreciar	evidentemente
prefiriendo	conocimiento de sí mismo	exigen	reciben
de vez en cuando	exigencias	no recuerdan	deja bien claro
fatigarse	vitales	destino	

1. _____, las mamás _____ su propia salud
   <small>Algunas veces</small>   <small>se olvidan de</small>

   y _____, _____ el bienestar de sus hijos.
     <small>necesidades</small>   <small>anteponiendo</small>

2. Pero lo que no _____ a pensar es que los niños necesitan mamás
                    <small>se ponen</small>

   _____.
   <small>sanas</small>

3. _____, amas a tus niños y harías todo por ellos, pero la vida
   <small>Por supuesto</small>

   _____ en dar.
   <small>se te va</small>

4. _____ un límite en qué tanto puede dar una mamá antes de
   <small>Existe</small>

   _____.
   <small>agotarse</small>

5. También podrás _____ que cuando estás 'vacía', tus niños
                   <small>darte cuenta de</small>

   _____ más de ti.
   <small>quieren</small>

6. Ellos _____ que no _____ nada de ti—porque
      sienten   obtienen

   no hay nada más que dar.

7. Y _____ , Seger _____ que el secreto para lograr
      de nuevo   hace hincapié en

   el _____ es el _____ y el imaginar el
      balance   autoanálisis

   _____ de nuestros hijos.
      futuro

¡No se olvide! El imperativo: tú

Commands, orders, instructions, and suggestions are expressed in Spanish with the imperative forms of the verb. The imperative is a mood, like the indicative, the subjunctive, and the conditional.

Affirmative tú commands

Affirmative commands for **tú** (informal, singular commands) are formed from the present indicative **tú** form minus the -**s**.

You can also remember the affirmative **tú** form as the third-person singular of the present indicative.

If the present indicative form has a stem change or an irregularity, the **tú** affirmative command will also have it. When needed, make sure to consult complete Spanish verb charts.

-ar verbs

(tú) **Llamas** a tu madre.	*You call your mother.*
> **Llama** a tu madre.	*Call your mother.*
(tú) **Piensas** en él.	*You think about him.*
> **Piensa** en él.	*Think about him.*

-er verbs

(tú) **Vendes** la casa.	*You sell the house.*
> **Vende** la casa.	*Sell the house.*
(tú) **Escoges** este curso.	*You choose this course.*
> **Escoge** este curso.	*Choose this course.*
(tú) **Vuelves** a casa.	*You go back home.*
> **Vuelve** a casa.	*Go back home.*

-ir verbs

(tú) **Escribes** el cuento.	*You write the story.*
> **Escribe** el cuento.	*Write the story.*
(tú) **Duermes** bien.	*You sleep well.*
> **Duerme** bien.	*Sleep well.*

Irregular affirmative tú commands

Eight Spanish verbs have irregular forms in the affirmative **tú** command. It's best to memorize these.

decir	**di**	salir	**sal**
hacer	**haz**	ser	**sé**
ir	**ve**	tener	**ten**
poner	**pon**	venir	**ven**

Sé egoísta.	*Be selfish.*
Haz la tarea.	*Do your homework.*
Di la verdad.	*Tell the truth.*

Negative tú commands

The negative **tú** command form is the same as the present subjunctive form for **tú** (second-person singular).

Take the first-person singular (**yo**) of the present indicative. Drop the final **-o** to get the stem. For **-ar** verbs, add **-es** to the stem. For **-er** and **-ir** verbs, add **-as** to the stem. With a few exceptions, this also applies to stem-changing and irregular verbs.

-ar verbs

No fum**es**.	*Don't smoke.*
No malgast**es** tu dinero.	*Don't waste your money.*

-er verbs

No enciend**as** la lámpara.	*Don't turn on the lamp.*
No vuelv**as** tarde.	*Don't get back late.*

-ir verbs

No escrib**as** el correo.	*Don't write the e-mail.*
No mient**as**.	*Don't lie.*

Irregular negative tú commands

Four Spanish verbs have irregular forms in the negative **tú** command. It's best to memorize these.

dar   **des**

No des este regalo.	*Don't give this gift.*

estar   **estés**

No estés molesto.	*Don't be upset.*

ser   **seas**

No seas egoísta.	*Don't be selfish.*

ir   **vayas**

No vayas al restaurante.	*Don't go to the restaurant.*

Verbs ending in **-car**, **-gar**, and **-zar** have a spelling change in the negative **tú** command.

-car   **c > qu** (tocar)

No to**ques** la guitarra.	*Don't play the guitar.*

-gar   **g > gu** (llegar)

No lle**gues** tarde.	*Don't arrive late.*

-zar   **z > c** (comenzar)

No comien**ces** primero.	*Don't start first.*

Commands with pronouns

Affirmative **tú** commands

Direct and indirect object pronouns, as well as reflexive pronouns, are attached to the affirmative form of the imperative. A written accent mark maintains the normal stress of the verb form in a multi-syllable command.

Da**me** este libro. Dá**melo**.	*Give me this book. Give it to me.*
Cálla**te**. Siénta**te**.	*Quiet (down). Sit down.*
Tóma**te** tiempo para ti.	*Take time for yourself.*

Negative **tú** commands

All object pronouns (direct, indirect, and reflexive) precede the verb in a negative command.

No me des ese libro. **No me lo des.**	*Don't give me that book. Don't give it to me.*
No hagas la tarea. **No la hagas.**	*Don't do the homework. Don't do it.*
No le digas nada a Juan.	*Don't tell Juan anything.*
No te acuestes.	*Don't go to bed.*

Other ways to give advice

In addition to the imperative forms, advice and suggestions in Spanish are often given in other ways.

- With the verb **deber** *to have to, must* + infinitive

  The conditional form of **deber** is often used in this construction.

Deberías disfrutar la vida.	*You ought to enjoy life.*
Se debería hacer un esfuerzo.	*One should make an effort.*

- With the expressions **hacer falta** + infinitive and **tener que** + infinitive

  Hacer falta is impersonal; it remains in the third-person singular. **Tener que** is conjugated.

Hace falta recordar lo que es importante.	*One needs to remember what is important.*
Tendremos que buscarlo.	*We will have to look it up.*

- With impersonal expressions—often **es** + adjective—followed either by an infinitive or **que** + the subjunctive

Es imperativo tomarse tiempo para disfrutar como adulta.	*It's imperative that you take time to enjoy yourself as an adult.*
Es esencial que las madres **se tomen** tiempo para ellas mismas.	*It's essential that mothers take time for themselves.*

- With sentences of "will" or "influence" that have two subjects and use the subjunctive

Quiero que (tú) **salgas** más a menudo.	*I want you to go out more.*
Deseamos que **lleguen** al mismo tiempo.	*We'd like all of you to arrive at the same time.*

List (a) each Imperative form with **tú** in the following excerpts from the reading, and give (b) its infinitive. Then use the same imperative form to (c) create another suggestion or command.

1. Pregúntate a ti misma si es así como quieres que sean tus hijos cuando se conviertan en adultos.

    a. _____ b. _____

    c. _____

2. Recuerda que te observan e imitarán lo que hagas.

    a. _____ b. _____

    c. _____

3. Tómate tiempo para comer bien, ejercitarte y divertirte.

    a. _____ b. _____

    c. _____

4. Tómate descanso.

    a. _____ b. _____

    c. _____

5. Llena tu vida.

    a. _____ b. _____

    c. _____

6. Sé egoísta.

    a. _____ b. _____

    c. _____

7. Supera culpa.

    a. _____ b. _____

    c. _____

8. Tómate tiempo para ti y para tu esposo.

    a. _____ b. _____

    c. _____

9. Sé una madre que provea a los niños y a ti misma de alimentos saludables.

    a. _____ b. _____

    c. _____

10. Apaga el televisor.

   a. _____   b. _____

   c. _____

11. Realiza actividades con tus hijos.

   a. _____   b. _____

   c. _____

¡Vaya más lejos!

◆ Busque en línea más **consejos para un estilo de vida saludable**. Utilice por ejemplo, www.google.es.

◆ Busque también en línea más **consejos de crianza de niños**. ¿Ve usted algunos consejos distintos de los que cabría esperar (*you'd expect*)?

◆ Busque en línea la respuesta a esta pregunta: ¿Existe en España y en Latinoamérica el fenómeno de los **padres** (no madres) **que se quedan en casa**, ocupándose a tiempo completo del cuidado de los hijos menores?

La chía, un súper alimento con pasado y mucho futuro

Yazmín Evia y Rolando Lino (México)

El uso **alimenticio** de la chía o **Salvia hispanica se remonta** a 3 mil 500 años. Es **endémica** de México, y se le consideraba un alimento principal entre mayas y aztecas. Su **consumo** era tan importante que se pagaba tributo al **imperio mexica** con estas minúsculas **semillas**, que eran ofrecidas a los **dioses** durante las ceremonias religiosas.

¿Estamos listos?

1. ¿Qué toma usted normalmente en el desayuno? ¿A qué hora desayuna?

   Tomo... pan, panecillos, tostadas, medialunas/cruasanes, mantequilla, mermelada, cereales, queso, yogurt, huevos, jugo de fruta, fruta, bananas, naranjas, melones, bayas (*berries*), arándanos (*blueberries*), fresas (*strawberries*), toronjas (*grapefruit*), piña (*pineapple*), mangos, café (con leche), té, chocolate...

2. ¿Qué toma en el almuerzo? ¿A qué hora come?

   Tomo... ensaladas, sándwiches/bocadillos (de jamón, de queso, de atún, de pollo, de pavo (*turkey*), de verduras...), tacos, enchiladas, pasta, frijoles, frijoles negros, garbanzos, soja...

3. ¿Qué toma en la cena?

   Tomo... sopas (de legumbres, de verduras, de fideos (*noodles*), de hongos (*mushrooms*), de frijoles...), carne de vaca (de res), pollo, pavo, pescado, mariscos (*seafood*), tofu, pasta, arroz, papas/patatas, legumbres, zanahorias (*carrots*), brócoli, verduras, col (*cabbage*), col rizada (*kale*), acelgas (*chard*), espinacas, postres, nueces (*nuts*), pasteles (*cakes*), galletas (*cookies*), helados (*ice cream*), dulces...

4. ¿Selecciona ciertos alimentos en vez de otros? ¿Evita algunos alimentos? ¿Por qué?

   Porque... tengo preferencias, tengo alergias, tengo razones de salud, soy vegetariano/a, soy vegano/a, prefiero los productos orgánicos/locales, prefiero los productos de comercio justo (*fair trade*), el costo es importante...

5. Por razones de salud, ¿qué alimentos deberíamos todos evitar o tomar en moderación?

   Incluyen, por ejemplo,... las bebidas alcohólicas, alimentos grasosos, alimentos azucarados, comida frita, comida muy salada (*salty*), bocados (*snack foods*), papas fritas, caramelos, chocolate, helados, refrescos (*sodas*), batidos (*shakes*)...

¡Leamos!

La importancia de la chía **radica** en los increíbles aspectos nutricionales que **posee**, **ya que** su **ingesta** contribuye a la prevención de **afecciones** cardiovasculares; **mejora** la función cerebral; y favorece el tratamiento de ciertos tipos de depresión.

La chía **aporta** altos **contenidos** de fibra dietética y Omega 3; es rica en antioxidantes, proteínas, y contiene una gran cantidad de minerales. **No en vano**, las semillas de chía han sido calificadas como uno de los mejores complementos alimenticios naturales. **Por si fuera poco**, no posee **contraindicaciones**.

Las semillas de chía contienen minerales esenciales como fósforo, manganeso, calcio, sodio y potasio. Es también abundante en antioxidantes, moléculas que inhiben el proceso de oxidación en las células, **por lo que** reduce los signos del **envejecimiento** y el **riesgo** de **padecer** ciertas enfermedades, incluyendo varios tipos de cáncer.

Una porción de 28 gramos de semillas de chía contiene **casi** el 9 por ciento de la ingesta diaria recomendada de proteínas; 13 por ciento de la ingesta recomendada para el porcentaje de **grasa**; y 42 de la ingesta diaria **aconsejada** de fibra dietética.

El consumo de las semillas de chía es fácil y **a menudo** requiere poca o ninguna preparación. Las semillas de chía se pueden **espolvorear** en ensaladas, sopas o yogurt, como si fuera **nuez** o **cualquier** otra semilla. También **se añaden** a los productos **horneados** como **molletes**, pan, **galletas** y **pasteles**. Hay quienes **se las agregan** al agua de cítricos o **tamarindo**; cereales para el desayuno; o **mezclas** de nueces y semillas. [...]

En Estados Unidos, el consumo de chía **se está volviendo bastante** común. [...]

La cantidad de trabajos científicos que **dan cuenta de** las **ventajas** nutricionales de la chía sobre las otras **fuentes** de Omega 3, **así como** la comercialización de productos que la incluyen, están creciendo rápidamente alrededor del mundo. [...]

Algunos **datos insólitos** acerca de la chía:

- Contiene más ácidos grasos Omega 3 que el salmón. Contiene más fibra que las semillas de **lino**.
- La planta floreciente puede **retoñar** en cuestión de días, y es tolerante a la **sequía**.
- La palabra *chía* proviene del **náhuatl**, cuyo significado es "**aceitoso**". Se utilizó para producir un aceite como base para pinturas **corporales** y decorativas.
- El estado de Chiapas debe su nombre a la chía. Etimológicamente, la palabra *Chiapas* proviene del náhuatl que significa "en el río de la chía". Su **glifo** indica que desde tiempos muy remotos en las **orillas** del río Grijalva se cultivaba la chía.
- Durante la época prehispánica **se ofrendaba** a los dioses por lo que su consumo, venta y producción fue prohibido y **castigado** durante la colonia en la **Nueva España**. Casi desapareció por 500 años y sólo se podía encontrar en unos cuantos pueblos de México.
- Está documentado que los **guerreros** aztecas podían subsistir alimentándose únicamente con chía durante sus batallas y expediciones. Las cantidades que consumían eran **sumamente** pequeñas: **tan sólo** el equivalente a una **cucharada** era suficiente para la marcha de todo un día.
- Los aztecas imponían a sus pueblos **tributarios** una **aportación** de hasta 15 mil **toneladas** anuales.

Yazmín Evia and Rolando Lino, excerpt from *E-Consulta: Periódico Digital*, http://www.e-consulta.com.

alimenticio [ADJ.]	*nutritional, food*	(los) pasteles	*cakes*
salvia	*sage (plant)*	se las agregan [agregarse]	*they are added*
se remonta [remontarse]	*go back, date back*	tamarindo	*tamarind (fruit)*
endémica	*native, indigenous*	mezclas	*mixtures*
consumo	*consumption*	se está volviendo [volverse]	*is becoming*
imperio mexica	*Aztec Empire*		
semillas	*seeds*	bastante	*rather, fairly*
(los) dioses	*gods*	dan [dar] cuenta de	*show*
radica [radicar]	*is based, is rooted*	ventajas	*advantages*
posee [poseer]	*possesses, has*	(las) fuentes	*sources*
ya que	*since*	así como	*as well as*
ingesta	*consumption, eating*	datos	*facts*
(las) afecciones	*ailments, illnesses*	insólitos	*unusual*
mejora [mejorar]	*improves*	lino	*flax*
aporta [aportar]	*contributes*	retoñar	*(to) sprout*
contenidos	*content(s)*	sequía	*drought*
no en vano	*it's not surprising that*	(el) náhuatl [MEX., CENT. AM.]	*Nahuatl language*
por si fuera [ser] poco	*what's more, not only that*		
(las) contraindicaciones	*reasons to avoid use*	aceitoso	*oily*
por lo que	*as a consequence*	corporales [ADJ.]	*body*
envejecimiento	*aging*	glifo	*glyph, symbol*
riesgo	*risk*	orillas	*riverbanks*
padecer	*falling victim to, suffering from*	se ofrendaba [ofrendarse]	*were given as an offering*
casi	*almost*	castigado	*punished*
grasa	*fat*	Nueva España	*New Spain (Spanish colonies in the New World)*
aconsejada	*recommended*		
a menudo	*often*		
espolvorear	*be sprinkled*	guerreros	*warriors*
(la) nuez (las nueces)	*nut(s), walnut(s)*	sumamente	*extremely*
cualquier	*any*	tan sólo	*only, just*
se añaden [añadirse]	*are added*	cucharada	*spoonful*
horneados	*baked*	tributarios [ADJ.]	*taxed, owing tribute*
(los) molletes	*muffins*	(la) aportación	*contribution*
galletas	*cookies*	toneladas	*(metric) tons*

¿De qué se trata? *Who might say the following? Choose* **N** *for* **un nutricionista** (a nutritionist), **A** *for* **un amigo** (a friend), *or* **AA** *for* **un antiguo azteca** (an ancient Aztec).

	N	A	AA
1. ¡Ay! Me falta energía; me parece perder la memoria.	☐	☐	☐
2. Dos toneladas, dice, o los dioses nos harán perder la batalla.	☐	☐	☐
3. ¿Qué preparación necesita la chía?	☐	☐	☐
4. La chía es rica en fibra, Omega 3, antioxidantes, proteínas y minerales.	☐	☐	☐
5. Reduce los signos del envejecimiento y el riesgo de ciertas afecciones.	☐	☐	☐
6. ¿Tienen los sacos de chía? ¡Entonces, pongámonos en marcha!	☐	☐	☐
7. ¿Cenamos juntos esta noche? ¡Mi vinagreta de chía es estupenda!	☐	☐	☐

Opciones *Choose the phrase or phrases that correctly complete each sentence. Include all correct responses.*

1. La planta es tolerante a

   a. las semillas.   b. la sequía.   c. las orillas.

2. Se añaden las semillas de chía a

   a. los pasteles.   b. las ensaladas.   c. los cereales.

3. Durante la colonia en la Nueva España, el consumo, la venta y la producción de la chía fueron

   a. prohibidos.   b. castigados.   c. reprimidos.

4. Se dice que los guerreros aztecas podían subsistir con cantidades de chía que fueron

   a. voluminosas.   b. pequeñas.   c. minúsculas.

5. El nombre *Chiapas* quiere decir "en el río de la chía". "Chía" significa

   a. delgado.   b. azucarado.   c. aceitoso.

6. Los nahuas usaban su aceite como base para

   a. pinturas corporales.   b. pinturas murales.   c. aderezos para ensaladas.

¿Cierto o falso? *Indicate whether each statement is true or false, using* **C** *for* **cierto** *(true) or* **F** *for* **falso** *(false). If a statement is false, provide a corrected statement in Spanish.*

1. C F   La chía contiene mucha fibra y muchos ácidos grasos.

   _____

2. C F   La *Salvia hispanica* es muy difícil de cultivar.

   _____

3. C F   Se cultivaba la chía desde tiempos remotos en las orillas del río Grijalva.

   _____

4. C F   Los españoles de la Nueva España favorecían y protegían el cultivo de la chía.

   _____

5. C F   Las semillas de chía nunca se añaden al pan.

   _____

6. C F   Un guerrero azteca necesitaba grandes cantidades de chía durante cada marcha.

   _____

Reflexiones *Consider the following themes and questions, and discuss them in Spanish.*

1. ¿Sigue usted (o intenta seguir) una dieta especial? Descríbala. ¿Quizás tiene alergias?

   _____

   _____

   _____

2. Para usted, ¿hay una conexión entre la salud y la comida? Explique.

   _____

   _____

   _____

3. ¿Cree que existe un súper alimento? Si es así, ¿cuál es? ¿Lo consume habitualmente o a veces?

   _____

   _____

   _____

4. Describa los efectos del consumo de su(s) súper alimento(s).

_____

_____

_____

Mi vocabulario *Select the word or phrase that does not belong in each group.*

1. a. disfrutar   b. poseer   c. tener   d. donar

2. a. cocinados   b. fritos   c. crudos   d. horneados

3. a. molletes   b. gallinas   c. pasteles   d. panes

4. a. cotidianos   b. raros   c. bizarros   d. insólitos

5. a. agregar   b. agravar   c. incorporar   d. añadir

6. a. disminuir   b. ampliar   c. crecer   d. alargar

7. a. guerrero   b. militar   c. soledad   d. soldado

8. a. dar cuenta de   b. mostrar   c. exponer   d. esconder

Contrarios *Match each word or phrase with its opposite.*

1. _____ extranjero   a. endémico

2. _____ a menudo   · b. mejorar

3. _____ empeorar   . c. inundaciones

4. _____ ventajas   d. envejecimiento

5. _____ sequía   . e. inconvenientes

6. _____ rejuvenecimiento   · f. pocas veces

7. _____ insólito   g. datos

8. _____ mitos   . h. normal

Equivalentes *Complete each sentence by substituting words or phrases from the following list for the words or phrases in small type.*

además	enfermedades	prohibiciones	aumenta
es basada en	recomendada	ayuda	por consiguiente
sufrir de	consumo	la posibilidad	tiene
cotidiana			

1. La importancia de la chía _____ en los increíbles aspectos nutricionales
   _{radica}

   que _____, ya que su _____ contribuye a la
   _{posee} _{ingesta}

   prevención de _____ cardiovasculares; _____ la
   _{afecciones} _{mejora}

   función cerebral; y _____ el tratamiento de ciertos tipos de depresión.
   _{favorece}

2. _____, no posee _____.
   _{Por si fuera poco} _{contraindicaciones}

3. Es también abundante en antioxidantes... _____ reduce los signos
   _{por lo que}

   del envejecimiento y _____ de _____ ciertas
   _{el riesgo} _{padecer}

   enfermedades.

4. Una porción de 28 gramos contiene 42 por ciento de la ingesta _____
   _{diaria}

   _____ de fibra dietética.
   _{aconsejada}

¡No se olvide! El presente progresivo

The Spanish present progressive tense, like the present progressive in English, emphasizes the current, ongoing, or continuous nature of an action.

The present progressive is constructed like its English counterpart: **Estoy caminando.** *I am walking.* The verb **estar** *to be* is followed by a present participle or gerund form: in Spanish, **-ando** for **-ar** verbs, **-iendo** for **-er** and **-ir** verbs; in English, *-ing*. The Spanish present participle ends in **-yendo** when the verb stem is a vowel (**leer** > **leyendo**).

Note that the Spanish present tense also conveys a progressive meaning: **Camino.** *I walk.* or *I am walking.* The Spanish progressive tense is used less often than it is in English. When used, its meaning is quite emphatic.

No podemos salir; **estamos estudiando.**   *We can't go out; we're studying.*

¡Ojo!

Object pronouns and reflexive pronouns precede the form of **estar** in this construction. Alternatively, they may be attached to the present participle. When the pronoun is attached, an accent is added to the antepenultimate vowel of the participle.

La estoy escuchando.
Estoy escuchándola. } *I am listening to her.*

Examples from the passage follow.

Los trabajos científicos... **están creciendo** rápidamente alrededor del mundo. — *Scientific studies are rapidly increasing around the world.*

En Estados Unidos, el consumo de chía **se está volviendo** bastante común. — *In the United States, consumption of chia seeds is becoming quite common.*

The Spanish progressive is also used in past tenses, as well as in the future, the conditional, and the subjunctive. These forms are easy to recognize. An example of the imperfect progressive follows.

Le estábamos hablando al profesor.
Estábamos hablándole al profesor. } *We were speaking to the professor.*

EJERCICIO 6·8

Change the following sentences from the present to the present progressive.

1. Los trabajos científicos crecen rápidamente.

   _____

2. Su dieta equilibrada mejora su salud.

   _____

3. ¿Comes menos alimentos salados?

   _____

4. ¿La cena? La preparo ahora.

   _____

5. Se añaden a los productos horneados.

   _____

¡Vaya más lejos!

◆ Busque la **chía** (*Salvia hispanica*), con sus recetas y sus usos.

◆ Busque la historia del **imperio mexica** (imperio azteca).

◆ Busque la lengua **náhuatl** y los pueblos que la hablan.

Consejos para mejorar nuestra memoria

(Unión Europea)

¿Lleva usted una vida súper complicada? ¿Se le olvidan a veces cosas importantes? Usted puede dejar de preocuparse. Hay técnicas fáciles para **fortalecer** su memoria y **potenciar** su capacidad intelectual.

¿Estamos listos?

1. ¿Se le olvidan a veces cosas importantes? ¿Qué cosas?

   Se me olvida(n) a veces... los nombres, citas (*appointments*), promesas, deberes (*duties*), tareas, fechas, cumpleaños, aniversarios, mis llaves, mis gafas, mi celular, mi cartera o bolsa, artículos que iba a comprar (en las tiendas)...

2. ¿Duerme usted bien? ¿Cuántas horas duerme por la noche normalmente?

   Duermo... ocho/diez/seis horas más o menos.

3. ¿Duerme a veces la siesta/siestita durante el día? ¿Por qué?

   Me siento cansado/a a las... dos/tres/cuatro porque...

4. ¿Hace ejercicio? ¿Qué tipo de ejercicio hace?

   Hago deportes, juego tenis, juego fútbol, practico la natación, hago el footing, hago caminatas, voy de excursión, doy un paseo con el perro, ando en bicicleta, bailo, cultivo el jardín...

5. En su opinión, ¿su rutina diaria es demasiado estresante? ¿Por qué?

   En mi vida hay... tráfico, malas comunicaciones (*connections*) de viaje, mal tiempo...

   Tengo... horas extras, tareas aburridas, preocupaciones profesionales, obligaciones familiares, problemas financieros, problemas de salud...

¡Leamos!

Mejore su memoria! ¿Cuáles de los remedios siguientes practica usted? ¿Cuáles le gustaría practicar?

1. Hacer ejercicio y mantener nuestro **cuerpo** en movimiento: el ejercicio no sólo **ejercita** el cuerpo, también ayuda a ejercitar nuestro **cerebro**.

2. Eliminar los factores de estrés y buscar ayuda para la depresión (en caso necesario). Cualquier cosa que nos genere un gran estrés, como **ira** o la **ansiedad**, empezará con el tiempo a **engullir** las partes de nuestro cerebro responsables de la memoria.

3. Dormir bien por la noche y **echar alguna cabezada** durante el día: **disfrutar de** unas 7–8 horas **seguidas** de **sueño** cada noche aumentará nuestra memoria. Durante el sueño, el cerebro **asienta** los **recuerdos** de la información adquirida recientemente y dormir lo suficiente nos ayudará a pasar por todo el **espectro** de los ciclos nocturnos que son esenciales para un funcionamiento óptimo del cerebro y el cuerpo durante las **horas de vigilia**.

4. **Anotarlo**: si hay algo que queremos **recordar**, escribirlo puede ayudar.

5. Escuchar música: las investigaciones muestran que ciertos tipos de música son muy útiles para evocar recuerdos. La información que se aprende mientras se escucha una canción en particular o una **colección** a menudo se puede evocar pensando en la canción o "**tocándola**" mentalmente.

6. **Alimentar** el cerebro: entre un 50 y un 60 por ciento del **peso** total del cerebro es pura **grasa**, que se utiliza para **aislar** sus miles de millones de células nerviosas. **Cuanto mejor aislada** está una célula, **más rápido** podrá enviar mensajes y más rápido pensaremos. Por eso precisamente se recomienda a los **padres** que alimenten a sus hijos con leche **entera** cuando son pequeños y **que se eviten** las dietas, **ya que** sus cerebros necesitan grasa para **crecer** y funcionar adecuadamente. **Escatimar** en grasas puede ser devastador, **incluso** para un cerebro adulto. **Por lo tanto**, tomar alimentos que contengan una **mezcla saludable** de grasas es de vital importancia para la memoria **a largo plazo**.

7. Visualizar los conceptos: con el **fin** de recordar las cosas, muchas personas necesitan visualizar la información que están estudiando. **Prestar atención** a las fotografías, **gráficos** y otras imágenes que puedan aparecer en nuestro libro de texto o **tratar de** hacer una imagen mental de lo que **intentamos** recordar.

8. **Enseñar** a otra persona: se ha demostrado que leer un material **en voz alta** mejora significativamente la capacidad de recordar el material.

9. Hacer **crucigramas**, leer o jugar a las cartas: los estudios han demostrado que practicar alguna de estas actividades **a diario** no sólo mantiene activo nuestro cerebro, sino que también ayuda a **retrasar** la **pérdida de memoria**, especialmente en las personas que **desarrollan** demencia [...]

10. **Desayunar** bien y **asegurarse** de incluir un huevo: los huevos contienen vitaminas B que ayudan a las células nerviosas a **quemar** glucosa, antioxidantes que protegen contra el **daño** de las neuronas y ácidos grasos omega-3 que mantienen las células nerviosas funcionando a una velocidad óptima. Otros alimentos que se deben **agregar** al desayuno son frutas, verduras y proteínas **magras**. Evitar las grasas trans y el **jarabe de maíz** rico en fructosa.

From Euroresidentes.com, http://como-estudiar.estudiantes.info.

VOCABULARIO

fortalecer	*to strengthen*	ya que	*since*
potenciar	*to reinforce, enhance*	crecer	*to grow*
mejore [mejorar]	*improve*	escatimar	*skimping on,*
cuerpo	*body*		*to skimp on*
ejercita [ejercitar]	*exercises*	incluso	*even, including*
cerebro	*brain*	por lo tanto	*so, therefore*
ira	*anger*	mezcla	*mixture*
(la) ansiedad	*anxiety*	saludable	*healthy, healthful*
engullir	*to swallow*	a largo plazo	*in the long run*
echar alguna cabezada	*take a cat nap*	(el) fin	*objective, goal*
disfrutar de	*enjoy*	prestar atención	*(to) pay attention*
seguidas	*continuous*	gráficos	*graphics,*
sueño	*sleep*		*illustrations*
asienta [asentar]	*stabilizes, fixes*	tratar de	*(to) try to*
recuerdos	*memories*	intentamos [intentar]	*we are trying to*
espectro	*spectrum*	enseñar	*teach*
horas de vigilia	*waking hours*	en voz alta	*out loud, aloud*
anotarlo	*write it down*	(los) crucigramas	*crossword puzzles*
recordar	*to remember*	a diario	*daily, on a daily*
(la) colección	*album*		*basis*
tocándola [tocar]	*playing it*	retrasar	*to postpone, delay*
alimentar	*feed, nourish*	pérdida de memoria	*memory loss*
peso	*weight*	desarrollan [desarrollar]	*are developing*
grasa	*fat*	desayunar	*(have) breakfast*
aislar	*to insulate*	asegurarse	*make sure*
cuanto mejor aislada...	*the better insulated . . .*	quemar	*to burn*
más rápido...	*the more rapidly . . .*	daño	*damage*
(los) padres	*parents*	agregar	*(to) add*
entera	*whole*	magras	*lean, low-fat*
que se eviten [evitarse]	*that they avoid*	(el) jarabe de maíz	*corn syrup*

¿De qué se trata? *Match the beginning of each sentence with the phrase that correctly completes it. There may be more than one correct answer for some items.*

1. _____ El ejercicio   a. la depresión.

2. _____ Eliminar los   b. aumentará la memoria.

3. _____ Buscar ayuda para   c. factores de estrés.

4. _____ Dormir bien   d. lo que queremos recordar.

5. _____ Unas 7–8 horas de sueño   e. ejercita el cuerpo y el cerebro.

6. _____ Anotar   f. pensando en una canción.

7. _____ La información se puede evocar   g. alimenten a los niños con leche entera.

8. _____ Se recomienda que   h. y echar alguna cabezada durante el día.

Opciones *Choose the phrase or phrases that correctly complete each sentence. Include all correct responses.*

1. El movimiento regular ejercita

   a. el cerebro.   b. el cuerpo.   c. la ira.

2. Los factores de estrés pueden conducir a la

   a. depresión.   b. ayuda.   c. pérdida de memoria.

3. Durante el sueño, el cerebro asienta

   a. la información adquirida.   b. los recuerdos.   c. la ansiedad.

4. Dormir lo suficiente nos ayudará a

   a. ponernos más guapos/   b. completar los ciclos   c. aumentar la memoria.
      guapas.   nocturnos.

5. Para evocar recuerdos, sabemos que es útil

   a. tomar notas.   b. escuchar música.   c. "tocar" mentalmente una canción.

6. Según el autor, la comida más importante es

   a. el desayuno.   b. la cena.   c. la comida.

7. Es quizás sorprendente que lo que constituya el elemento más esencial para alimentar el cerebro son

   a. las vitaminas.   b. las grasas.   c. los pescados.

8. Se necesita evitar

   a. las grasas trans.   b. el jarabe de maíz.   c. los huevos.

¿Cierto o falso? *Indicate whether each statement is true or false, using **C** for **cierto** (true) or **F** for **falso** (false). If a statement is false, provide a corrected statement in Spanish.*

1. C F La ira y la ansiedad podrían servir para fortalecer una memoria defectuosa.

   _____

   _____

2. C F Necesitamos pasar por todo el espectro de los ciclos nocturnos esenciales.

   _____

   _____

3. C F Para muchas personas los conceptos se asientan con la visualización.

   _____

   _____

4. C F Enseñar a otra persona siempre ayuda a esta persona a recordar el material.

   _____

   _____

5. C F Los huevos son ricos en vitamina C.

   _____

6. C F Se recomienda que los niños tomen leche descremada.

   _____

7. C F Los crucigramas, lecturas y juegos ayudan a retrasar la pérdida de memoria.

   _____

   _____

8. C F Los ácidos grasos omega-3 mantienen las células nerviosas.

   _____

Reflexiones *Consider the following themes and questions, and discuss them in Spanish.*

1. ¿Ya tiene usted estrategias para compensar las actividades más frenéticas?

_____

_____

_____

2. ¿Hay algunas personas que escogen salidas insalubres o dañinas para remediar sus problemas (por ejemplo, el alcohol, el tabaco, la droga, el juego (*gambling*), los videojuegos)?

_____

_____

_____

3. Discuta las mejores soluciones o las soluciones más efectivas para usted y sus conocidos.

_____

_____

_____

Mi vocabulario *Select the word or phrase that does not belong in each group.*

1. a. tener pensado   b. tratar de   c. intentar   d. transferir

2. a. mejorar   b. forrar   c. fortalecer   d. potenciar

3. a. repostar ·   b. descansar   c. tomar una siesta   d. echar una cabezada

4. a. escatimar   b. ahorrar   c. escarmentar   d. economizar

5. a. fantasma   b. espectro   c. gama   d. repertorio

6. a. anotar   b. recordar   c. escribir   d. apuntar

7. a. engrillar   b. engullir   c. devorar   d. comer

8. a. retrasar   b. posponer   c. aplazar   d. aplastar

9. a. rompecabezas   b. crucigramas   c. cruceros   d. acertijos

10. a. mezcla   b. mezquita   c. conjunto   d. unión

Contrarios *Match each word or phrase with its opposite.*

1. _____ gordo   a. interrumpido

2. _____ seguido   b. sueño

3. _____ quitar   c. magro

4. _____ disminuir   d. jamás

5. _____ vigilia   e. poner

6. _____ a diario   f. no hacer caso

7. _____ prestar atención   g. evitar

8. _____ atraer   h. agregar

9. _____ saludable   i. dañino

Equivalentes *Complete each sentence by substituting words or phrases from the following list for the words or phrases in small type.*

a la larga	competencia	manual	acordarse de
disminuir	objetivo	aprender	encontrarse
se ha probado	aprendiendo	enfocarse en	ruinoso
aumenta	incluyan	tienen que	beneficiosa
luego	tratamos de	combinación	

1. _____ en grasas puede ser _____, incluso para un
   Escatimar   devastador

   cerebro adulto.

2. _____, tomar alimentos que _____ una
   Por lo tanto   contengan

   _____ _____ de grasas es de vital importancia para
   mezcla   saludable

   la memoria _____.
               a largo plazo

3. Visualizar los conceptos: con el _____ de _____ las cosas,
                                     fin   recordar

   muchas personas _____ visualizar la información que están
                    necesitan

   _____.
   estudiando

4. _____ las fotografías, gráficos y otras imágenes que puedan
   Prestar atención a

_____ en nuestro _____ o tratar de hacer una imagen
   aparecer   libro de texto

mental de lo que _____ recordar.
                     intentamos

5. _____ a otra persona: _____ que leer un material en voz
   Enseñar   se ha demostrado

alta _____ significativamente la _____ de recordar el
        mejora   capacidad

material.

¡No se olvide! El infinitivo

The basic, unconjugated form of a verb is called an infinitive. Spanish infinitives end in **-ar**, **-er**, or **-ir**. They have many uses, including the following.

- As the subject of a verb or a sentence. Here, the infinitive functions as a masculine noun. The definite article (**el**) is often omitted.

  Escuchar música es agradable.   *Listening to music is pleasurable.*

- Following verbs of obligation, desire, intentionality, or ability. Some verbs (**deber, necesitar, querer, desear, esperar, dejar, poder**) are followed directly by the infinitive. Other verbs (**ayudar a, tratar de, enseñar a, empezar a**) require a preposition (**a, de, para**) before the infinitive. These usually need to be memorized.

  Debe terminar su trabajo.   *She has to finish her work.*
  Quisiera acostarme temprano.   *I'd like to go to bed early.*
  Podríamos llegar a las seis.   *We would be able to arrive at six o'clock.*
  ¿Sabes nadar?   *Do you know how to swim?*
  Trataron de recordar los hechos.   *They tried to remember the facts.*

- Following prepositions in general (**de, a, para, por, sin**), as the object of the preposition.

  Trabajo **para vivir**.   *I work in order to live.*
  Asistió a la reunión **sin hablar**.   *He attended the meeting without speaking.*
  Gracias **por ayudarme**.   *Thank you for helping me.*

- To express obligation with **tener que** and **hay que**. **Tener que** + infinitive is personal; **hay que** + infinitive is impersonal.

  Tengo que mover el carro.   *I have to move the car.*
  Hay que respetar a los profesores.   *It is necessary to respect the teachers.*

- After a verb of motion (**ir, venir**) followed by the preposition **a**. **Ir a** + infinitive also expresses the near future.

  Vamos a visitar a los vecinos.   *We are going to visit the neighbors.*
  Venían a hablar con mi padre.   *They used to come to speak with my father.*

♦ After verbs of perception (**oír, ver**) in the past. In other tenses, verbs of perception may be followed by a gerund (the -**ando**/-**iendo** form).

| Lo **vi partir**. | *I saw him leave.* |
| Las **oímos cantar**. | *We heard them sing.* |

♦ After **al** (meaning *upon*) to show a certain causality.

| **Al oír** la canción, recordó su juventud. | *Upon hearing the song, he remembered his youth.* |
| **Al despertarme** ayer, llamé a mis amigos. | *Upon waking up yesterday, I phoned my friends.* |

♦ As an impersonal command or suggestion, in the negative or the affirmative. The infinitive often replaces the command form in recipes and other instructions.

Pelar y **picar** finamente la cebolla.	*Peel and finely chop the onion.*
Eliminar los factores de estrés.	*Eliminate stress factors.*
Anotarlo.	*Write it down.*
No fumar en la playa.	*No smoking on the beach.*

EJERCICIO
7·8

List each infinitive in these excerpts, then explain its use, using the explanations in ¡**No se olvide!**

1. Hacer ejercicio y mantener nuestro cuerpo en movimiento.

_____ _____

_____ _____

2. El ejercicio no sólo ejercita el cuerpo, también ayuda a ejercitar nuestro cerebro.

_____ _____

3. Cualquier cosa que nos genere un gran estrés... empezará... a engullir las partes de nuestro cerebro responsables de la memoria.

_____ _____

4. Disfrutar de unas 7–8 horas seguidas de sueño cada noche aumentará nuestra memoria.

_____ _____

5. Si hay algo que queremos recordar, escribirlo puede ayudar.

_____ _____

_____ _____

_____ _____

6. Ciertos tipos de música son muy útiles para evocar recuerdos.

_____ _____

7. Cuanto mejor aislada está una célula, más rápido podrá enviar mensajes.

_____ _____

8. Escatimar en grasas puede ser devastador.

_____   _____

_____   _____

9. Visualizar los conceptos: con el fin de recordar las cosas.

_____   _____

_____   _____

10. Muchas personas necesitan visualizar la información que están estudiando.

_____   _____

11. Tratar de hacer una imagen mental de lo que intentamos recordar.

_____   _____

_____   _____

_____   _____

12. Otros alimentos que se deben agregar al desayuno son frutas, verduras y proteínas magras.

_____   _____

¡Vaya más lejos!

- Haga tarjetas personales para el nuevo vocabulario español.
- Haga tarjetas mnemotécnicas para otras materias que esté estudiando.
- Busque sitios en internet de **crucigramas fáciles** en español. Inténtelos.
- Busque sitios en internet de **juegos de memoria** o **entrenamiento de la memoria** en español. Intente algunos juegos.

La granada
Juan Ramón Jiménez (España)

Juan Ramón Jiménez Mantecón (1881, Moguer, Huelva, España–1958, San Juan de Puerto Rico) fue un poeta español, ganador del Premio Nobel de Literatura en 1956. Su obra más destacada es la narración lírica *Platero y yo: Elejía andaluza* (1914–1917). Siempre **dirigiéndose** a Platero, su querido burro, el narrador-poeta evoca con nostalgia la vida en su pueblecito **natal** de Andalucía.

¿Estamos listos?

1. ¿Le gustan las frutas? ¿Toma mucha fruta? ¿Cuáles prefiere?

   Prefiero la(s)/los... manzanas, naranjas, toronjas (*grapefruit*), limones, limas, bananas, peras, uvas (*grapes*), cerezas (*cherries*), duraznos (*peaches*) [LAT. AM.], melocotones (*peaches*) [SP.], ciruelas (*plums*), nectarinas, albaricoques (*apricots*), piña (*pineapple*), bayas (*berries*), fresas (*strawberries*), frambuesas (*raspberries*), arándanos (*blueberries*), moras (*blackberries*)...

2. Según usted, ¿qué frutas son "exóticas" o inusuales? ¿Puede comprarlas cerca? ¿Las toma a veces?

   He probado... mangos, papayas, plátanos (*plantains*), caquis [M.] (*persimmons*), granadas (*pomegranates*), chirimoyas (*pawpaws*), lichis, quinotos (*kumquats*), maracuyás [M.] (*passion fruit*), nopal [M.] (*prickly pear*)...

3. Si un manzano produce manzanas y un naranjo produce naranjas, ¿puede usted nombrar otros árboles y plantas que producen frutas comunes?

   Hay... el granado (granadas), el cerezo (cerezas), el toronjo (toronjas), el ciruelo (ciruelas), el plátano (plátanos), el duraznero (duraznos), el arándano (arándanos), el mango (mangos), el bananero (bananas), el albaricoquero (albaricoques), el limonero (limones), el limero (limas), el melocotonero (melocotones), el peral (peras), el ananá (piñas), las vides (uvas)...

4. ¿Cómo describimos las frutas? ¿Qué adjetivos utilizamos?

   Usamos adjetivos que describen su color (rojo/a, amarillo/a, verde, anaranjado/a, azul, morado/a (*purple*), de color púrpura, de color marrón...), su aspecto (hermoso/a, feo/a, grande, pequeño/a, redondo/a (*round*), esférico/a, largo/a (*long*), con/sin semillas (*with/without seeds*), con/sin piel (*skin/skinless*)...), su textura (blando/a (*soft*), duro/a, maduro/a (*ripe*), verde, inmaduro/a (*unripe*), liso/a (*smooth*), áspero/a, rugoso/a (*rough*), espinoso/a (*prickly*), grueso/a (*thick*), seco/a, húmedo/a (*damp*), mojado/a (*wet*)...), su gusto/sabor (jugoso/a (*juicy*), dulce, fresco/a, amargo/a (*bitter*), ácido/a, agrio/a, con sabor a limón...), sus usos (comidas, jugos, ensaladas, bebidas, medicamentos, pasteles, conservas...)...

¡Leamos!

Platero y yo: Capítulo 96

¡Qué hermosa esta granada, Platero! Me la ha mandado Aguedilla, **escogida** de lo mejor de su **arroyo** de las Monjas. Ninguna fruta me hace pensar, como ésta, en la **frescura** del agua que la **nutre**. **Estalla de** salud fresca y fuerte. ¿Vamos a comérnosla?

¡Platero, qué **grato** gusto amargo y seco el de la piel, dura y **agarrada** como una **raíz** a la tierra! Ahora, el primer **dulzor**, **aurora** hecha breve rubí, de los **granos** que **se vienen pegados** a la piel. Ahora, Platero, el núcleo **apretado**, sano, completo, con sus **velos** finos, el exquisito tesoro de **amatistas** comestibles, jugosas y fuertes, como el corazón de no sé qué **reina** joven. ¡Qué llena está, Platero! Ten, come. ¡Qué rica! ¡Con qué **fruición** se pierden los dientes en la abundante **sazón** alegre y roja! Espera, que no puedo hablar. Da al gusto una sensación como la del ojo perdido en el laberinto de colores **inquietos** de un calidoscopio. **¡Se acabó!**

Yo ya no tengo granados, Platero. Tú no viste los del **corralón** de la **bodega** de la calle de las Flores. Íbamos por las tardes... Por las **tapias caídas** se veían los **corrales** de las casas de la calle del Coral, cada uno con su encanto, y el **campo**, y el río. Se oía el **toque** de las **cornetas** de los **carabineros** y la **fragua de Sierra**... Era el descubrimiento de una parte nueva del pueblo que no era la mía, en su plena poesía diaria. Caía el sol y los granados **se incendiaban** como ricos tesoros, junto al **pozo en sombra** que **desbarataba** la **higuera** llena de **salamanquesas**...

¡Granada, fruta de Moguer, **gala** de su **escudo**! ¡Granadas abiertas al sol **grana** del **ocaso**! ¡Granadas del **huerto** de las Monjas, de la **cañada** del Peral, de Sabariego, con los reposados valles **hondos** con arroyos donde se queda el cielo rosa, como en mi pensamiento, hasta bien entrada la noche!

Juan Ramón Jiménez, capítulo 96 from *Platero y yo: Elejía andaluza* (Madrid: Editorial Calleja, 1917).

VOCABULARIO			
dirigiéndose [dirigirse]	*addressing, speaking to*	velos	*veils (membranes)*
natal	*native*	amatistas	*amethysts*
escogida	*chosen*	reina	*queen*
arroyo	*stream*	(la) fruición	*delight*
frescura	*freshness*	(la) sazón	*ripeness*
nutre [nutrir]	*nourishes*	inquietos	*lively, restless*
estalla [estallar] de	*(it) is bursting with*	se acabó [acabarse]	*it's finished, that's that!*
grato	*agreeable, pleasant*	(el) corralón	*large dooryard*
agarrada	*clutched tight*	bodega	*wine shop, bar*
(la) raíz	*root*	tapias	*low walls*
(el) dulzor	*sweetness*	caídas	*crumbling, fallen*
aurora	*dawn*	(los) corrales	*courtyards*
granos	*seeds*	campo	*fields, countryside*
se vienen [venirse] pegados	*are clinging*	(el) toque	*(bugle) call*
		cornetas	*bugles*
apretado	*tiny, compact*	carabineros	*national police* [SP.]

fragua de Sierra	*traditional iron forge in the Sierra Morena*	salamanquesas	*lizards*
		gala	*ornament*
se incendiaban [incendiarse]	*caught fire* [FIG.]	escudo	*shield, coat of arms*
		grana	*deep red*
pozo	*(water) well*	ocaso	*sunset*
en sombra	*shaded*	huerto	*orchard*
desbarataba [desbaratar]	*was ruining, was damaging*	cañada	*valley, ravine*
higuera	*fig tree*	hondos	*deep*

EJERCICIO 8·1

¿De qué se trata? *Match each item with its description.*

1. _____ Aguedilla
2. _____ Moguer
3. _____ Platero
4. _____ Juan Ramón Jiménez
5. _____ el arroyo de las Monjas
6. _____ El Peral y Sabariego
7. _____ la fragua de Sierra

a. el autor de este cuento
b. el sitio donde crecen los granados
c. la fábrica de hierro en las montañas
d. varios lugares andaluces
e. la vecina que ha mandado la granada
f. el burro del narrador
g. la aldea natal del autor

EJERCICIO 8·2

Opciones *Choose the phrase or phrases that correctly complete each sentence. Include all correct responses.*

1. La amiga que le ha mandado al narrador una bella granada se llama

   a. Sierra.   b. Aguedilla.   c. Platero.

2. La granada le parece

   a. hermosa.   b. fresca.   c. saludable.

3. Según el autor, la frescura de esta granada viene

   a. de la piel.   b. de su color.   c. del arroyo de la Monjas.

4. Existe un gran contraste entre la piel dura y seca y

   a. las "amatistas" jugosas.   b. los granos rojos.   c. el gusto amargo.

5. En su juventud el narrador iba por las tardes a

   a. mirar la puesta del sol.　　　　b. la calle del Coral.　　　　c. admirar el encanto del
   　　　　　　　　　　　　　　　　　　　　　　　　　　　　　　　　barrio antiguo.

6. Por esas tardes, lo que el narrador puede oír cerca de la bodega es

   a. las cornetas de los carabineros.　　b. las salamanquesas.　　c. la fragua de Sierra.

7. Por las mismas tardes, el narrador veía

   a. los granados rojos brillantes.　　b. el ocaso del sol.　　c. las tapias caídas.

EJERCICIO
8·3

¿Cierto o falso? *Indicate whether each statement is true or false, using* **C** *for* **cierto** *(true) or* **F** *for* **falso** *(false). If a statement is false, provide a corrected statement in Spanish.*

1.　C　F　El burro y el narrador comparten la fruta con gran placer.

   _____

2.　C　F　El narrador no tiene buenos recuerdos de esos sentimientos y sensaciones.

   _____

3.　C　F　El autor tiene todavía un huerto importante de granados.

   _____

4.　C　F　Afirma que el calidoscopio era su juguete preferido.

   _____

5.　C　F　En el pasado le gustaba al autor pasear por la vieja calle de las Flores.

   _____

6.　C　F　La higuera estaba dañando el pozo de ese barrio.

   _____

7.　C　F　Para él, la granada representa mucho más que un simple alimento.

   _____

   _____

EJERCICIO

8·4

Reflexiones *Consider the following themes and questions, and discuss them in Spanish.*

1. ¿Qué sentidos evoca el narrador? Según usted, ¿cuál de las evocaciones es la más exitosa (*successful*)? ¿Puede saborear, ver, oír, tocar, sentir lo que describe Jiménez?

_____

_____

_____

_____

2. ¿Hay en su vida un lugar que le trae sentimientos o sensaciones similares? ¿Recuerda usted un alimento o plato asociado a este lugar?

_____

_____

_____

_____

EJERCICIO

8·5

*Read the following passage out loud, paying particular attention to the hard **c** sound (before **a**, **o**) as well as the sound **que** (another form of hard **c**). Then explain whether or not you think this passage is poetic.*

Por las tapias **ca**ídas se veían los **co**rrales de las **ca**sas de la **ca**lle del **Co**ral, **ca**da uno **co**n su en**ca**nto, y el **ca**mpo, y el río. Se oía el to**que** de las **co**rnetas de los **ca**rabineros y la fragua de Sierra.

_____

_____

_____

_____

EJERCICIO

8·6

Mi vocabulario *Select the word that does not belong in each group.*

1. a. alba   b. pueblo   c. aldea   d. ciudad

2. a. tapias   b. muros   c. paredes   d. parejas

3. a. huerto   b. huelga   c. campo   d. jardín

4. a. amatistas   b. rubís   c. auroras   d. diamantes

5. a. grato   b. agradable   c. simpático   d. agarrado

6. a. cuenca   b. cuento   c. cañada   d. valle

7. a. higuera   b. granado   c. peral   d. pera

EJERCICIO 8·7

Contrarios *Match each word with its opposite.*

1. _____ ocaso   a. altos

2. _____ jugoso   b. dolor

3. _____ grueso   c. madrugada

4. _____ áspero   d. tranquilos

5. _____ hondos   e. liso

6. _____ fruición   f. seco

7. _____ inquietos   g. dulce

8. _____ amargo   h. delicado

EJERCICIO 8·8

Equivalentes *Match each expression from Jiménez's story with its more mundane equivalent. Two expressions are covered by the same answer.*

1. _____ aurora hecha breve rubí

2. _____ el corazón de no sé qué reina joven

3. _____ el exquisito tesoro de amatistas comestibles

4. _____ Espera, que no puedo hablar.

5. _____ Ten, come.

6. _____ ¡Qué rica!

7. _____ ¡Se acabó!

8. _____ arroyos donde se queda el cielo rosa

a. Te ofrezco esta granada.

b. El jugo de granada es de sangre real.

c. Es deliciosa.

d. Ya está consumada.

e. Ya estoy comiendo.

f. La puesta del sol colorea de rosa los arroyos.

g. Las semillas parecen piedras preciosas.

¡No se olvide! El participio pasado (I)

The Spanish past participle (when used with conjugated forms of the auxiliary verb **haber**) forms the present perfect tense. The present perfect expresses a completed past action relatively close to the present.

Ya **he comido**.	*I've already eaten.*
Me la **ha mandado** Aguedilla.	*Aguedilla sent it to me.*

To form the past participle of -**ar** verbs, add -**ado** to the stem (**pagar** > **pagado**); for -**er** and -**ir** verbs add -**ido** (**comer** > **comido, dirigir** > **dirigido**). Some verbs have irregular past participles: **abrir** > **abierto, decir** > **dicho, escribir** > **escrito, hacer** > **hecho, morir** > **muerto, poner** > **puesto, romper** > **roto, ver** > **visto, volver** > **vuelto**. Compound forms of these verbs also have irregular past participles: **describir** > **descrito, prever** > **previsto**.

Most past participles can also be used as adjectives (for example, **aurora *hecha* breve rubí, el núcleo *apretado***). These normally follow the noun and agree with it in gender and number. (See Chapter 25 for more uses of the past participle.)

EJERCICIO
8·9

In the following examples from the reading, identify (a) the past participle used as an adjective, (b) its infinitive, and (c) the infinitive's English equivalent.

1. escogida de lo mejor de su arroyo de las Monjas

   a. _____   b. _____   c. _____

2. dura y agarrada como una raíz

   a. _____   b. _____   c. _____

3. aurora hecha breve rubí

   a. _____   b. _____   c. _____

4. los granos que se vienen pegados a la piel

   a. _____   b. _____   c. _____

5. el núcleo apretado, sano, completo

   a. _____   b. _____   c. _____

6. una sensación como la del ojo perdido en el laberinto

   a. _____   b. _____   c. _____

7. Por las tapias caídas se veían los corrales.

   a. _____   b. _____   c. _____

8. ¡Granadas abiertas al sol grana del ocaso!

   a. _____   b. _____   c. _____

9. con los reposados valles hondos

a. _____ b. _____ c. _____

10. hasta bien entrada la noche

a. _____ b. _____ c. _____

¡Vaya más lejos!

- Busque información sobre **Andalucía**, España.
- Busque información sobre **Juan Ramón Jiménez** y su obra.
- Visite un mercado al aire libre en su ciudad y pruebe algunas frutas nuevas.

VIDA COTIDIANA

Cómo conducir de forma eficiente, en diez consejos

Josep Camós (Unión Europea)

Cualquiera que sea nuestra experiencia en conducir y en **coches, tendemos todos a darlos por sentados**. De vez en cuando hay que volver a lo básico.

¿Estamos listos?

1. ¿Conduce usted? ¿Cuándo aprendió a conducir? ¿Quién le enseñó a conducir? ¿Sabe manejar un carro mecánico (con cambio manual)? ¿O conduce únicamente coches con cambio automático? ¿Tiene coche?

   Sí, necesito un coche porque... estoy muy ocupado/a, no hay transporte público, el transporte no es práctico, hace mal tiempo, trabajo lejos de mi casa, tengo que recoger a mis hijos, vivo en el campo, necesito el coche para mi trabajo...

2. Si conduce, por ejemplo, al trabajo o a la universidad, ¿toma generalmente calles de la ciudad? ¿la carretera (*highway*)? ¿la autopista (*freeway*)?

3. ¿Ya ha conducido hoy? Si ha conducido, ¿cuáles de estas acciones no ha hecho usted hoy día?

   Hoy, no (me) he... entrado/subido al coche/carro, colocado/abrochado el cinturón de seguridad, arrancado (*start*), girado a la derecha, girado a la izquierda, dado un giro total (*U-turn*), tomado la autopista, cambiado/pasado de marcha (*change gears*), acelerado, frenado (*brake*), detenido/parado (*stop*), llenado el tanque, pasado/rebasado a otro vehículo, cambiado de carril (*lane*), bajado del coche...

4. ¿Qué mantenimiento periódico necesita su coche? ¿Le dio un mantenimiento recientemente? ¿Va usted regularmente a un mecánico? ¿Le gusta a usted hacer sus propias reparaciones?

   Se debe periódicamente revisar... el nivel de aceite (*oil*), la presión de los neumáticos, los frenos (*brakes*), las bujías (*spark plugs*), la batería, el limpiaparabrisas (*windshield wipers*), la correa de distribución (*timing belt*), los fluidos y líquidos, el refrigerante...

5. ¿Qué partes de su coche necesitaron reparaciones últimamente?

   Últimamente tuve que reparar... el motor, la batería, el carburador, las ruedas (*wheels*), los frenos, los neumáticos, el volante (*steering wheel*), la caja de cambios (*gear box*), la transmisión manual o automática, el silenciador (*muffler*), el aire acondicionado, la calefacción (*heating*), el radiador, el maletero (*trunk*), el capó/toldo (*hood*), el portaequipajes (*roof rack*), el equipo de sonido, el sistema eléctrico, el sistema informático...

¡Leamos!

1. Observe las instrucciones de mantenimiento de su coche y **revise** periódicamente el **nivel** de **aceite**.

   Porque un coche mal cuidado es un coche que consume más y contamina mucho más. Cada motor **merece** un programa de mantenimiento, unas **revisiones**, unos cambios de aceite. Cada coche tiene un libro de mantenimiento donde **se especifica** qué **plazos** deben **transcurrir** entre revisión y revisión. **No llevar** este mantenimiento **al día** es exponerse a **gastar** más y a **quedarse tirado en el momento menos pensado**.

2. Revise la presión de los neumáticos cada mes.

   Porque unos neumáticos con una presión inferior a la **marcada** por el fabricante pueden aumentar el consumo hasta en un 4% según **datos** de la Agencia Internacional de la Energía, además de ser un **pasaporte** para el **desgaste** prematuro e irregular del único punto de contacto del vehículo con el **suelo**.

3. Retire **peso** innecesario del maletero o de los **asientos traseros**.

   Porque **cuanto más cargado** vaya el coche, más tendrá que trabajar el motor para **arrastrarlo** y más **carburante** consumirá. En un maletero **no pintan nada** las cosas de la playa cuando en la calle **está granizando**, de la misma forma que no tenemos por qué **acarrear** una **lata** de aceite si el coche no tiene **pérdidas**. Diez cosas que pesan "un **kilillo** de nada" **suman** 10 Kg.

4. Cierre las ventanas, sobre todo cuando circule a alta velocidad y retire el portaequipajes cuando lo lleve **vacío**.

   Porque así se reduce la resistencia al aire y se puede disminuir el consumo de carburante y las emisiones de CO_2 hasta en un 10%, según datos de la Comisión Europea. Circular por carretera o autopista con las ventanas abiertas o con la **baca montada** equivale a **cargarse** buena parte de los estudios de aerodinámica que **se llevan a cabo** cuando se diseña el vehículo.

5. Utilice el aire acondicionado sólo cuando sea necesario.

   Porque el uso excesivo de aire acondicionado aumenta el consumo de carburante y las emisiones de CO_2 hasta en un 5%, según datos de la Comisión Europea. **Claro que**, **puestos a elegir**, circulando a alta velocidad siempre será mejor utilizar el aire acondicionado que las ventanas abiertas.

6. **Inicie la marcha en cuanto encienda** el motor y **apáguelo** cuando **esté detenido** durante más de un minuto.

   Porque los motores modernos están diseñados para ser más eficientes cuando el conductor comienza el trayecto en cuanto enciende el motor. **Atrás** quedaron los tiempos del "enciéndelo ya y **deja que se vaya calentando**". Hoy en día la inyección de **combustible** se realiza considerando, entre otros muchos parámetros, la temperatura del motor. Y porque gastar con el coche **parado** es **de tontos**. Se apaga cuando no hace falta, se enciende cuando se necesita y **ya está**.

7. Conduzca a velocidades razonables y, sobre todo, hágalo **con suavidad**.

   Porque cada vez que aceleramos bruscamente el motor consume más carburante y produce más CO_2. Porque cada vez que **frenamos** bruscamente **sometemos** a un **sobreesfuerzo** tonto a los sistemas de **frenado** y de suspensión y a las ruedas y neumáticos.

Y porque acelerar fuertemente para **acabar frenando al cabo de un suspiro** es **tirar el dinero**. No vale la pena. **A corto plazo**, la suavidad al volante es economía para nuestro **bolsillo**. **A largo plazo**, la suavidad al volante es vida para el vehículo.

8. Intente anticiparse al tráfico.

   Porque de esta manera nos evitaremos los extremos a los que refiere el punto anterior. Para anticiparse es **básico** mantener siempre una distancia razonable en relación con el resto de vehículos, observar y entender lo que nos **rodea** y decidir y **actuar** cuanto antes, para evitar que las situaciones **nos pillen con el paso cambiado**.

9. **Cambie de marcha cuanto antes** mejor.

   Porque las marchas largas (4ª, 5ª y 6ª) son las que menos carburantes consumen, según datos de la Comisión Europea. Claro que de nada servirá pasar a una marcha larga si **nos empeñamos en** acelerar bruscamente para recuperar velocidad a toda costa tras haber cambiado de marcha. La idea es que pasemos de marcha para **relajar** el motor, haciéndolo trabajar al mínimo régimen de **vueltas** posible.

10. Considere la posibilidad de **compartir** coche para ir a trabajar o durante su tiempo libre.

    Porque de esta manera se reduce el tráfico y el consumo de carburante. Cuando varias personas comparten una necesidad de movilidad, lo inteligente es economizar **recursos**. Buscar excusas **peregrinas** es lo más parecido a **enrocarse** en el consumo irracional. Si se puede hacer y todos los ocupantes son gente **honrada**, **limpia** y **aseada**, ¿por qué no compartir el viaje? Consejos de bolsillo para beneficio de nuestro bolsillo. Ni más ni menos.

Josep Camós, excerpt from Circula Seguro, http://www.circulaseguro.com.

---

cargarse	*destroy, ruin*	tirar el dinero	*throwing money*
se llevan [llevarse] a cabo	*are carried out, conducted*	a corto plazo	*down the drain* *in the short run*
claro que	*it's obvious that*	bolsillo	*pocketbook*
puestos a elegir	*given the choice*	a largo plazo	*in the long run*
inicie [iniciar] la marcha	*start driving*	básico	*basic*
en cuanto (+ SUBJ.)	*as soon as (+ VERB)*	rodea [rodear]	*surrounds*
encienda [encender]	*turns on, starts*	actuar	*to act, react*
apáguelo [apagar]	*turn it off*	nos pillen [pillar] con el paso cambiado	*take us by surprise*
esté [estar] detenido	*you are stopped*		
atrás	*in the past*	cambie [cambiar] de marcha	*change gears*
deja [dejar] que se vaya [ir] calentando [calentarse]	*let it warm up*	cuanto antes	*as soon as possible*
(el) combustible	*fuel*	nos empeñamos [empeñarse] en	*persist in*
parado	*stopped*	relajar	*to ease, relax*
de tontos	*foolish, crazy*	vueltas	*revolutions*
ya está [estar]	*there you have it, that's it*	compartir	*sharing*
		recursos	*resources*
con suavidad	*gently, smoothly*	peregrinas	*ridiculous, dumb*
frenamos [frenar]	*we brake*	enrocarse	*to trap or "castle" yourself*
sometemos [someter]	*we subject*		
sobreesfuerzo	*overexertion*	honrada	*honest*
frenado	*braking*	limpia	*clean*
acabar frenando	*to end up braking*	aseada	*neat, clean*
al cabo de un suspiro	*in a heartbeat, in the blink of an eye*		

EJERCICIO
9·1

¿De qué se trata? *Match the beginning of each sentence with the phrase that correctly completes each driving tip, as given in the reading. There may be more than one correct answer for some items.*

1. _____ Observe las instrucciones   a. la presión de los neumáticos.

2. _____ Cierre las ventanas   b. encienda el motor.

3. _____ Retire el portaequipajes   c. cuando esté detenido más de un minuto.

4. _____ Revise cada mes   d. a velocidades razonables y con suavidad.

5. _____ Inicie la marcha en cuanto   e. al tráfico.

6. _____ Apague el motor   f. de mantenimiento de su coche.

7. _____ Considere la posibilidad   g. de compartir coche.

8. _____ Retire peso innecesario del   h. cuando circule a alta velocidad.

9. _____ Intente anticiparse   i. cuando lo lleve vacío.

10. _____ Conduzca   j. maletero y de los asientos traseros.

EJERCICIO

9·2

Opciones *Choose the phrase or phrases that correctly complete each sentence. Include all correct responses.*

1. Todos los coches merecen

    a. unas revisiones.   b. un mantenimiento.   c. el aceite.

2. Los neumáticos con una presión inferior pueden

    a. tocar el suelo.   b. desgastarse muy pronto.   c. aumentar el consumo.

3. El motor tendrá que trabajar más si

    a. el maletero está vacío.   b. hay peso innecesario.   c. el coche tiene portaequipajes.

4. Tenemos que acarrear una lata de aceite si el motor

    a. está bien cuidado.   b. es viejo.   c. tiene pérdidas.

5. Es mejor cerrar las ventanas

    a. para reducir las emisiones.   b. cuando circule a alta velocidad.   c. para disminuir el uso de carburante.

6. Cuando circule a alta velocidad será mejor

    a. usar el aire acondicionado.   b. abrir las ventanas.   c. cerrar las ventanas.

7. No frenar bruscamente para

    a. prolongar la vida del coche.   b. tirar el dinero.   c. comprar un bolsillo.

8. Compartir coche es una práctica

    a. peregrina.   b. extravagante.   c. económica.

EJERCICIO

9·3

¿Cierto o falso? *Indicate whether each statement is true or false, using* **C** *for* **cierto** *(true) or* **F** *for* **falso** *(false). If a statement is false, provide a corrected statement in Spanish.*

1. C F No hay que leer el libro de mantenimiento de su coche.

    _____

2. C F Los neumáticos con una presión inferior a la marcada por el fabricante pueden disminuir el consumo de carburante.

    _____

    _____

3. C F Conducir con suavidad alarga la vida del coche.

    _____

4. C F Circulando a alta velocidad siempre será mejor utilizar el aire acondicionado que las ventanas abiertas.

_____

_____

5. C F Gastar carburante con el coche parado es razonable.

_____

6. C F Cada vez que aceleramos bruscamente el motor produce más CO_2.

_____

_____

7. C F Las marchas largas (4ª, 5ª y 6ª) son las que más carburante consumen.

_____

_____

8. C F Es mejor cambiar de marcha sin acelerar bruscamente después.

_____

_____

EJERCICIO
9·4

Reflexiones *Consider the following themes and questions, and discuss them in Spanish.*

1. En su opinión, en el futuro, ¿los coches particulares serán el medio de transporte preferido? ¿Por qué? ¿Por qué no?

_____

_____

_____

_____

2. Y, ¿qué hay de países como China e India, donde el índice de propiedad de automóviles sigue creciendo?

_____

_____

_____

_____

3. Si pudiera, ¿renunciaría a su coche? ¿En qué circunstancias?

_____

_____

_____

_____

4. ¿Puede a veces compartir un auto con sus amigos o colaboradores? ¿Ya ha intentado usar un servicio de coche compartido? ¿Qué le ha parecido?

_____

_____

_____

_____

5. ¿Tiene usted experiencia con los automóviles híbridos o eléctricos? ¿Qué opinión tiene de ellos?

_____

_____

_____

_____

EJERCICIO 9·5

Mi vocabulario *Select the word or phrase that does not belong in each group.*

1. a. incumplimiento   b. mantenimiento   c. atención   d. cuidado

2. a. automóvil   b. carro   c. coche   d. carroza

3. a. merecer   b. merendar   c. ser digno de   d. valer

4. a. atascado   b. tirado   c. parado   d. arrastrado

5. a. combustible   b. gasolina   c. comestible   d. carburante

6. a. tiempo   b. plaza   c. plazo   d. período

7. a. sobreesfuerzo   b. sobredicho   c. lucha   d. laboriosidad

8. a. desgastes   b. ruedas   c. neumáticos   d. llantas

9. a. rejilla   b. portaequipajes   c. mejilla   d. baca

10. a. carretera   b. calle   c. autopista   d. carreta

11. a. manejar   b. pilotar   c. manear   d. conducir

12. a. reducir   b. acordar   c. disminuir   d. acortar

Contrarios *Match each word or phrase with its opposite.*

1. _____ apagar
2. _____ atrás
3. _____ ahorrar
4. _____ peregrino
5. _____ acelerar
6. _____ enfriarse
7. _____ aseado
8. _____ vacío
9. _____ detenerse

a. gastar
b. cargado
c. frenar
d. calentarse
e. encender
f. más adelante
g. ordinario
h. descuidado
i. actuar

Equivalentes *Complete each sentence by substituting words or phrases from the following list for the words or phrases in small type.*

calmar	se desconecta	mantenido	cambiemos
detenido	no tienen sentido	carburante	estúpido
ocurre	se conecta	fugas	poluciona
consumir	gasta	un contenedor	otras muchas reglas generales
llevar	rotaciones		

1. Porque un coche mal _____ es un coche que _____
   <small>cuidado</small>   <small>consume</small>

   más y _____ mucho más.
   <small>contamina</small>

2. En un maletero _____ las cosas de la playa cuando... está granizando,
   <small>no pintan nada</small>

   de la misma forma que no tenemos por qué _____
   <small>acarrear</small>

   _____ de aceite si el coche no tiene _____.
   <small>una lata</small>   <small>pérdidas</small>

3. Hoy en día la inyección de _____ _____
   <small>combustible</small>   <small>se realiza</small>

   considerando, entre _____, la temperatura del motor.
   <small>otros muchos parámetros</small>

4. Y porque _____ con el coche _____ es
   <small>gastar</small>   <small>parado</small>

   _____.
   <small>de tontos</small>

5. _____ cuando no hace falta, _____ cuando
   Se apaga   se enciende

   se necesita y ya está.

6. La idea es que _____ de marcha para _____
   pasemos   relajar

   el motor, haciéndolo trabajar al mínimo régimen de _____ posible.
   vueltas

¡No se olvide! El presente de subjuntivo

Unlike English, where the subjunctive mood is considered formal speech, in Spanish it is natural, everyday usage. In reading, the present subjunctive is easy to recognize if you keep in mind its basic forms and the typical sentence patterns that require it.

Forms of the present subjunctive

For -**ar** verbs, the present subjunctive is conjugated by changing **a** to **e**, using the forms of the present indicative. In addition, the first-person singular (**yo**) and third-person singular (**él, ella, usted**) forms are identical. Context generally clarifies the subject.

-**ar** VERBS **hablar** *to speak, talk*	
que (yo) habl**e** español	*that I speak Spanish*
que (tú) habl**es** español	*that you* [FAM.] *speak Spanish*
que (él, ella, usted) habl**e** español	*that he/she/you* [FORM.] *speak Spanish*
que (nosotros/as) habl**emos** español	*that we speak Spanish*
que (vosotros/as) habl**éis** español	*that you* [FAM. PL.] [SP.] *speak Spanish*
que (ellos, ellas, Uds.) habl**en** español	*that they/you speak Spanish*

For -**er** and -**ir** verbs, both **e** and **i** in the present indicative forms are changed to **a** in the present subjunctive. The first-person singular (**yo**) form is identical to the third-person singular (**él, ella, usted**) form.

-**er** AND -**ir** VERBS		
	comer *to eat*	**vivir** *to live*
que (yo)	com**a**	viv**a**
que (tú)	com**as**	viv**as**
que (él, ella, usted)	com**a**	viv**a**
que (nosotros/as)	com**amos**	viv**amos**
que (vosotros/as)	com**áis**	viv**áis**
que (ellos, ellas, Uds.)	com**an**	viv**an**

Consult a verb chart for a complete list of stem-changing and irregular verbs in the present subjunctive.

* Stem-changing verbs (-**ar**, -**er**, and -**ir**) in the present indicative have the same changes in the present subjunctive, for example, **pensar** > **piense, entender** > **entienda, dormir** > **duerma.**

- Verbs that have an irregularity in the **yo** form of the present indicative, for example, **conocer (conozco), decir (digo), hacer (hago), poner (pongo), salir (salgo), tener (tengo), ver (veo)**, have the same irregularity in all persons of the present subjunctive: **conozca, diga, haga, ponga, salga, tenga, vea**.

- **Dar** and **estar** are regular, except for the addition of accent marks: **dé (dar)** and **esté, estéis**, and **estén (estar)**.

- Four verbs have irregular stems in the present subjunctive, though their endings are regular: **haber (hay-)** > **haya, ir (vay-)** > **vaya, saber (sep-)** > **sepa, ser (se-)** > **sea**.

- If the stem of an **-ar** verb ends in **c**, **g**, or **z**, all forms of the present subjunctive show the following changes: **c > qu, g > gu**, and **z > c**. Endings are the regular present subjunctive endings.

buscar *to look for*	que (yo) **busque**, que (tú) **busques**, etc.
llegar *to arrive*	que (yo) **llegue**, que (tú) **llegues**, etc.
empezar *to begin*	que (yo) **empiece**, que (tú) **empieces**, etc.

- If the stem of an **-er** or **-ir** verb ends in **g**, **gu**, or **c**, all forms of the present subjunctive show the following changes: **g > j, gu > g**, and **c > z**. Endings are the regular present subjunctive endings.

recoger *to gather*	que (yo) **recoja**, que (tú) **recojas**, etc.
seguir *to follow*	que (yo) **siga**, que (tú) **sigas**, etc.
vencer *to defeat*	que (yo) **venza**, que (tú) **venzas**, etc.

Uses of the present subjunctive

The present subjunctive is typically seen in a dependent (noun) clause that follows a verb in the indicative + **que**. The main clause and the dependent clause have different subjects: **Quiero que te vayas**. *I want you to leave.*

The main clause expresses the speaker's or writer's feelings about an action or state of being which usually has not yet occurred. (This explains why the English equivalent is often in the future tense.) The main clause often has an impersonal subject. Main clauses that determine the subjunctive can be roughly divided into three categories.

- Expressions of doubt, uncertainty, and expectation

Dudamos que venga.	{ *We doubt (that) she is coming.* *We doubt (that) she will come.*
Espero que llueva.	*I hope it will rain.*
No es seguro que tengamos éxito.	*It isn't certain that we'll succeed.*

- Requests, recommendations, advice, demands, and needs

¿Deseas que pague?	*Do you want me to pay?*
Es preferible que lleguen temprano.	*It's preferable that they arrive early.*

- Verbs of emotion or attitude

Temo que haga demasiado frío.	*I'm afraid it will be too cold.*
Se alegra que sea viernes.	*She's happy it's Friday.*

¡Ojo!

The verb in the main clause determines the present subjunctive. It is usually in the present indicative; it can also be in the present perfect, the future, or the imperative.

Conjunctions with the subjunctive

Conjunctions in adverbial clauses followed by the subjunctive include expressions of time. The subjunctive is used in the dependent clause when the main clause refers to a future action or state, or when it is in the imperative, and when the action in the dependent clause is planned, under way, or has not yet occurred: **Llámame cuando llegues.** *Call me when you arrive.* Conjunctions of time include the following.

así que	*as soon as*	hasta que	*until*
cuando	*when*	luego que	*as soon as*
después (de) que	*after*	tan pronto (como)	*as soon as*
en cuanto	*as soon as*		

When adverbial clauses, such as these expressions of time, are followed by the subjunctive, the subject of both clauses can be the same.

Inicie la marcha **en cuanto encienda** el motor.	*Get into gear as soon as you turn on the motor.*
Trabajaré hasta que me llamen.	*I'll work until they call me.*
Cierre las ventanas **cuando circule** a alta velocidad.	*Close the windows when you drive at high speed.*

Note that the conjunction **cuando** *when* is followed by the indicative when the action has already been completed or could continue.

Recuerdo **cuando aprendí** a conducir.	*I remember when I learned to drive.*
Cuando varias personas **comparten** una necesidad de movilidad, lo inteligente es economizar recursos.	*When several people share transportation needs, it is smart to save resources.*

EJERCICIO
9·8

Complete each sentence with the correct form of the present subjunctive, using the infinitive provided.

1. Porque cuanto más cargado (ir) _____ el coche, más tendrá que trabajar el motor para arrastrarlo.

2. Cierre las ventanas, sobre todo cuando (circular) _____ a alta velocidad

    y retire el portaequipajes cuando lo (llevar) _____ vacío.

3. Utilice el aire acondicionado sólo cuando (ser) _____ necesario.

4. Inicie la marcha en cuanto (encender) _____ el motor y apáguelo

    cuando (estar) _____ detenido durante más de un minuto.

5. Atrás quedaron los tiempos del "enciéndelo ya y deja que (irse) _____ calentando".

6. Para anticiparse es básico mantener siempre una distancia razonable en relación con el resto de vehículos, observar y entender lo que nos rodea y decidir y actuar cuanto antes, para evitar que las situaciones nos (pillar) _____ con el paso cambiado.

7. La idea es que nosotros (pasar) _____ de marcha para relajar el motor, haciéndolo trabajar al mínimo régimen de vueltas posible.

8. Cualquiera que (ser) _____ nuestra experiencia en conducir y en coches, tendemos todos a darlos por sentados.

¡Vaya más lejos!

◆ Busque **club del automóvil** (países latinoamericanos) o **RAAC** (España) para información sobre los servicios ofrecidos a los conductores.

◆ Busque **guía de mantenimiento** + [**el nombre de su coche**] para ver si su manual existe en internet.

◆ Busque **servicios de coche compartido**. ¿En qué ciudades los encuentra?

Zapatos
Juan José Millás (España)

A veces, ocurre que la vida cotidiana **se entrelaza** con lo sobrenatural... ¿Cuál de las dos realidades es la verdadera?

¿Estamos listos?

1. ¿Qué ropa se pone usted todos los días?

    Yo me pongo generalmente... calcetines [M. PL.] (*socks*), medias (*stockings*), ropa interior (calzoncillos (*briefs*), boxers [M. PL.], bragas (*underpants*), sostén [M.] (*bra*)), zapatos, zapatillas (*sneakers*), tacones altos (*high heels*), pantalón [M.], jeans [M. PL.], vaqueros, falda (*skirt*), vestido (*dress*), camisa (*shirt*), camiseta (*T-shirt*), pulóver [M.], suéter [M.], chaqueta, chaleco (*vest*), abrigo (*overcoat*), sombrero, guantes [M. PL.] (*gloves*)...

2. ¿Qué partes del cuerpo cubren los calcetines y los zapatos? ¿Qué partes del cuerpo protege usted con sombrero?

    La ropa cubre/protege... los pies, los dedos, los talones (*heels*), los tobillos (*ankles*), la planta (*sole*) del pie, las uñas (*nails*) del pie, la cabeza, el pelo (*hair*), las orejas, la nariz, la boca, las mejillas (*cheeks*), la frente, el mentón (*chin*), el cuello (*neck*)...

3. En casa, ¿cómo lava y seca sus prendas de vestir? ¿Cómo lava los platos?

    Los/Las lavo... en la lavadora, en la secadora, en el tendedero (*clothesline*), en el lavaplatos, a mano en el fregadero (*sink*)...

4. ¿Dónde guarda los alimentos frescos?

    Los guardo... en el frigorífico, en el refrigerador...

5. ¿Qué utiliza para cocinar?

    Utilizo... la estufa (*stove*), ollas (*pots*), cazuelas (*casseroles*), sartenes [M.] (*frying pans*)...

6. ¿Duerme usted bien, por lo general? ¿Sueña con frecuencia? ¿Sueña todas las noches? ¿Recuerda sus sueños? ¿Con qué sueña? ¿Tiene a veces pesadillas (*nightmares*)? ¿pesadillas recurrentes?

    Anoche vi en sueños... a mis amigos, a mis parientes, mi trabajo, mi escuela, mis clases, mi universidad, a mis profesores, mis vacaciones, a mis animales domésticos, mi casa, mi ciudad, mis lugares favoritos, situaciones extrañas o desagradables, a personas o animales amenazadores (*threatening*)...

95

¡Leamos!

El caso es que empezaron a desaparecer mis **calcetines** preferidos. **Desmonté** la **lavadora** por si se hubieran quedado atrapados en el filtro, **revisé** los **cajones** de toda la casa, le pregunté a la vecina de abajo si por casualidad **se había desatado** una **lluvia** de calcetines sobre su **tendedero**. Nada, no había **rastro** de ellos en ningún sitio. Me compré más y **a los quince días se habían vuelto a evaporar**.

En esto, una noche me desperté con la boca seca. Abrí los ojos y **recibí** un **roce** sutil sobre la **moqueta**. **Al encender** la luz vi que un calcetín de **lana** negro **estaba siendo succionado** por el zapato correspondiente al pie derecho. Más de la **mitad** del calcetín **permanecía aún fuera**, pero **se deslizaba** sin pausa hacia el interior oscuro del **calzado**. En ese momento hice un ruido y la actividad **engullidora** cesó. Tiré del **extremo** libre del calcetín y **arrastré** con él el zapato, como el **sedal** arrastra al **pez** que ha mordido el **cebo**. Preferí pensar que **se trataba de** una **pesadilla** y me volví a dormir. Al día siguiente el calcetín había desaparecido.

Empecé a dejar los calcetines fuera de los zapatos al acostarme y cesaron las desapariciones, pero se ve que ahora **pasan tanta hambre** que se los comen cuando **los tengo puestos**. **A lo mejor** estoy hablando por teléfono y **de repente** siento un **cosquilleo pantorrilla abajo**; miro, que **casi no me atrevo**, y veo descender la **manga** en dirección a los **tobillos**. Es muy incómodo.

Siempre **desconfié de** los zapatos, esas **cajas** donde se guardan los pies con sus **dedos** y todo. Parecen **osarios** o **ataúdes**. Y luego que también **tienen algo de** túnel sin forma. En realidad, es muy difícil llegar a ver el extremo de la **puntera** dentro; ahí, seguramente, reside su estómago. Conocí a **uno** que se durmió con los zapatos puestos y desapareció. Precisamente fue **por estas fechas**.

Felices Pascuas.

Juan José Millás, from *Algo que te concierne, algo que te concierne está sucediendo sin parar aunque no sabes dónde, quizá entre las páginas de este volumen* (Madrid: El País/Aguilar, 1995). Reprinted with the permission of Agencia Literaria Casanovas & Lynch, Barcelona. Many thanks to Ana Lucía de Bastos.

VOCABULARIO			
se entrelaza [entrelazarse]	*is interwoven with*	se habían vuelto a [volverse a] evaporar	*(they) had vanished again*
(los) calcetines	*socks*	en esto	*in this (situation)*
desmonté [desmontar]	*took apart, dismantled*	recibí [recibir]	*heard, sensed*
lavadora	*washing machine*	(el) roce	*brushing, grazing*
revisé [revisar]	*went through, inspected*	moqueta	*carpet*
(los) cajones	*(dresser) drawers*	al encender	*on turning on*
se había desatado [desatarse]	*had been released or unloosed*	lana	*wool*
		estaba siendo succionado [succionar]	*was being sucked up*
lluvia	*deluge*		
tendedero	*clothesline, drying rack*	(la) mitad	*half*
rastro	*sign, trace*	permanecía [permanecer]	*remained*
a los quince días	*within two weeks*	aún	*still*

fuera	*outside (the shoe)*	cosquilleo	*tickle*
se deslizaba [deslizarse]	*(it) was slipping, (it) was sliding*	pantorrilla abajo	*lower part of my calf*
		casi	*almost, nearly*
calzado	*shoe, footwear*	no me atrevo [atreverse]	*I do not dare*
engullidora	*gobbling*	manga	*top of (my) sock*
extremo	*opposite end*	tobillos	*ankles*
arrastré [arrastrar]	*I dragged*	desconfié [desconfiar] de	*I distrusted*
(el) sedal	*fishing line*	cajas	*boxes, crates*
(el) pez	*fish*	dedos	*toes*
cebo	*bait*	osarios	*burial urns*
se trataba de [tratarse de]	*it was (all about)*	(los) ataúdes	*coffins*
pesadilla	*nightmare*	tienen [tener] algo de	*bear some similarity to*
pasan [pasar] tanta hambre	*they are so hungry*	puntera	*toe (of a shoe)*
los tengo [tener] puestos	*I have them on*	uno	*someone*
a lo mejor	*chances are, say*	por estas fechas	*this time of year*
de repente	*suddenly*	Felices Pascuas	*Happy Easter*

EJERCICIO

10·1

¿De qué se trata? *Match the beginning of each sentence with the phrase that correctly completes it to retell the narrator's experience.*

1. _____ Empezaron a

2. _____ Le preguntó a su vecina

3. _____ Se compró más

4. _____ Una noche

5. _____ Cuando los dejó fuera de los zapatos

6. _____ La manga de su calcetín

7. _____ Está convencido de que

a. pero volvieron a desaparecer.

b. descendía hacia los tobillos.

c. desaparecer sus calcetines preferidos.

d. los zapatos tienen estómago.

e. los comieron cuando los tenía puestos.

f. si había visto una gran cantidad de calcetines.

g. vio un calcetín deslizarse hacia el interior del zapato derecho.

Opciones *Choose the phrase or phrases that correctly complete each sentence. Include all correct responses.*

1. El narrador vive en

   a. un apartamento.   b. una casa.   c. un piso.

2. La vecina vive

   a. en el piso de arriba.   b. en el piso de al lado.   c. en el piso de abajo.

3. Él pierde continuamente

   a. sus zapatos.   b. sus calcetines.   c. su calzado.

4. Una noche se esforzó por

   a. discutir con la vecina.   b. recuperar un calcetín.   c. luchar con el zapato.

5. Él esperaba que se tratara de

   a. una pesadilla.   b. un estado permanente.   c. la realidad.

6. En la opinión del narrador, los zapatos tienen algo de

   a. ataúd.   b. túnel sin forma.   c. osario.

7. Al final el narrador parece

   a. resignado.   b. desconfiado.   c. furioso.

¿Cierto o falso? *Indicate whether each statement is true or false, using* **C** *for* **cierto** *(true) or* **F** *for* **falso** *(false). If a statement is false, provide a corrected statement in Spanish.*

1. C F   El narrador no sabe desmontar una lavadora.

   _____

2. C F   La vecina de abajo robaba regularmente las prendas del narrador.

   _____

3. C F   A veces los calcetines se caían sobre el tendedero de la vecina.

   _____

4. C F   Incluso fuera de los zapatos, los calcetines continúan evaporándose.

   _____

5. C F   Casi no se atreve a observar sus propios tobillos.

   _____

6. C F   El narrador conoce a un señor que desapareció, después de dormirse con los zapatos puestos.

_____

_____

7. C F   A partir de ahora ya no va a ponerse calcetines.

_____

Reflexiones *Consider the following themes and questions, and discuss them in Spanish.*

1. Para el narrador, ¿se trata de un sueño recurrente? ¿O hay más?

_____

_____

_____

2. En su opinión, ¿el narrador parece muy enojado con su situación? ¿Continuará tolerándola? ¿Qué puede hacer?

_____

_____

_____

3. ¿Qué acciones emprende contra esta amenaza?

_____

_____

_____

4. ¿Qué sucede después? Dé un final posible.

_____

_____

_____

5. ¿Por qué dice el narrador "Felices Pascuas"? (Juan José Millás escribe para los periódicos.)

_____

_____

_____

6. Entre el sueño y la vigilia, ¿tiene usted a veces alucinaciones? ¿Ha experimentado un incidente de este tipo? ¿En qué circunstancias? ¿Qué vio usted?

_____

_____

_____

_____

Mi vocabulario *Select the word that does not belong in each group.*

1. a. lavadora   b. cosquilleo   c. secadora   d. lavaplatos

2. a. desarmar   b. desmoralizar   c. desmantelar   d. desmontar

3. a. alfombra   b. tapiz   c. moqueta   d. piso

4. a. mallas   b. calcetines   c. pantorrillas   d. medias

5. a. madera   b. lana   c. algodón   d. seda

6. a. aventurarse   b. osar   c. atravesar   d. atreverse

7. a. traza   b. rastro   c. signo   d. rastrillo

8. a. remonté   b. tiré   c. arrastré   d. remolqué

Contrarios *Match each word with its opposite.*

1. _____ incómodo   a. desconfiar

2. _____ desmontar   b. extinguir

3. _____ arrastrar   c. ruido

4. _____ silencio   d. acostarse

5. _____ creer   e. construir

6. _____ encender   f. extremo

7. _____ comienzo   g. derecho

8. _____ izquierdo   h. empujar

9. _____ despertarse   i. confortable

Equivalentes *Read the following sentences. Then substitute each underlined word or phrase with its equivalent from the following list.*

se acabó	desarmé	golosa	súbitamente
busqué por	enredados	habían desaparecido otra vez	zapato
cincuenta por ciento	entendí	se parecen a un	cuando iba a la cama
se resbalaba	se quedaba		

1. _____ la lavadora por si se hubieran quedado

Desmonté

   _____ en el filtro, _____ los cajones de toda

atrapados · revisé

   la casa.

2. Me compré más y a los quince días _____.

se habían vuelto a evaporar

3. Abrí los ojos y _____ un roce sutil sobre la moqueta.

recibí

4. Más de _____ del calcetín _____ aún fuera,

la mitad · permanecía

   pero _____ sin pausa hacia el interior oscuro del

se deslizaba

   _____.

calzado

5. En ese momento hice un ruido y la actividad _____

engullidora

   _____.

cesó

6. Empecé a dejar los calcetines fuera de los zapatos _____ y cesaron

al acostarme

   las desapariciones.

7. Estoy hablando por teléfono y _____ siento un cosquilleo pantorrilla

de repente

   abajo.

8. Y luego que también _____ túnel sin forma.

tienen algo de

¡No se olvide! El pluscuamperfecto

The Spanish past perfect (or pluperfect) is a compound tense, as it is in English. It narrates a completed action in the past that preceded another past action. In the English equivalent, the auxiliary verb is always *had*: **(Ya) había llegado.** *I had (already) arrived.*

To form the past perfect tense, use the imperfect forms of the auxiliary **haber**, followed by the past participle of the verb.

	llegar *to arrive*	**ponerse** *to put on*
yo	**había** llegado	**me había** puesto
tú	**habías** llegado	**te habías** puesto
él, ella, usted	**había** llegado	**se había** puesto
nosotros/as	**habíamos** llegado	**nos habíamos** puesto
vosotros/as	**habíais** llegado	**os habíais** puesto
ellos, ellas, Uds.	**habían** llegado	**se habían** puesto

EJERCICIO
10·8

Refer to the reading, if necessary, to find the indicator of past action that precedes the past perfect action in bold in the following excerpts. List (a) the preceding past action, and (b) the explanation for the use of the past perfect tense in the excerpt.

1. Le pregunté a la vecina de abajo si por casualidad **se había desatado** (*had been released/ unloosed*) una lluvia de calcetines sobre su tendedero.

   a. _____   b. _____

2. Me compré más y a los quince días **se habían vuelto a evaporar** (*they had vanished again*).

   a. _____   b. _____

3. Al día siguiente el calcetín **había desaparecido** (*had disappeared*).

   a. _____   b. _____

EJERCICIO
10·9

Complete each sentence with the correct form of the past perfect indicative, using the infinitive provided.

1. Rosa ya (irse) _____ cuando me desperté.

2. Llegamos a tiempo, pero los artesanos ya (cumplir) _____ el trabajo.

3. Estaba lloviendo ese tarde; el tiempo (cambiarse) _____ sin aviso alguno.

4. Quería comprar ese coche usado, pero (ser vendido) _____ el día antes.

5. ¿Qué dijiste cuando descubriste que (ellos / casarse) _____?

¡No se olvide! El pluscuamperfecto de subjuntivo

The past perfect subjunctive is used like the past perfect indicative, to indicate a "past past" action.

In the main clause, past tense verbal expressions such as hoping and wishing focus on a past event or action, expressed by the past perfect subjunctive in the dependent clause. The past perfect subjunctive also follows conjunctions such as **para que**, **antes que**, and **como si**.

The past perfect subjunctive is formed with the imperfect subjunctive of **haber**, plus the past participle.

	llegar *to arrive*	**ponerse** *to put on*
yo	**hubiera** llegado	**me hubiera** puesto
tú	**hubieras** llegado	**te hubieras** puesto
él, ella, usted	**hubiera** llegado	**se hubiera** puesto
nosotros/as	**hubiéramos** llegado	**nos hubiéramos** puesto
vosotros/as	**hubierais** llegado	**os hubierais** puesto
ellos, ellas, Uds.	**hubieran** llegado	**se hubieran** puesto

In the following example from the story, the expression **por si** *whether, if, in case* requires the subjunctive in the dependent clause.

Desmonté la lavadora *por si* **se hubieran quedado** atrapados en el filtro.

I disassembled the washing machine in case they had gotten caught in the filter.

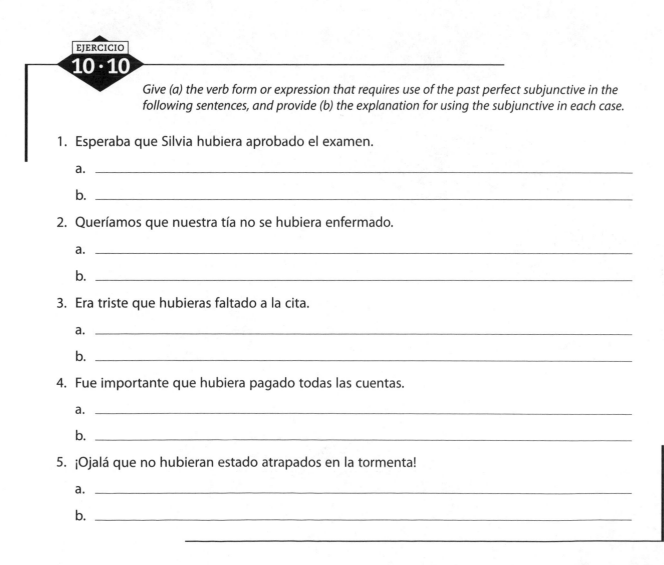

EJERCICIO

10·10

Give (a) the verb form or expression that requires use of the past perfect subjunctive in the following sentences, and provide (b) the explanation for using the subjunctive in each case.

1. Esperaba que Silvia hubiera aprobado el examen.

    a. _____

    b. _____

2. Queríamos que nuestra tía no se hubiera enfermado.

    a. _____

    b. _____

3. Era triste que hubieras faltado a la cita.

    a. _____

    b. _____

4. Fue importante que hubiera pagado todas las cuentas.

    a. _____

    b. _____

5. ¡Ojalá que no hubieran estado atrapados en la tormenta!

    a. _____

    b. _____

¡Vaya más lejos!

- Busque en línea otros cuentos modernos en español.
- Vaya a algunos sitios web de empresas o grandes almacenes (utilice, por ejemplo, www .google.es) donde se compran **prendas de vestir**. Busque varios artículos que le interesan a usted.

¿Diferencias culturales?
Ariel Dorfman
(Chile/Estados Unidos)

En 1969, después de pasar un año en California, el escritor y profesor chileno Ariel Dorfman volvió con su familia a reinstalarse en Santiago, Chile. Él ya tenía algunas **costumbres** muy californianas. Este es fragmento de *Rumbo al sur, deseando el norte* (1998).

¿Estamos listos?

1. ¿Hace ejercicio o deportes? ¿Qué actividades le gustan?

   Me gusta(n)... las caminatas (*walks*), el jogging/footing, el tenis, el balonmano, el ciclismo, el ping-pong, el patinaje (*skating*), el esquí, la gimnasia, el yoga, la natación (*swimming*), levantar pesas (*weights*), montar a caballo, navegar...

2. ¿Sus actividades deportivas son normales, cotidianas? ¿o son originales? ¿Hacen las mismas actividades los miembros de su familia, sus amigos, sus vecinos?

3. ¿Dónde hace ejercicio?

   Voy... al aire libre, adentro, al gimnasio, por un sendero (*path, trail*), por un camino, a un campo o a una cancha (*field, court*), a una pista de patinaje (*rink*), a una piscina (*pool*), a la playa (*beach*)...

4. ¿Qué prendas se pone usted para hacer ejercicio?

   Me pongo... camiseta, shorts, chándal [M.] (*tracksuit*), culotes [M.] (*bike shorts*), traje de baño [M.], casco (*helmet*), parka, pantalones de esquí [M.]...

5. ¿Hay que tener equipo especial para practicar su deporte?

   Necesito... calzado (*footwear*) especial, una raqueta, una bicicleta, un casco, balones, patines, esquís, pesas, equipo de ejercicio, un velero (*sailboat*), un caballo...

6. ¿Cómo se siente antes de hacer ejercicio? ¿durante el ejercicio? ¿después de practicar deportes?

   Me siento... entusiasta, perezoso/a, cansado/a, exhausto/a, sin aliento (*out of breath*), enérgico/a, tenso/a, relajado/a, adolorido/a (*in pain*), alegre, feliz, tranquilo/a...

7. ¿Hay ejercicios o deportes que estarían desaprobados por sus vecinos, si usted los practicara afuera?

¡Leamos!

Quizá la mejor manera de examinar los obstáculos, físicos y culturales, que **se me aparecieron** sea describir lo que **me sucedió apenas** comencé a hacer jogging en las calles de Santiago. Era un hábito, el de correr todas las mañanas que había adoptado de mis **saludables** amigos californianos [...]

Y salí a demostrar que, en efecto, las calles **pertenecían** al **pueblo**, a los pueblos.

Los indignados **ladridos** de los perros le permitieron a **Angélica** seguir mi progreso por el **barrio**. Jamás esos perros ni sus **dueños** habían visto un espectáculo **parecido**: un **gringo** con sus **anteojos bamboleantes** y **piernas como zancudos** y **mechas rubias** al aire, trotando frente a sus **pudientes** residencias, **armando un lío del carajo**. Las calles eran para los **mendigos**, los vagabundos, quienes **carecían de un hogar**, o en último caso, para plácidas abuelas supervisando los primeros pasos de sus nietos o para empleadas domésticas en sus **almidonados** uniformes yendo a comprar pan a la tienda de la **esquina**. Y no para alguien que **atravesara** el **vecindario** en ropa atlética **impúdica**, perturbando la paz en forma intolerable.

Ese era el punto de vista de Angélica cada vez que yo volvía al hogar, **sudoroso** y feliz de hacer mis ejercicios **deportivos**. Estaba preocupada entonces (y todavía lo está) de que **no me ubicaba**, y detrás de lo que ella llamaba mi constante **desubicación** se juzgaba mi conducta habitual como un **ultraje** a las buenas costumbres, las reglas bastante rígidas con que ella **se había criado** y que permiten a alguien pasar **desapercibido** y evitar líos. Su inquietud ante **el hecho de que** yo me pusiera a correr y **traspirar a plena luz** representaba la perspectiva chilena típica y tradicional: no hay que mostrarse, todo en forma moderada, a **esconder** las extravagancias, no le **expongas** a nadie tu **ser** privado y secreto. Al pasar los días, sin embargo, sin que nada calamitoso ocurriera, ella pareció aceptar que mi democrática apropiación de las calles era inofensiva, después de todo, y hasta declaró que había comenzado a **gozar** del hecho de que podía, desde su cama **somnolienta**, **trazar** la ruta que estaba tomando por la forma en que **se acrecentaban** o disminuían los ladridos de los perros.

Cierta mañana, si se hubiera puesto a escuchar con especial atención, **se habría dado cuenta de que** los ladridos **habían alcanzado** una **fiereza** inhabitual.

Había una casa en particular donde un **can** excepcionalmente feo daba **señas** de verdadera antipatía ante mis **correrías**, lo que me llevó a pasar **a propósito** por esa calle, casi como una provocación.

Ese día, alguien había dejado la **verja** abierta **a sabiendas de que** el perro, cuando yo pasara, **me asaltaría** furiosamente, **mordiendo** mis pantalones de jogging. Traté de **zafar** mi **vestimenta** de sus dientes, pero **no me soltaba** por nada. **Siguió gruñendo** y salivando hasta que un hombre en una **bata de levantarse** de execrable **gusto** apareció en la puerta, mandando al **despreciable** animal que me dejara tranquilo. Cosa que no hizo el dueño, **puesto que** se puso a insultarme: qué me creía, **molestándolo** a él, a su perro, a su familia, a su abuela y quién sabe a quién más. [...]

Ariel Dorfman, excerpts from *Rumbo al sur, deseando el norte, un romance en dos lenguas*. Reprinted with the permission of The Permissions Company, Inc., on behalf of Seven Stories Press, www.seven stories.com. Many thanks to Frederick T. Courtright.

(las) costumbres	*habits, customs*	se había criado [criarse]	*had been raised*
se me aparecieron [aparecerse]	*confronted me*	desapercibido	*unnoticed, unseen*
me sucedió [suceder]	*happened to me*	el hecho de que	*the fact that*
apenas	*hardly, barely*	traspirar	*to sweat*
saludables	*healthy*	a plena luz	*in broad daylight*
pertenecían [pertenecer]	*belonged*	esconder	*to hide, conceal*
		expongas [exponer]	*to expose*
pueblo	*people*	(el) ser	*being, self*
ladridos	*barks (dog)*	gozar	*to enjoy*
Angélica	*the author's wife*	somnolienta	*drowsy, sleepy*
barrio	*neighborhood*	trazar	*trace, draw*
dueños	*owners*	se acrecentaban [acrecentarse]	*increased*
parecido	*similar, like this one*		
gringo [SLANG]	*foreigner, non-Hispanic*	se habría dado [darse] cuenta de que	*(she) would have noticed*
anteojos	*(eye)glasses*		
bamboleantes	*wobbling, bouncing*	habían alcanzado [alcanzar]	*had reached*
piernas como zancudos	*skinny legs like a mosquito*	fiereza	*ferocity, savagery*
mechas rubias	*shaggy blond locks*	(el) can	*hound, dog*
pudientes	*wealthy, affluent*	señas	*signs, clues*
armando [armar] un lío del carajo [VULGAR]	*kicking up a helluva fuss*	correrías	*incursions*
		a propósito	*on purpose*
		verja	*iron gate, grill*
mendigos	*beggars*	a sabiendas de que	*knowing full well*
carecían [carecer] de un hogar	*were homeless, were lacking shelter*	me asaltaría [asaltar]	*would attack me*
		mordiendo [morder]	*biting*
almidonados	*starched*	zafar	*to remove*
esquina	*corner*	vestimenta	*clothing*
atravesara [atravesar]	*would cross, would go through*	no me soltaba [soltar]	*didn't let me go*
vecindario	*neighborhood*	siguió gruñendo [gruñir]	*kept on growling*
impúdica	*shameless, immodest*		
sudoroso	*sweaty*	bata de levantarse	*bathrobe*
deportivos	*athletic*	gusto	*taste (style)*
no me ubicaba [ubicarse]	*I didn't fit in*	despreciable	*despicable*
		puesto que	*since*
desubicación	*uprooting*	molestándolo [molestar]	*bothering him, annoying him*
(el) ultraje	*outrage*		

¿De qué se trata? *Who might say or think the following? Choose **N** for **el narrador** (the narrator), **A** for **Angélica** (Angelica), or **V** for **un vecino** (a neighbor). Include all correct responses.*

	N	A	V
1. "Es mi saludable hábito californiano."	☐	☐	☐
2. "Las calles son para los mendigos, las abuelas y las empleadas."	☐	☐	☐
3. "Tú nunca te ubicarás."	☐	☐	☐
4. "Éstas eran las reglas de mi abuela..."	☐	☐	☐
5. "Ya llega ese loco; cariño, abre la verja para que el perrito pueda salir."	☐	☐	☐
6. "Ahora tengo que comprarme nuevos shorts..."	☐	☐	☐

Opciones *Choose the phrase or phrases that correctly complete each sentence. Include all correct responses.*

1. Al narrador le gusta

   a. hacer jogging.   b. alimentar a los perros.   c. correr en las calles.

2. Le gusta también

   a. provocar a cierto perro.   b. molestar a los vecinos.   c. dormir hasta tarde.

3. Ariel había aprendido ese hábito deportivo

   a. en Chile.   b. en los Estados Unidos.   c. de niño.

4. Su esposa

   a. dormía hasta más tarde que él.   b. estaba avergonzada por su conducta.   c. hacía jogging.

5. En este barrio, era inaceptable

   a. transpirar en la calle.   b. soltar a los perros.   c. supervisar a los nietos.

6. En ese momento, al narrador, la gente chilena le parecía

   a. plácida.   b. rígida.   c. hostil.

7. El dueño del perro malicioso

   a. acusó a Ariel del ataque.   b. estaba simpático.   c. había abierto su verja.

¿Cierto o falso? *Indicate whether each statement is true or false, using **C** for **cierto** (true) or **F** for **falso** (false). If a statement is false, provide a corrected statement in Spanish.*

1. C F   Cada mañana Angélica se le unía a su esposo para correr.

_____

2. C F   Angélica podía, finalmente, trazar la ruta de Ariel por los ladridos próximos.

_____

3. C F   En Chile, las costumbres exigen moderación, discreción y privacidad.

_____

4. C F   A Ariel le gusta siempre correr con su perro.

_____

5. C F   Los vecinos desaprobaban el aspecto informal de Ariel.

_____

Reflexiones *Consider the following themes and questions, and discuss them in Spanish.*

1. ¿Quién tiene razón sobre hacer jogging en Santiago? ¿Ariel o Angélica?

_____

_____

_____

_____

2. En el fondo, ¿le gusta a Ariel molestar a los residentes de su barrio? ¿Por qué? ¿Según usted, debería él hacer concesiones para vivir en esa ciudad? ¿o seguir sus propios deseos?

_____

_____

_____

_____

3. ¿Era relevante que ese incidente sucediera en Santiago? ¿Podría ocurrir en otros lugares?

_____

_____

_____

_____

4. ¿Cómo reacciona usted ante una persona que tiene hábitos o costumbres diferentes de los suyos?

_____

_____

_____

_____

5. ¿Ha experimentado una situación similar? ¿En viajes? ¿Cuándo se mudó a otra ciudad?

_____

_____

_____

_____

Mi vocabulario *Select the word or phrase that does not belong in each group.*

1. a. somnolienta   b. alerta   c. cansada   d. adormilada

2. a. quitar   b. zafar   c. sacar   d. poner

3. a. cortesía   b. ultraje   c. desprecio   d. ofensa

4. a. echar raíces   b. instalarse   c. marcharse   d. ubicarse

5. a. bata   b. pantufla   c. kimono   d. pijama

6. a. barrio   b. distrito   c. vecindario   d. vecino

7. a. vestido   b. ropa   c. vestimenta   d. vestigio

8. a. impúdicos   b. pudientes   c. poderosos   d. ricos

Contrarios *Match each word or phrase with its opposite.*

1. _____ esconder   a. plácidas

2. _____ desapercibido   b. se acrecentaban

3. _____ a plena luz   c. despreciable

4. _____ admirable   d. mendigos

5. _____ inquietas   e. obvio

6. _____ fiereza   f. dulzura

7. _____ prósperos   g. exponer

8. _____ se reducían   h. por la noche

Equivalentes *Complete each sentence by substituting words or phrases from the following list for the words or phrases in small type.*

barrio	de los habitantes	ocurrió	debí enfrentar
indecente	recorriera	domicilio	indigentes
semejante	eran	necesitaban	señalar

1. Quizá la mejor manera de examinar los obstáculos... que _____ sea

se me aparecieron

   describir lo que me _____ apenas comencé a hacer jogging.

sucedió

2. Y salí a _____ que... las calles _____

demostrar   *pertenecían*

   _____.

al pueblo

3. Jamás... habían visto un espectáculo _____.

parecido

4. Las calles eran para los _____ ... quienes _____

mendigos   *carecían de*

   un _____.

hogar

5. Y no para alguien que _____ el _____ en ropa atlética

travesara   *vecindario*

   _____.

impúdica

¡No se olvide! El imperfecto de subjuntivo

The imperfect subjunctive is used in a dependent clause (starting with **que** or another conjunction) where the subjunctive is required by a verb in the main clause that is in a past tense—either the preterit or the imperfect. Use of the present conditional in the main clause also requires the use of the imperfect subjunctive in a dependent clause.

As a learner, you will read these forms far more often than you'll need to write them. They are easy to recognize; all endings show the characteristic **-ra** combination.

Era posible que Ud. **viniera**.	*It was possible that you came.*
Yo **quise** que tú **te fueras**.	*I wanted you to leave.*
Preferiría que María **trabajara**.	*He would prefer that María work.*

The stem of all imperfect subjunctive forms, both regular and irregular, is the stem of the third-person singular of the preterit tense: **llegar** > **llegó** (**lleg-**), **comer** > **comió** (**com-**), **entender** > **entendió** (**entend-**), **ser** > **fue** (**fu-**). Refer to complete verb charts to review irregular preterit forms. Note that **-er** verbs and **-ir** verbs have the same endings.

	hablar *to speak, talk*	**comer** *to eat*	**salir** *to leave, go out*
yo	habl**ara**	com**iera**	sal**iera**
tú	habl**aras**	com**ieras**	sal**ieras**
él, ella, usted	habl**ara**	com**iera**	sal**iera**
nosotros/as	habl**áramos**	com**iéramos**	sal**iéramos**
vosotros/as	habl**arais**	com**ierais**	sal**ierais**
ellos, ellas, Uds.	habl**aran**	com**ieran**	sal**ieran**

In your reading, you will see the imperfect subjunctive in cases such as the following.

♦ After verbs of volition (wishes, preferences, orders, commands)

Yo **quería que** el profesor **explicara** más.   *I wanted the professor to explain more.*

♦ After verbs of emotion and hope

Se alegró que llegara.   *She was happy he arrived.*

♦ After verbs expressing uncertainty or doubt

Era dudoso que dijeran la verdad.   *It was doubtful they were telling the truth.*

♦ In the clause after certain conjunctions, usually indicating anticipation (for example, **antes de que**, **a pesar de que**, **cuando**, **después de que**, **en caso de que**, **hasta que**, **para que**, **sin que**)

Trabajaba **hasta que vinieran**.   *She worked until they arrived.*

♦ In a dependent adjective clause where the object or person being sought does not (yet) exist

Busqué un empleado **que conociera** ese software.   *I looked for an employee who was familiar with that software.*

♦ After **si** *if* in the **si**-clause of a conditional sentence

Podría viajar **si tuviera** suficiente dinero.   *I would be able to travel if I had enough money.*

Note that the **si**-clause may also begin the sentence.

Read the following excerpts from the reading, then (a) list each verb form in the imperfect subjunctive, (b) identify its infinitive, and (c) explain the reason for its use.

1. y no para alguien que atravesara el vecindario en ropa atlética impúdica

   a. _____   b. _____

   c. _____

2. su inquietud ante el hecho de que yo me pusiera a correr y traspirar a plena luz

   a. _____   b. _____

   c. _____

3. sin que nada calamitoso ocurriera

   a. _____   b. _____

   c. _____

4. Si se hubiera puesto a escuchar..., se habría dado cuenta de que los ladridos habían alcanzado una fiereza inhabitual.

   a. _____   b. _____

   c. _____

5. Alguien había dejado la verja abierta a sabiendas de que el perro, cuando yo pasara, me asaltaría.

   a. _____   b. _____

   c. _____

6. Un hombre... apareció en la puerta, mandando al despreciable animal que me dejara tranquilo.

   a. _____   b. _____

   c. _____

¡Vaya más lejos!

- Busque información sobre la vida y las obras de **Ariel Dorfman**.
- Busque información sobre la ciudad de **Santiago, Chile**, su geográfica y su historia.
- Busque información sobre los **deportes populares** hoy en día en Chile.

NIÑEZ Y JUVENTUD

El canario vuela •
El canario se muere
Juan Ramón Jiménez (España)

He aquí otros capítulos extraídos de *Platero y yo*. (Ver también el capítulo 8.) El narrador y los niños de la vecindad—su burro Platero incluido—están muy **apegados** a una pequeña **mascota** sin nombre.

¿Estamos listos?

1. ¿Tiene usted mascotas (animales domésticos)? ¿Cuántos? ¿Qué tipos de animales?

   Tengo... un perro, un labrador, un golden retriever, un caniche (*poodle*), un perro salchicha, un chihuahua, un gato, un pájaro, un canario, un periquito, un loro (*parrot*), un lagarto (*lizard*), un conejo (*rabbit*), un cobayo (*guinea pig*), un caballo...

2. ¿Dónde vive(n) su(s) mascota(s)?

   Vive(n) en... la casa, el apartamento, una caseta para perros, el jardín, un corral, una jaula (*cage*), una pajarera, un acuario, un terrario, una conejera...

3. ¿Cuántos años tiene su mascota? Para ese animal, ¿es viejo o joven? ¿Es grande o pequeño? ¿Qué color(es) tiene?

4. Describa la personalidad de su mascota.

   Mi perro/gato/mascota es... tranquilo/a, activo/a, nervioso/a, lento/a, rápido/a, inteligente, cariñoso/a, distante, independiente...

5. De niño, ¿tenía mascotas? ¿Cuáles tenía en aquella época?

6. Describa la mascota que quería de niño, pero nunca tuvo.

7. ¿Se le escapó alguna vez una mascota? ¿Volvió sola? Si se la encontró, ¿quién la encontró? ¿En qué circunstancias?

8. ¿Qué papel juegan las mascotas en su vida? ¿en la vida de sus amigos y los miembros de su familia?

   Para mí, las mascotas son... amigos, compañeros, defensores, cazadores, auxilios...

9. Si una mascota se muere, ¿la reemplaza inmediatamente o espera durante algún tiempo? ¿Por qué?

¡Leamos!

Platero y yo, Capítulo 30: El canario vuela

Un día el canario verde, no sé cómo ni por qué, voló de su **jaula**. Era un canario viejo, **recuerdo** triste de una muerta, al que yo no había dado libertad **por miedo de que** se muriera de hambre o de frío, o de que se lo comieran los gatos.

Anduvo toda la mañana entre los **granados** del **huerto**, en el **pino** de la **puerta**, por las **lilas**. Los niños estuvieron, toda la mañana también, sentados en la **galería, absortos** en los breves **vuelos** del **pajarillo amarillento**. Libre, Platero **holgaba** junto a los **rosales**, jugando con una **mariposa**.

A la tarde, el canario se vino al **tejado** de la casa grande, y allí se quedó largo tiempo, **latiendo** en el **tibio** sol que declinaba. De pronto, y sin saber nadie cómo ni por qué, apareció en la jaula, otra vez alegre.

¡Qué **alborozo** en el jardín! Los niños **saltaban**, tocando las palmas, **arrebolados** y **rientes** como **auroras**; Diana, loca, los seguía, **ladrándole** a su propia y riente **campanilla**; Platero, **contagiado**, en un **oleaje de carnes de plata**, igual que un **chivillo**, **hacía corvetas**, **giraba** sobre sus **patas**, en un **vals tosco**, y **poniéndose en las manos**, **daba coces** al aire claro y **suave**.

Juan Ramón Jiménez, capítulo 30 from *Platero y yo: Elejía andaluza* (Madrid: Editorial Calleja, 1917).

VOCABULARIO

apegados [apegarse]	*attached to*	alborozo	*joy*
mascota	*pet*	saltaban [saltar]	*jumped up and down*
jaula	*cage*	arrebolados [arrebolar]	*red-cheeked*
recuerdo	*memento, gift*	rientes	*laughing*
por miedo de que	*fearing that*	auroras	*sunrises, dawns*
granados	*pomegranate trees*	ladrándole [ladrar]	*barking at*
huerto	*orchard*	campanilla	*little bell*
pino	*pine tree*	contagiado [contagiar]	*infected (with joy)*
puerta	*gate*	(el) oleaje	*swell (as of waves)*
lilas	*lilacs*	de carnes de plata	*of silvery flesh*
galería	*veranda*	chivillo	*little goat*
absortos	*fascinated*	hacía [hacer] corvetas	*(he) pranced*
vuelos	*flights*	giraba [girar]	*(he) twirled/spun*
pajarillo	*little bird*	patas	*legs (of animal)*
amarillento	*yellowish, chartreuse*	(el) vals	*waltz*
holgaba [holgar]	*idled, loafed around*	tosco	*rough, crude*
(los) rosales	*rosebushes*	poniéndose [ponerse] en las manos	*kicking up his hooves*
mariposa	*butterfly*		
tejado	*roof*	daba [dar] coces	*kicked up*
latiendo [latir]	*beating (his wings)*	suave	*sweet, gentle*
tibio	*lukewarm*		

¡Leamos!

Platero y yo, Capítulo 83: El canario se muere

Mira, Platero, el canario de los niños **ha amanecido hoy muerto** en su jaula de **plata**. Es verdad que el pobre estaba ya muy viejo... El invierno último, tú te acuerdas bien, lo pasó silencioso, con la cabeza **escondida** en el **plumón**. Y al entrar esta primavera, cuando el sol hacía jardín la **estancia abierta** y abrían las mejores rosas del patio, él quiso también **engalanar** la vida nueva, y cantó pero su voz era **quebradiza** y asmática, como la voz de una **flauta cascada**.

El mayor de los niños, que **lo cuidaba**, viéndolo **yerto** en el fondo de la jaula, **se ha apresurado, lloroso**, a decir:

—¡**Puej no l'a faltao na**: ni comida, ni agua!

No. No le ha faltado nada, Platero. "Se ha muerto **porque sí**", diría **Campoamor**, otro canario viejo...

Platero, ¿habrá un paraíso de los pájaros? ¿Habrá un **vergel** verde sobre el cielo azul, todo en flor de rosales **áureos**, con **almas** de pájaros blancos, rosas, **celestes**, amarillos?

Oye, a la noche, los niños, tú y yo **bajaremos** el pájaro muerto al jardín. La luna está ahora llena, y a su pálida plata, el pobre **cantor**, en la mano **cándida** de Blanca, parecerá el pétalo **mustio** de un **lirio** amarillento. Y lo **enterraremos** en la tierra del rosal grande.

A la primavera, Platero, **hemos de** ver al pájaro salir del corazón de una rosa blanca. El aire fragante **se pondrá canoro**, y habrá por el sol de abril un **errar** encantado de **alas** invisibles y un **reguero** secreto de **trinos** claros de **oro** puro.

Juan Ramón Jiménez, capítulo 83 from *Platero y yo: Elejía andaluza* (Madrid: Editorial Calleja, 1917).

VOCABULARIO

ha amanecido [amanecer] hoy muerto	*was found dead this morning, turned up dead this morning*	porque sí	*just because*
		Campoamor	*19th century Spanish poet/philosopher*
plata	*silver(-colored)*	(el) vergel	*orchard, garden*
escondida	*hidden*	áureos	*golden*
(el) plumón	*down, plumage*	almas	*souls*
estancia abierta	*outdoor room, sunroom*	celeste	*sky blue*
engalanar	*to decorate, adorn*	bajaremos [bajar]	*we'll carry down*
quebradiza	*frail, fragile*	(el) cantor	*singer*
flauta	*flute*	cándida	*naïve, gentle*
cascada	*worn-out, broken*	mustio	*withered, shrunken*
lo cuidaba [cuidar]	*took care of him*	lirio	*iris (flower)*
yerto	*stiff, rigid*	enterraremos [enterrar]	*we'll bury*
se ha apresurado [apresurarse] a decir	*quickly said*	hemos de [haber de]	*we should, we have to*
		se pondrá [ponerse] canoro	*will become tuneful*
lloroso	*tearful*	(el) errar	*movement, wandering*
Puej no l'a faltao na (Pues, no le ha faltado nada) [REGIONAL]	*But he had everything!*	alas	*wings*
		reguero	*trail, track, trace*
		trinos	*trills, bird songs*
		oro	*gold*

¿De qué se trata? *Match the beginning of each sentence with the phrase that correctly completes it to retell the story "El canario vuela."*

1. _____ Un día el canario verde

2. _____ Era un canario viejo al que no había dado libertad

3. _____ Los niños estuvieron

4. _____ Platero holgaba junto a los rosales

5. _____ A la tarde, se vino al tejado

6. _____ De pronto,

7. _____ Platero... hacía corvetas...

a. por miedo de que se muriera.

b. y se quedó largo tiempo.

c. apareció en la jaula, alegre.

d. jugando con una mariposa.

e. voló de su jaula.

f. y... daba coces al aire claro y suave.

g. absortos en los vuelos del pájaro.

Opciones *Choose the phrase or phrases that correctly answer each question. Include all correct responses.*

1. ¿Qué o quién se escapó?

   a. el canario verde   b. Diana   c. un niño

2. ¿Quién sabe cómo o por qué se escapó?

   a. los niños   b. nadie   c. el narrador

3. ¿Cuántos años tiene el canario?

   a. cuatro años   b. tiene la misma edad que Platero   c. no se sabe, pero es viejo

4. ¿Cómo obtuvo el narrador el pájaro?

   a. fue el recuerdo de una muerta   b. lo encontró en el huerto   c. los niños lo compraron

5. ¿Por qué el narrador no puso en libertad al canario?

   a. la vida fuera es peligrosa   b. el pájaro no quería salir   c. temía la muerte del canario

6. ¿Sabían cómo regresó el canario a la jaula?

   a. se bajó del tejado   b. no, no lo sabían   c. Platero lo persiguió

7. ¿Cómo reaccionaron todos ante la reaparición del pajarillo?

   a. ladraban   b. saltaban   c. daban coces al aire

¿Cierto o falso? *Indicate whether each statement is true or false, using* **C** *for* **cierto** *(true) or* **F** *for* **falso** *(false). If a statement is false, provide a corrected statement in Spanish.*

1. C   F   La dueña del canario había muerto.

_____

2. C   F   El narrador se había decidido a no poner en libertad al canario.

_____

3. C   F   Uno de los niños abrió la jaula.

_____

4. C   F   Diana es un burro como Platero.

_____

5. C   F   Ya no lo vieron más al canario.

_____

6. C   F   Platero parecía entender la gran alegría de todos.

_____

Mi vocabulario *Select the word that does not belong in each group.*

1. a. presente   b. recuerdo   c. regalo   d. rechazo

2. a. olmo   b. roble   c. rosal   d. pino

3. a. distintos   b. absortos   c. encantados   d. distraídos

4. a. holograma   b. disfrutaba   c. holgaba   d. se divertía

5. a. patas   b. piernas   c. pescados   d. pezuñas

6. a. roznando   b. maullando   c. roncando   d. ladrando

Contrarios *Match each word or phrase with its opposite.*

1. _____ suave
2. _____ rientes
3. _____ aurora
4. _____ suelo
5. _____ muy caliente
6. _____ tristeza

a. tejado
b. alborozo
c. tibio
d. tosco
e. llorosos
f. puesta del sol

Equivalentes *Complete each sentence by substituting words or phrases from the following list for the words or phrases in small type.*

alegres   descansaba   veranda   aplaudiendo
enrojecidos   voló   danzaban   se escapó

1. Un día el canario verde... _____ de su jaula.
   _{voló}

2. _____ toda la mañana entre los granados del huerto.
   _{Anduvo}

3. Los niños estuvieron... sentados en la _____.
   _{galería}

4. Libre, Platero _____ junto a los rosales.
   _{holgaba}

5. Los niños _____, _____,
   _{saltaban}   _{tocando las palmas}
   _____ y _____.
   _{arrebolados}   _{rientes}

¿De qué se trata? *Who might say this? Choose* **N** *for* **el narrador** (the narrator),
M *for* **el mayor niño** (the oldest boy), **C** *for* **Campoamor** (Campoamor), **B** *for* **Blanca**
(Blanca), *or* **P** *for* **Platero** (Platero). *Include all correct responses for* "El canario se muere."

	N	M	C	B	P
1. "El pobre estaba ya muy viejo."	☐	☐	☐	☐	☐
2. "Se ha muerto porque sí."	☐	☐	☐	☐	☐
3. "¡Puej no l'a faltao na: ni comida, ni agua!"	☐	☐	☐	☐	☐
4. "No. No le ha faltado nada, Platero."	☐	☐	☐	☐	☐
5. "¿Yo podría tenerlo en la mano?"	☐	☐	☐	☐	☐
6. "¡No veo alas, pero oigo sus trinos!"	☐	☐	☐	☐	☐

Opciones *Choose the phrase or phrases that correctly answer each question. Include all
correct responses for* "El canario se muere."

1. ¿Qué pasó una mañana?

   a. la jaula se rompió   b. el canario se murió   c. el canario se escapó

2. ¿Quién vio primero al canario yerto en la jaula?

   a. Blanca   b. el mayor de los niños   c. Platero

3. ¿Qué o quién es Campoamor?

   a. otro pajarillo   b. otra mascota   c. un poeta-filósofo español

4. ¿Por qué Campoamor diría "porque sí"?

   a. conoce los pájaros   b. no entiende la situación   c. es viejo también

5. ¿Dónde enterrarán al canario verde?

   a. al lado del rosal grande   b. en el jardín   c. en el huerto

6. ¿Quién lo llevará?

   a. Blanca   b. Campoamor   c. una mariposa

7. A la primavera siguiente, ¿qué pasará, según el narrador?

   a. Campoamor se morirá   b. el aire se volverá melodioso   c. el canario saldrá de una rosa

¿Cierto o falso? *Indicate whether each statement is true or false, using* **C** *for* **cierto** *(true) or* **F** *for* **falso** *(false). If a statement is false, provide a corrected statement in Spanish.*

1. C F   Esa mañana el canario estaba realmente vivo.

   _____

2. C F   Era un canario muy viejo.

   _____

3. C F   Había indicios anteriores de que el pájaro era débil y enfermo.

   _____

4. C F   Todos los niños cuidaban al canario.

   _____

5. C F   El narrador muestra Campoamor como filosófico.

   _____

6. C F   Todos creían que se les perdería el canario para siempre.

   _____

Mi vocabulario *Select the word that does not belong in each group.*

1. a. lila   b. granada   c. lirio   d. rosa
2. a. plata   b. oro   c. rubí   d. cobre
3. a. viola   b. flauta   c. oboe   d. trompeta
4. a. alas   b. trinos   c. plumón   d. dientes
5. a. mustia   b. cansada   c. cascada   d. fresca

Contrarios *Match each word or phrase with its opposite.*

1. _____ maliciosa   a. fuerte

2. _____ lo abandonaba   b. cándida

3. _____ bajaremos   c. escondida

4. _____ lloroso   d. levantaremos

5. _____ quebradiza   e. de buen humor

6. _____ descubierta   f. lo cuidaba

Equivalentes *Complete each phrase or sentence by substituting words or phrases from the following list for the words or phrases in small type.*

azules   y no hay motivo   tumbado   débil
se ha precipitado trazo   ha aparecido   recuerdas

1. El canario de los niños _____ hoy muerto.
   <small>ha amanecido</small>

2. El invierno último, tú _____ bien.
   <small>te acuerdas</small>

3. pero su voz era _____ y asmática
   <small>quebradiza</small>

4. El mayor de los niños, viéndolo _____ en el fondo de la jaula,
   <small>yerto</small>

   _____ a decir —¡Puej no l'a faltao na!
   <small>se ha apresurado</small>

5. Se ha muerto _____.
   <small>porque sí</small>

6. con almas de pájaros blancos, rosas, _____, amarillos
   <small>celestes</small>

7. y un _____ secreto de trinos claros de oro puro
   <small>reguero</small>

Reflexiones *Consider the following themes and questions, and discuss them in Spanish.*

1. ¿Qué le parece el comportamiento de Platero? ¿Es creíble?

_____

_____

_____

2. Según usted, en los cuentos de Juan Ramón Jiménez, ¿cuál es el verdadero papel de Platero?

_____

_____

_____

Figuras retóricas *Rephrase the following expressions in a less poetic style of writing.*

1. el símil = figura de comparación

   a. "arrebolados y rientes como auroras"

   _____

   b. "igual que un chivillo"

   _____

2. la metáfora = substitución de palabras o expresiones

   "un oleaje de carnes de plata"

   _____

¡No se olvide! El tiempo futuro simple

The simple future tense is used for actions, thoughts, and states that will take place in the future. To express the near future, many Spanish speakers use **ir** + **a** + infinitive: **Voy a salir.** *I am going to go out.* Sometimes the simple present tense of the verb is used: **Llegan mañana.** *They'll arrive tomorrow.*

The formation of the future tense is easy. For **-ar**, **-er**, and **-ir** verbs, use the infinitive as the stem, adding these endings: **(yo)** -**é**, **(tu)** -**ás**, **(él, ella, usted)** -**á**, **(nosotros/as)** -**emos**, **(vosotros/as)** -**éis**, **(ellos, ellas, ustedes)** -**án**.

¡Ojo!

The Spanish **futuro simple** is a one-word verb form, while the English future is a compound form that includes *will* or *shall*.

Llegar**án** la semana próxima.	*They will arrive next week.*
Le escribir**é** a Jorge.	*I shall write to Jorge.*
Comer**emos** en la cafetería.	*We'll eat in the cafeteria.*

About a dozen Spanish verbs have irregular stems. Endings are identical to those for regular verbs in the future: **decir** (**dir-**), **haber** (**habr-**), **hacer** (**har-**), **poder** (**podr-**), **poner** (**pondr-**), **querer** (**querr-**), **saber** (**sabr-**), **salir** (**saldr-**), **tener** (**tendr-**), **valer** (**valdr-**), **venir** (**vendr-**).

El futuro de probabilidad

Forms of the future tense in Spanish may also indicate probability. Such guessing or conjecture usually refers to states or events in the present. Compare the English equivalents in the following examples.

Platero, ¿**habrá** un paraíso de los pájaros?	*Platero, might there be a heaven for birds?*
—No vino; ¿**estará** enferma?	*She didn't come; is she perhaps sick?*
—Ella **partirá** ahora.	*She's probably leaving now.*

EJERCICIO 12·15

Each of the following verbs appears in the simple future tense in the reading. Create a new sentence in the simple future using each verb.

1. haber

_____

2. bajar

_____

3. parecer

_____

4. enterrar

_____

5. poner

_____

¡Vaya más lejos!

- Busque información sobre el número y tipo de **mascotas en los países hispanohablantes**. ¿Qué animales tienden a preferir los habitantes?

- Busque información sobre **Juan Ramón Jiménez**. (Ver también el capítulo 8.)

- Busque en línea el audiolibro (¡gratis!) para escuchar capítulos narrados de *Platero y yo*.

Jíbara
Esmeralda Santiago (Puerto Rico)

Esmeralda Santiago nació en Santurce, San Juan de Puerto Rico, en 1948. Creció **humildemente** en Puerto Rico y luego en Nueva York adonde se había mudado a los trece años con su madre y sus hermanos. Con una **licenciatura** (B.A.) de Harvard University, Santiago se hizo actriz, cineasta (de documentales), **dramaturga**, **periodista** y escritora. Sus publicaciones incluyen memorias, novelas, obras teatrales, antologías y ensayos. La autobiografía *Cuando era puertorriqueña* fue su primer libro, de donde esta selección, **Jíbara**, proviene.

¿Estamos listos?

1. ¿Dónde nació usted? ¿Dónde nacieron sus padres? ¿sus abuelos?

2. ¿Qué orígenes étnicos, nacionales y religiosos hay en su familia?

   Somos... europeos, ingleses, irlandeses, escoceses, franceses, alemanes, austriacos, italianos, españoles, suizos, belgas; norteafricanos, marroquís, argelinos (*Algerian*), tunecinos, libios; rusos, checos, húngaros, rumanos, ucranianos; hispanos/latinos, mexicanos, salvadoreños, cubanos, puertorriqueños, chilenos, venezolanos, colombianos, brasileños; asiáticos, chinos, japoneses, coreanos, vietnamitas, indios; nativos de América, turcos, saudíes, egipcios, iraquíes, afganis, sirios, libaneses, israelíes, palestinos; afroamericanos, africanos...

   Y nosotros somos (originalmente)... cristianos, protestantes, cuáqueros, unitarios, mormones, católicos, judíos, musulmanes, budistas, confucianos, hindúes, espiritistas, ateos, agnósticos...

3. ¿Cómo fue criado?

   Mis padres eran... tranquilos, relajados, comprensivos, nerviosos, exigentes, difíciles, pacientes, impacientes, inquietos, preocupados, cómicos, pobres, ricos, de la clase media...

4. ¿De niño cómo era?

   Yo era... curioso/a, contento/a, bromista (*playful*), activo/a, serio/a, inteligente, atlético/a, estudioso/a, apático/a, rebelde...

5. ¿De niño dónde vivía? ¿Cómo era su casa, apartamento o piso? En su opinión, ¿su vivienda tenía defectos o problemas?

   Nuestro hogar (*home*) era (demasiado)... pequeño, grande, moderno, viejo, anticuado, nuevo, elegante, confortable, sencillo, gastado, remoto, aislado, ruidoso, tranquilo...

6. ¿Hoy día vive de manera diferente de cuando era niño/a? ¿Sus circunstancias actuales son distintas o similares?

¡Leamos!

Llegamos a **Macún** cuando yo tenía cuatro años. Nuestro nuevo hogar, un rectángulo de zinc elevado en **pilotes** sobre un círculo de tierra **rojiza**, parecía una versión enorme de las **latas** de **manteca** en las que Mami traía agua de la **pluma** pública. Las ventanas y puertas también eran de zinc, y cuando toqué la **pared** al entrar, **me quemé los dedos**.

—Eso es **pa' que** aprendas —me **regañó** Mami— que nunca se toca una pared donde le dá [sic] el sol.

Rebuscó dentro de un **bulto** lleno de ropas y **pañales** y **sacó** su Vick's, con el cual me **embarró** los dedos. Por el resto del día me **ardieron** las **yemas** de los dedos, y esa noche **no me pude chupar el pulgar**. —Ya tú estás muy grande pa' eso —me dijo.

El **piso de madera** estaba **remendado** con **tablas** irregulares que formaban una **joroba** en el medio de la casa, sus **costados** inclinados hacia los **umbrales brillosos** y bien **gastados**. Papi puso nuevas tablas bajo la **máquina de coser** de Mami y debajo de la cama, pero el piso todavía **crujía** y **se empinaba** hacia las **esquinas**, hasta que parecía que la menor brisa nos **tumbaría** la casa **encima**.

—Voy a **arreglar** el piso —afirmó Papi—. Pero **mientras tanto**, tendremos que vivir con un piso de tierra...

Mami miró hacia sus pies y **se frotó los brazos**. Alguien nos había dicho que en las casas con piso de tierra los **alacranes** y las **culebras se salen** de sus **huecos** y se meten dentro de la casa. Mami no sabía si eso era **mentira** o no, y yo, siendo niña, todavía no comprendía que no todo lo que se decía era verdad. **Así que** reaccionamos a nuestra manera: Si ella le **tenía miedo** a algo, a mí me fascinaba, y lo que más me **atemorizaba** a mí, a ella le **entusiasmaba**. **Al levantar ella** sus pies al **travesaño** del **mecedor** y **sobarse los escalofríos** de los brazos, imaginé un mundo de criaturas serpentinas trazando círculos debajo de la casa.

El día que Papi **desprendió** el piso, yo le acompañé, llevando un **pote** donde él ponía **clavos** que todavía se podían utilizar. Los dedos me **picaban** del **polvo mohoso**, y cuando lo **probé**, un **sabor** seco y metálico me **rizó** la punta de la **lengua**. Mami, **parada** en el umbral, **rascándose el tobillo** con las **uñas** del otro pie, nos observaba.

—**Negi**, ven acá. Vamo' a buscar **leña** pa'l **fogón**.

—Ahora no, Mami, que estoy trabajando con Papi.

En mi voz traté de poner un **ruego** para que él me pidiera que me quedara. Pero Papi siguió **de rodillas** sacando clavos del piso con la **horquilla del martillo**, **tarareando** su cha-cha-chá favorito.

—Vénte [sic] conmigo —ordenó Mami. Papi mantuvo su **espalda** hacia nosotras. **Tiré** el pote lleno de clavos contra el piso para que Papi me oyera y me dijera que me quedara con él, pero no lo hizo. **Haroneando** detrás de Mami, bajamos los tres **escalones** hacia el **batey**. Delsa y Norma, mis dos hermanas menores, jugaban en un **columpio** que Papi **había colgado** de las **ramas** de un mangó.

—¿Por qué no le dices a ellas que ayuden con la leña?

—¡**No me faltes el respeto**! —me dio un **cocotazo**— Ustedes **no se acerquen a** la casa mientras su papá está trabajando —**advirtió** cuando pasábamos cerca de mis hermanas.

Mami **se metió por** un **matorral** que había al otro lado de la **letrina**. Ramitas secas **crepitaban** bajo mis pies **descalzos, puyándome las plantas**. Una **reinita** voló hasta la rama **espinosa** de un **limón** y miró de lado a lado. Contra las paredes verdes del **boscaje**, puntitas de sol bailaban entre las ramas **cargadas** con **vainas** de **gandules**, la tierra cubierta de **chamarasca, moriviví** y **cohitre** de **florecillas** azules. Mami **canturreaba** un **danzón**. [...]

Una mariposa roja se le acercó y voló alrededor de su cabeza. Ella **se asustó** y le dio un **golpazo** que **mandó** a la mariposa contra el **suelo**.

—¡Huy! Parecía como que se me metía al cerebro —murmuró con una **sonrisa turbada**.

VOCABULARIO

humildemente	*poor*	costados	*sides*
licenciatura	*bachelor's degree (B.A.)*	(los) umbrales	*doorsteps*
dramaturga	*playwright*	brillosos	*shiny*
periodista [M., F.]	*journalist*	gastados	*worn-out*
jíbara [jíbaro] [PEJ.] [P.R.]	*peasant, Jivaro (tribe) native*	máquina de coser	*sewing machine*
		crujía [crujir]	*creaked*
Macún	*barrio in the Toa Baja Pueblo on the north coast of Puerto Rico*	se empinaba [empinarse]	*slanted upwards*
		esquinas	*corners*
(los) pilotes	*pilings, stilts*	tumbaría [tumbar]	*would knock over*
rojiza	*reddish*		
latas	*cans, tins*	encima	*on top of (us)*
manteca	*lard*	arreglar	*repair, fix*
pluma	*fountain*	mientras tanto	*meanwhile*
(la) pared	*wall*	se frotó [frotarse] los brazos	*rubbed her arms, shivered*
me quemé [quemarse] los dedos	*I burned my fingers*	(los) alacranes	*scorpions*
pa' que (para que)	*so, so that*	culebras	*snakes*
regañó [regañar]	*scolded, yelled at*	se salen [salirse]	*pop out, escape*
rebuscó [rebuscar]	*she rummaged*	huecos	*hollows, burrows*
bulto	*bundle, bag*	mentira	*lie, falsehood*
(los) pañales	*diapers*	así que	*and so, thus*
sacó [sacar]	*took out*	tenía [tener] miedo	*was afraid*
embarró [embarrar]	*(she) smeared*	atemorizaba [atemorizar]	*terrified*
ardieron [arder]	*burned*		
yemas	*tips*	entusiasmaba [entusiasmar]	*excited*
no me pude [poder] chupar el pulgar	*I couldn't suck my thumb*	al levantar ella	*as she lifted*
piso de madera	*wood floor*	travesaño	*rung (of a chair)*
remendado [remendar]	*patched*	(el) mecedor	*rocking chair*
tablas	*boards, planks*	sobarse los escalofríos	*(as she) kneaded the shivers*
joroba	*hump*		

desprendió [desprender]	*dismantled*	no se acerquen [acercarse] a	*don't go near*
(el) pote	*pot, tub*	advirtió [advertir]	*she warned*
clavos	*nails*	se metió [meterse] por	*went into, entered*
picaban [picar]	*stung*		
polvo	*dust*	(el) matorral	*brush, thicket*
mohoso	*moldy*	letrina	*outhouse, latrine*
probé [probar]	*tasted*	crepitaban [crepitar]	*crackled*
(el) sabor	*taste, flavor*	descalzos	*barefoot*
rizó [rizar]	*curled up*	puyándome [puyar] las plantas	*pricking the soles of my feet*
lengua	*tongue*		
parada	*standing*	reinita	*bananaquit (common bird of Puerto Rico)*
rascándose [rascarse] el tobillo	*scratching her ankle*		
		espinosa	*thorny*
uñas	*toenails*	(el) limón	*lemon tree*
Negi (Negrita)	*nickname, term of endearment*	(el) boscaje	*thicket, grove*
		cargadas	*loaded, heavy*
leña	*firewood*	vainas	*pods*
(el) fogón	*(cooking) fire*	(los) gandules	*pigeon peas*
ruego	*plea, supplication*	chamarasca	*brush, kindling*
de rodillas	*on his knees*	(el) moriviví	*sensitive plant (Mimosa pudica)*
horquilla del martillo	*claw of the hammer*		
tarareando [tararear]	*humming*	(el) cohitre	*spiderwort (Trascendencia cultivula)*
espalda	*back*		
tiré [tirar]	*I dropped*	florecillas	*little flowers, florets*
haroneando [haronear]	*dawdling*	canturreaba [canturrear]	*was humming*
(los) escalones	*steps*		
(el) batey	*sugar workers' compound*	(el) danzón	*dance form (originally Cuban)*
columpio	*(child's) swing*	se asustó [asustarse]	*got scared*
había colgado [colgar]	*had hung*	golpazo	*thump, whack*
ramas	*branches*	mandó [mandar]	*sent*
¡No me faltes [faltar] el respeto!	*Don't talk back! / Do what I say!*	suelo	*ground*
		sonrisa	*smile*
cocotazo	*slap*	turbada	*fearful, distraught*

¿De qué se trata? *Match the beginning of each sentence with the phrase that correctly completes it to retell the story from the reading.*

1. _____ Llegamos a Macún
2. _____ Nuestro nuevo hogar
3. _____ Cuando toqué la pared
4. _____ Mientras Papi arreglaba el piso
5. _____ Mami se frotó los brazos
6. _____ Yo prefería ayudar a Papi
7. _____ Mis hermanas menores
8. _____ Una mariposa roja

a. me quemé los dedos.

b. teníamos que vivir con un piso de tierra.

c. que recoger la leña del fogón.

d. cuando yo tenía cuatro años.

e. jugaban en un columpio colgado de las ramas.

f. no sobrevivió al miedo de Mami.

g. parecía una versión de las latas de manteca.

h. porque tenía miedo de las criaturas del piso.

Opciones *Choose the phrase or phrases that correctly answer each question. Include all correct responses.*

1. En este pasaje, ¿cuántos años tiene Negi, la narradora?

    a. más de cuatro años
    b. menos de cuatro años
    c. catorce años

2. ¿Cómo se sabe que esta familia no es rica?

    a. cocina con fuego de leña
    b. no tiene agua corriente
    c. las niñas están descalzas

3. ¿Por qué la casa está en pilotes?

    a. hay dos pisos
    b. está en la playa
    c. los umbrales están gastados

4. ¿Qué hace el padre?

    a. le pide ayuda a su esposa
    b. arregla el piso
    c. trabaja en la casa

5. ¿Cómo es la madre?

    a. inquieta
    b. tranquila
    c. preocupada

6. ¿Qué hace la madre?

    a. se va a recoger leña
    b. regaña a su hija mayor
    c. recoge los clavos

7. En el matorral, ¿qué observa Negi?

   a. las flores   b. las malas hierbas   c. una reinita

8. La madre se asusta cuando siente los movimientos de algo. ¿Qué es?

   a. una culebra   b. un alacrán   c. una mariposa

EJERCICIO
13·3

¿Cierto o falso? *Indicate whether each statement is true or false, using **C** for **cierto** (true) or **F** for **falso** (false). If a statement is false, provide a corrected statement in Spanish.*

1. C F   La familia ya vive en esta casa desde hace algunos años.

   _____

2. C F   Negi es una niña curiosa y activa.

   _____

3. C F   El piso de la casa está gastado y desigual.

   _____

4. C F   No es posible arreglar el piso.

   _____

5. C F   Papi quiere que Negi le ayude a hacerlo.

   _____

6. C F   Mami se fue a recoger leña para el fogón.

   _____

7. C F   Delsa y Norma también ayudan a sus padres.

   _____

8. C F   Las criaturas del campo aterrorizan a la madre de Negi.

   _____

Reflexiones *Consider the following themes and questions, and discuss them in Spanish.*

1. En su opinión, ¿este pasaje expresa bien las circunstancias de una familia humilde?
   ¿Cómo y con qué detalles?

   _____

   _____

   _____

2. Mami y Papi reaccionan ante las actividades de su hija mayor de diferente manera.
   Describa la reacción de cada uno. ¿Es lógica?

   _____

   _____

   _____

3. ¿Recuerda usted unos hábitos de su infancia? ¿Lo tocaba usted todo? ¿Lo probaba todo?
   ¿Se chupaba el pulgar? ¿Cuándo dejó usted de chuparse el pulgar? ¿Recuerda cómo lo
   hizo?

   _____

   _____

   _____

4. Esmeralda Santiago fue la mayor de los once hijos de su madre. Trabajó duro para obtener
   una buena educación secundaria y universitaria. Se hizo actriz, autora, cineasta y activista.
   En su opinión, ¿es un factor importante el orden de nacimiento del individuo?

   _____

   _____

   _____

Mi vocabulario *Select the word that does not belong in each group.*

1. a. rueda   b. solicitud   c. demanda   d. ruego

2. a. maestría   b. bachillerato   c. licenciatura   d. liceo

3. a. remendar   b. reparar   c. arreglar   d. dañar

4. a. destornillador   b. martillo   c. clavo   d. sierra

5. a. huecos   b. agujeros   c. aberturas   d. agujas

6. a. manteca   b. aceituna   c. mantequilla   d. aceite

7. a. canes   b. culebras   c. cocodrilos   d. lagartos

8. a. escalones   b. escalofríos   c. grados   d. travesaños

9. a. regalar   b. regañar   c. reprender   d. amonestar

10. a. boscaje   b. chamarasca   c. matorral   d. chamarra

EJERCICIO 13·6

Contrarios *Match each word or phrase with its opposite.*

1. _____ nuevos   a. acercarse

2. _____ desprender   b. espinoso

3. _____ golpazo   c. entusiasmar

4. _____ mentira   d. tirar

5. _____ darse prisa   e. haronear

6. _____ levantar   f. parado

7. _____ alejarse   g. caricia

8. _____ liso   h. cielo

9. _____ atemorizar   i. juntar

10. _____ de rodillas   j. gastados

11. _____ suelo   k. verdad

EJERCICIO 13·7

Equivalentes *Complete each sentence by substituting words or phrases from the following list for the words or phrases in small type.*

crujían	sin zapatos	picándome	temerosa
aproximó	aleteó	del retrete	atemorizó
tarareaba	bosque	se me entraba	envió
entró en	la tierra	cocotazo	susurró

1. Mami _____ un _____ que había al otro lado

     <small>se metió por</small>   <small>matorral</small>

   _____.

<small>de la letrina</small>

2. Ramitas secas _____ bajo mis pies _____,

                 <small>crepitaban</small>   <small>descalzos</small>

   _____ las plantas.

<small>puyándome</small>

3. Mami _____ un danzón.
   canturreaba

4. Una mariposa roja se le _____ y _____ alrededor
   acercó voló

   de su cabeza.

5. Ella se _____ y le dio un _____ que
   asustó golpazo

   _____ a la mariposa contra _____.
   mandó el suelo

6. —¡Huy! Parecía como que _____ al cerebro —_____
   se me metía murmuró

   con una sonrisa _____.
   turbada

¡No se olvide! Verbos reflexivos

Reflexive verbs are very common in Spanish. Used in all tenses and verb structures, including command forms, they are called reflexive because the subject of the verb and its object (pronoun) are identical (the pronoun reflects back). They appear in the dictionary with the pronoun **se** attached to the infinitive: **bañarse** *to bathe (oneself)*, **divertirse** *to have a good time.*

Many verbs, considered idiomatic reflexives, do not include the element myself, yourself, etc. in the English equivalent: **dormirse** *to fall asleep*; **sentarse** *to sit down.*

1. The reflexive pronouns **me, te, se, nos, os, se** correspond to the six persons of the conjugation. The reflexive pronoun precedes the conjugated verb and follows the subject pronoun, if the subject pronoun is used: **(yo) me acuesto** *I go to bed.*

sentarse *to sit down* (PRESENT)		**vestirse** *to get dressed* (PRETERIT)	
me siento	**nos** sentamos	**me** vestí	**nos** vestimos
te sientas	**os** sentáis	**te** vestiste	**os** vestisteis
se sienta	**se** sientan	**se** vistió	**se** vistieron

2. When used with infinitives, the reflexive pronoun follows and is attached to the infinitive form.

   ¿Vas a levantar**te** a las siete?   *Are you going to get up at 7 o'clock?*

   However, in such verb + verb constructions, the reflexive pronoun can also be placed before the conjugated verb (but not before the infinitive). Note that the meaning is the same.

   ¿**Te** vas a levantar a las siete?   *Are you going to get up at 7 o'clock?*

3. With a present participle (the **-ando, -iendo** forms)—alone or with the progressive **estar** + present participle—the reflexive pronoun is attached to the participle. Alternatively, it may precede the conjugated verb. (When the pronoun is attached, a written accent appears on the antepenultimate syllable.)

   Nos estamos divirtiendo. ⎫
   Estamos divirtiéndo**nos**. ⎭   *We're having a good time.*

4. In constructions that include a part of the body or an article of clothing, the part of the body or article of clothing is preceded by **el**, **la**, **los**, or **las** and is considered the direct object of the verb. The reflexive pronoun then functions as the indirect object of that verb.

Negi **se** quemó **los dedos**.   *Negi burned her fingers.*
Sus hermanas no **se** ponían **los zapatos**.   *Her sisters didn't put on their shoes.*

5. The third-person **se** form, in both singular and plural, is often used to express a generality. This can be considered the equivalent of a passive voice in English.

No todo lo que **se decía** era verdad.   *Not everything (that was) said was true.*
Los vinos rojos **se beben** a temperatura   *Red wines are drunk at room temperature.*
ambiente.

EJERCICIO
13·8

Give the correct tense for the verb form in bold (command, imperfect, infinitive, present, present participle, preterit; passive voice if applicable) in each of the following phrases or sentences, then give the infinitive for each verb.

1. **Me quemé** los dedos.

_____   _____

2. Esa noche no **me pude chupar** el pulgar.

_____   _____

3. Pero el piso todavía crujía y **se empinaba** hacia las esquinas.

_____   _____

4. **Se frotó** los brazos.

_____   _____

5. Los alacranes y las culebras **se salen** de sus huecos y **se meten** dentro de la casa.

_____   _____

_____   _____

6. (al) **sobarse** los escalofríos de los brazos

_____   _____

7. Mami..., **rascándose** el tobillo con las uñas del otro pie, nos observaba.

_____   _____

8. **Vénte** conmigo.

_____   _____

9. Ustedes no **se acerquen** a la casa.

_____   _____

10. Mami **se metió** por un matorral que había al otro lado de la letrina.

_____   _____

11. Ella **se asustó** y le dio un golpazo.

_____   _____

12. Parecía como que **se me metía** al cerebro.

_____   _____

13. que nunca **se toca** una pared donde le dá el sol

_____   _____

14. No todo lo que **se decía** era verdad.

_____   _____

15. llevando un pote donde él ponía clavos que todavía **se podían utilizar**

_____   _____

¡Vaya más lejos!

- Busque información sobre la relación entre la isla de **Puerto Rico** y el territorio continental de los EE.UU. ¿Cuál es la ciudadanía de los puertorriqueños?

- En los Estados Unidos, ¿dónde se encuentra una gran población puertorriqueña?

- ¿Cómo evidencian estas ciudades la influencia puertorriqueña?

- Esmeralda Santiago llegó a **Macún** a los cuatro años, en 1952. Busque en un mapa esta región de Puerto Rico. En su investigación, ¿ve usted indicaciones de cambios en la región de **Toa Baja Pueblo**?

- Busque fotos de la **reinita** o _bananaquit,_ el ave más común de Puerto Rico, y de otros pájaros de las islas del Caribe.

MEDIO AMBIENTE

El hogar natural: Plantar una huerta
(España)

El cultivar una **huerta** es el pasatiempo más popular entre las personas que **disponen de** un **terreno** (pequeño o grande). Si usted no tiene jardín en el **hogar**, puede **arreglarse** con **jardineras** o **macetas**. Si le gustan los ingredientes frescos para cocinar o para una alimentación saludable, debería pensar en cultivar sus propias verduras.

¿Estamos listos?

1. ¿Les gustan a usted, a sus amigos y parientes los productos frescos? ¿Dónde se obtienen estos productos?

   Los obtengo en el/la/mi... supermercado, mercado de productos frescos, mercado agrícola (al aire libre), granja de la localidad, propia huerta...

2. ¿Ya ha cultivado una huerta? En su opinión, ¿qué verduras son las más deliciosas?

   Prefiero... las acelgas (*chard*), ajo (*garlic*), albahaca (*basil*), alcachofas (*artichokes*), apio (*celery*), berenjenas (*eggplants*), brócoli [M.], calabazas (*pumpkins*), calabacines [M.] (*zucchini*), cebollas (*onions*), champiñones [M.] (*mushrooms*), col [F.] (*cabbage*), col de Bruselas (*Brussels sprouts*), coliflor [F.], espárragos, espinacas, garbanzos, chiles [M.], guisantes [M.] (*peas*) [SP.], arvejas (*peas*) [LAT. AM.], chícharos (*peas*) [MEX.], judías verdes [F.] (*green beans*) [SP.], ejotes [M.] (*green beans*) [MEX.], lechuga (*lettuce*), maíz [M.] (*corn*), patatas, papas [LAT. AM.], pepinos (*cucumbers*), perejil [M.] (*parsley*), pimientos verdes/rojos (*green/red peppers*), puerros (*leeks*), rábanos (*radishes*), remolacha (*beets*), soja, tomates [M.], zanahorias (*carrots*)...

3. ¿Qué árboles frutales son fáciles de cultivar en una huerta doméstica? ¿en el clima donde vive?

   Hay... aguacates [M.] (*avocados*), albaricoques [M.] (*apricots*), bananas, caquis [M.] (*persimmons*), cerezas (*cherries*), ciruelas (*plums*), melocotones [M.] (*peaches*) [SP.], duraznos (*peaches*) [LAT. AM.], limones, manzanas, naranjas, piñas (*pineapples*), toronjas (*grapefruit*)...

4. ¿Y los arbustos frutales que producen bayas y otras frutas en la huerta familiar?

   Hay por ejemplo... arándanos (*blueberries*), moras (*blackberries*), frambuesas (*raspberries*), fresas (*strawberries*), grosellas rojas (*currants*), melón [M.], sandía (*watermelon*), uvas (*grapes*)...

¡Leamos!

Todo cuanto necesitamos para tener una pequeña huerta **familiar** es: una pequeña parcela, con buena tierra y agua, unos **sobres** de aquellas **semillas** que queramos plantar, **herramienta** adecuada y algunos conocimientos básicos. **Con ello** podrá tener, no sólo fruta y verdura fresca, **recogida** en el día, sino un entretenimiento agradable y relajante.

Primero deberíamos **realizar** un análisis del **suelo** para saber de qué tipo es y si es fértil. Si no fuera fértil sólo hay que enriquecerlo y **mejorarlo** con aquellos nutrientes **que le falten**. Después debería **cercarse** el terreno, para que los animales domésticos no pasaran y nos **estropearan** la labor realizada. La orientación también es importante, **aunque** por lo general para la huerta siempre utilizamos el lugar menos visto desde la entrada, una buena orientación sería al sur. Si la orientación es norte, deberemos poner muros o **setos** para protegerla del viento frío, siempre dejando **hueco** por donde entre bien el sol y la luz. Un seto vivo es una buena solución, pero no deberá ser muy alto para que **no dé** demasiada **sombra** a los **cultivos**. Un seto natural excelente son los arbustos de frutales como las frambuesas.

El **huerto** debe tener un acceso fácil y permitir el paso con una carretilla para el transporte del **abono**, y **si fuera grande**, caminos o **senderos** para poder pasar sin problemas.

Una parcela de 3 × 4 metros le permitirá hacer durante todo el año unas **cosechas** variadas. Para **proveer a** una familia (2–3 personas), el huerto deberá ser por lo menos de 100 m2. Como no se dispondrá **seguramente** de mucho espacio, deberemos pensar muy bien qué es lo que deseamos plantar, lo que ocupa cada planta y la cantidad de alimento que **nos proporcionará**. Afortunadamente las especies que ocupan menos volumen, también son las más **apetecibles**.

La **siembra** deberemos realizarla en **fajas** o **hileras** muy juntas, dejando un espacio de unos **30 ó 35** centímetros. para poder realizar las labores de mantenimiento y recolección. Las siembras con semillas en plena tierra se efectúan en línea con un **cordel**, en unos **surcos cavados** con el **rastrillo**. Las semillas más gordas se depositan 4 ó 5 en **agujeros** bien alineados, después rastrillar para cubrir los agujeros. Las siembras **crecerán** más rápidamente en **cajas vidriadas** que en la tierra (unas 3 ó 4 semanas más rápido). Cubrir las plantas jóvenes para protegerlas del frío, y colocar la caja en un sitio **soleado**, abrirla para ventilarla cuando el tiempo sea **cálido**.

Para evitar el **agotamiento** de la tierra, cada año se deberá alternar el emplazamiento de los cultivos. Las **verduras de raíces** (como las cebollas, zanahorias, etc.) son las que más agotan el suelo. **En cambio** las **verduras de semillas** son muy benéficas para el terreno. Las verduras de crecimiento rápido, podrán darle dos cosechas al año sobre una misma **superficie**.

Tampoco debe olvidar el tiempo que deberá dedicarle a tener el huerto **en condiciones, ya que** si no tiene tiempo suficiente, mejor será que se tengan cosechas más pequeñas.

Algunos días después de que las plantitas salgan, se deberá **pulverizar** con un fungicida sobre los **brotes**. Si el suelo se seca mucho en la superficie es necesario **regar en pulverización**, preferiblemente por la tarde o por la mañana temprano.

También tenemos que tener en cuenta el eliminar las **malas hierbas**, para ellos debemos **binar** dos veces al mes. Los herbicidas pueden atacar las plantas, por lo que es recomendable usar productos naturales y **arrancarlas** con la mano.

Otros enemigos son las **plagas**, que debemos combatir lo antes posible para que no se propaguen a todo el huerto. Leer bien todas las instrucciones de los productos que usemos, y no usar al menos 15 días antes de la cosecha.

En cuanto a la conservación de los productos, hay variedades **tardías** que se conservan muy bien hasta entrado el invierno, ya que la tierra protege las verduras de raíz (zanahorias,

nabos, remolacha), pero es conveniente cubrir el terreno con **hojas** o **paja** para evitar que el suelo se quede demasiado **duro**, con lo que no podríamos arrancarlas correctamente. Hay otros productos que en la **nevera** o el **congelador**, se conservarán por mucho tiempo.

Los **datos** son aproximados y **orientativos**, ya que todo influye y puede variar según muchas variables externas, como el clima más **autóctono**, el modo de plantar, etc... Las fechas son para el hemisferio norte, para fechas del hemisferio Sud se le deben añadir 6 meses.

Brócoli

Siembra y reproducción: en **semillero**. La semilla se cubre con una **capa** de tierra de 1–1.5 centímetros y se riega frecuentemente. A los 10 días empiezan a **brotar** y a los 45–55 días la planta está **desarrollada**. **Cuando alcance** 18–20 centímetros y unas 6–8 hojas, estará lista para el trasplante. Regar abundante y regularmente durante el crecimiento.

Fechas: otoño, invierno.

Recolección: cuando la longitud del **tallo** es de 5 ó 6 centímetros. Las **inflorescencias** deben estar cerradas y de color verde oscuro brillante y compacto.

Plagas y enfermedades: los **minadores** de hojas, la **mosca de la col**, y la **oruga de la col**.

Calabaza

Siembra y reproducción: por semilla en terreno definitivo, una vez haya pasado el peligro de **heladas**. Se puede **adelantar** la siembra en semillero protegido y luego trasplantar las **matitas** cuando tengan 2 ó 3 hojas. Requiere **exposición** soleada y estar **resguardada** del viento. **Riego** frecuente.

Fechas de siembra: febrero a junio.

Recolección: en otoño, dejando un poco de **pedúnculo para que se almacene** mejor.

Fecha de recolección: julio a octubre.

Plagas y enfermedades: su peor enemigo es la baja temperatura y los **hongos**.

From *El Hogar Natural*, http://www.elhogarnatural.com. Used with the permission of María Rosa González Gil and *El Hogar Natural*. Many thanks to María Rosa González Gil.

VOCABULARIO

huerta	*vegetable/kitchen garden*	suelo	*soil*
		mejorarlo	*to improve it*
disponen [disponer] de	*have (available)*	que le falten [faltar]	*that they need*
terreno	*plot, field*	cercarse	*(to) fence, enclose*
(el) hogar	*home*	estropearan [estropear]	*ruin*
arreglarse	*manage*	aunque	*although*
jardineras	*window boxes*	setos	*hedges*
macetas	*pots, containers*	hueco	*space, gap*
familiar	*family(-sized)*	no dé [dar]... sombra	*doesn't shade*
(los) sobres	*packets*	cultivos	*plants, crops*
semillas	*seeds*	huerto	*vegetable/kitchen garden*
herramienta	*(set of) tools*		
con ello [NEUTER PRON.]	*with that*	abono	*compost, fertilizer*
recogida	*harvested, gathered*	si fuera [ser] grande	*if it's big*
realizar	*to carry out*	senderos	*paths*

cosechas	crops, harvests	plagas	infestations
proveer a	to supply	tardías	late(-season)
seguramente	certainly, surely	nabos	turnips
nos proporcionará [proporcionar]	will give/supply us	hojas	leaves
		paja	straw
apetecibles	appetizing	duro	hard
siembra	sowing	nevera	refrigerator
fajas	furrows	(el) congelador	freezer
hileras	rows	datos	facts, information
30 ó 35	30 or 35	orientativos	illustrative
(el) cordel	cord, string	autóctono	local, native
surcos	furrows	semillero	seedbed, seed tray
cavados	dug (out)	capa	layer
rastrillo	rake	brotar	to sprout
agujeros	holes	desarrollada [desarrollar]	well-developed
crecerán [crecer]	will grow	cuando alcance [alcanzar]	when it reaches
cajas vidriadas	cold frames		
soleado	sunny	tallo	stalk, stem
cálido	warm, hot	inflorescencias	florets
agotamiento	depletion	(los) minadores	borers (insects)
verduras de raíces	root vegetables	mosca de la col	cabbage fly
en cambio	on the other hand	oruga de la col	cabbage caterpillar
verduras de semillas	seed vegetables	heladas	frost(s)
(la) superficie	area, space	adelantar	(to) advance, hurry along
tampoco debe olvidar	nor should you forget		
en condiciones	in good order	matitas	stalks, sprouts
ya que	since	(la) exposición	exposure
pulverizar	spray	resguardada [resguardar]	protected, sheltered
(los) brotes	shoots, sprouts	riego	watering
regar en pulverización	spray with water	pedúnculo	stem
malas hierbas	weeds	para que se almacene [almacenarse]	so that it will keep
binar	(to) hoe		
arrancarlas	to pull them out	hongos	fungi

EJERCICIO

14·1

¿De qué se trata? *Read the following statements, then suggest a list of plants or crops each person could grow. Use vocabulary from* **¿Estamos listos?** *and* **Vocabulario.**

1. Nos gustan muchísimo las tartas de fruta.

_____

2. Los veranos donde vivo son soleados y calurosos.

_____

3. En mi parcela el suelo está pobre y agotado.

_____

4. Las verduras son difíciles de cultivar; prefiero las frutas.

_____

5. Vivo en un apartamento, pero tengo un balcón y mi ventana es soleada.

_____

6. Todas las semanas nos gusta preparar una sopa de verduras.

_____

7. A mis hijos no les gustan las verduras de la familia de las coles. ¿Qué verduras debería cultivar?

_____

8. En nuestra casa necesitamos conservar las verduras durante mucho tiempo, a veces todo el invierno.

_____

Opciones *Choose the phrase or phrases that correctly complete each sentence. Include all correct responses.*

1. Todo cuanto necesitamos para tener una huerta familiar es

   a. unas semillas.   b. una parcela.   c. buena tierra y agua.

2. Los placeres del cuidado de un jardín residen en

   a. el entretenimiento.   b. los productos frescos. c. la herramienta.

3. El análisis del suelo se realiza para saber

   a. su color.   b. de qué tipo es.   c. si es fértil.

4. El terreno debe cercarse para

   a. decorarlo.   b. impedir que entren animales. c. usar madera.

5. Para proteger la huerta del viento frío, sería bueno poner

   a. setos vivos.   b. muros.   c. hileras.

6. Debemos sembrar las plantas en fajas muy

   a. profundas.   b. espaciadas.   c. juntas.

7. Las siembras crecerán rápidamente en cajas vidriadas porque estarán más

   a. protegidas.   b. cálidas.   c. frías.

8. Se alterna el emplazamiento de los cultivos cada año para

   a. evitar el agotamiento. b. mejorar el suelo.   c. obtener dos cosechas.

¿Cierto o falso? *Indicate whether each statement is true or false, using* **C** *for* **cierto** *(true) or* **F** *for* **falso** *(false). If a statement is false, provide a corrected statement in Spanish.*

1. C F   Las lechugas son las que más agotan el suelo.

   _____

2. C F   Las verduras de crecimiento rápido podrán darle dos cosechas al año.

   _____

3. C F   Es preferible regar en pulverización por la tarde o por la mañana temprano.

   _____

   _____

4. C F   No hay ningún problema con las herbicidas.

   _____

5. C F   Las plagas y las malas hierbas son enemigos de la huerta.

   _____

6. C F   Una buena orientación de la huerta sería al norte.

   _____

7. C F   Las verduras de raíz no se conservan bien.

   _____

8. C F   Las plantitas de la calabaza requieren sol y protección del viento.

   _____

   _____

   _____

Reflexiones *Consider the following themes and questions, and discuss them in Spanish.*

1. En su opinión, ¿por qué le gusta tanto a la gente la jardinería?

   _____

   _____

   _____

   _____

2. ¿Cuáles son las ventajas de cultivar una huerta? ¿Hay igualmente desventajas o aspectos negativos?

_____

_____

_____

_____

3. Planee o diseñe una huerta apropiada para su clima, en dos temporadas del año. ¿Qué cultivos son aptos para cada una?

_____

_____

_____

_____

4. Piense en los platos que le gusta comer o cocinar. ¿Qué frutas y verduras necesita para preparar sus recetas preferidas?

_____

_____

_____

_____

EJERCICIO
14·5

Mi vocabulario *Select the word that does not belong in each group.*

1. a. arboledas   b. senderos   c. arbustos   d. setos

2. a. abono   b. hueco   c. agujero   d. espacio

3. a. regar   b. rociar   c. pulverizar   d. desempolvar

4. a. recipiente   b. maceta   c. matita   d. envase

5. a. ranuras   b. pajas   c. surcos   d. fajas

6. a. recoger   b. coser   c. cosechar   d. recolectar

7. a. rastrillar   b. binar   c. estropear   d. cavar

8. a. terremoto   b. suelo   c. parcela   d. terreno

9. a. tallos   b. brotes   c. heladas   d. pedúnculos

10. a. protegido   b. sembrado   c. resguardado   d. defendido

Contrarios *Match each word or phrase with its opposite.*

1. _____ malas hierbas   a. duro
2. _____ siembra   b. inmaduro
3. _____ mejorar   c. autóctono
4. _____ cavado   d. cultivos
5. _____ desarrollado   e. nublado
6. _____ soleado   f. cosecha
7. _____ blando   g. amontonado
8. _____ extranjero   h. agotar
9. _____ apetecible   i. desagradable

Equivalentes *Complete each sentence by substituting words or phrases from the following list for the words or phrases in small type.*

encerrar	disposición	variedades	tendrá a su disposición
queremos	en buen estado	por suerte	vivero
consagrarle	los brotes	cubre	entraran
terreno	sabrosas	propagación	el trabajo acabado
progresar	irrigación	dará	la parcela
dañaran	recuerde bien	cogidas	considerar
protegida	necesita	las mascotas	

1. Como no _____ mucho _____, deberemos
    se dispondrá de espacio

   _____ muy bien qué es lo que _____ plantar,
   pensar deseamos

   lo que _____ cada planta y la cantidad de alimento que nos
    ocupa

   _____.
   proporcionará

2. _____ las _____ que ocupan menos volumen,
   Afortunadamente especies

   también son las más _____.
    apetecibles

3. Después debería _____ (cercarse) _____ (el terreno), para que _____ (los animales domésticos) no _____ (pasaran) y nos _____ (estropearan) _____ (la labor realizada). La _____ (orientación) también es importante.

4. _____ (Tampoco debe olvidar) el tiempo que deberá _____ (dedicarle) a tener el huerto _____ (en condiciones), ya que si no tiene tiempo suficiente, mejor será que se tengan _____ (cosechas) más pequeñas.

5. Se puede _____ (adelantar) la _____ (siembra) en _____ (semillero) protegido y luego trasplantar _____ (las matitas) cuando tengan 2 ó 3 hojas.

6. _____ (Requiere) exposición soleada y estar _____ (resguardada) del viento. _____ (Riego) frecuente.

¡No se olvide! El condicional

Like the indicative and the subjunctive, the conditional is technically a mood, not a tense. In most cases it is the equivalent of *would* + verb in English: *I **would join** you, if....*

To form the conditional in Spanish, add the endings of the imperfect tense of **-er** and **-ir** verbs to the infinitive. Regular and irregular **-ar**, **-er**, and **-ir** verbs all use the same endings.

-ar VERBS   **bailar** *to dance*

(yo) bailar**ía**	*I would dance*
(tú) bailar**ías**	*you* [FAM.] *would dance*
(él, ella, usted) bailar**ía**	*he/she/you* [FORM.] *would dance*
(nosotros/as) bailar**íamos**	*we would dance*
(vosotros/as) bailar**íais**	*you* [FAM. PL.] [SP.] *would dance*
(ellos, ellas, Uds.) bailar**ían**	*they/you would dance*

-er AND **-ir** VERBS

	conocer *to know*	**partir** *to leave*
yo	conocer**ía**	partir**ía**
tú	conocer**ías**	partir**ías**
él, ella, usted	conocer**ía**	partir**ía**
nosotros/as	conocer**íamos**	partir**íamos**
vosotros/as	conocer**íais**	partir**íais**
ellos, ellas, Uds.	conocer**ían**	partir**ían**

About a dozen Spanish verbs have irregular stems. The same stems are used in both the simple future tense and the conditional. In both, their endings are identical to those for regular verbs. These verbs in the conditional are **decir** (dir-) > **diría**, **haber** (habr-) > **habría**, **hacer** (har-) > **haría**, **poder** (podr-) > **podría**, **poner** (pondr-) > **pondría**, **querer** (querr-) > **querría**, **saber** (sabr-) > **sabría**, **salir** (saldr-) > **saldría**, **tener** (tendr-) > **tendría**, **valer** (valdr-) > **valdría**, **venir** (vendr-) > **vendría**.

The conditional is used as follows.

♦ To make a request, state a desire, or give a suggestion or advice (often with **deber**).

¿Yo **podría** cobrar este cheque aquí?	{ *May I cash this check here?* *Would I be able to cash this check here?*
Le **gustaría** a Isabel ver esta película.	*Isabel would like to see this movie.*
Debería realizar un análisis del suelo.	*You would need to carry out a soil analysis.*

♦ In indirect discourse in the past, after **que** + verb of communication (like **decir**) or **que** + verb of belief or understanding (like **creer**, **saber**).

Dije que no **iría**.	*I said I would not go.*
Creíamos que **contestarían**.	*We believed they would answer.*

♦ In the main clause of so-called contrary-to-fact sentences, preceded or followed by a clause starting with **si** *if* + a verb in the imperfect subjunctive. (See Chapter 11.)

¿Si tu amigo te invitara, **irías**?	*If your friend invited you, would you go?*
Si perdiera mi celular, lo **llamaría**.	*If I misplaced my cellphone, I would call it.*

♦ To express conjecture or probability in the past. An English sentence uses *probably* or *must have*.

Llegaron tarde; **habría** mal tiempo.	*They arrived late; the weather must have been bad.*
Estaría dormido; parecía confundido.	*He must have been asleep; he seemed confused.*
En esa foto, **tendrías** trece años.	*In that photo, you were probably thirteen.*

EJERCICIO
14·8

Each of the following phrases in bold appears in the reading. First (a) give an English equivalent of that phrase, then (b) create a new sentence in Spanish with the same conditional form of the verb.

1. **Primero deberíamos realizar** un análisis del suelo para saber de qué tipo es y si es fértil.

   a. _____

   b. _____

2. **Después debería cercarse** el terreno, para que los animales domésticos no pasaran y nos estropearan la labor realizada.

   a. _____

   b. _____

3. Para la huerta siempre utilizamos el lugar menos visto desde la entrada, **una buena orientación sería al sur.**

   a. _____

   b. _____

4. Pero es conveniente cubrir el terreno con hojas o paja para evitar que el suelo se quede demasiado duro, con lo que **no podríamos arrancarlas** correctamente.

   a. _____

   b. _____

EJERCICIO
14·9

Give a Spanish equivalent for each of the following statements or questions.

1. *Can you (Ud.) tell me where the pharmacy is?*

   _____

2. *I would like to see a classic movie tonight.*

   _____

3. *You (tú) should plant a vegetable garden this year.*

   _____

4. *She knew that we would not be able to do it.*

   _____

5. *Marina and Gloria said they would buy the seeds.*

   _____

6. *If you (Ud.) called Jorge, would he help us?*

   _____

7. *Would they eat spinach, if I picked (recoger) it?*

   _____

8. *He arrived late; it was probably snowing.*

   _____

9. *I see a message (mensaje); Silvia must have called.*

   _____

¡Vaya más lejos!

◆ Busque **diseño de un huerto** para recoger ideas de diseño.

◆ Busque **jardines célebres** o **jardines clásicos** o **jardines históricos** para ver fotos e imágenes.

◆ Busque **El Hogar Natural** y su publicación en línea **Cibernaturaleza**. Lea algunos artículos.

◆ Busque el sitio **www.jardinitis.com**. Vea las fotos y examine algunas categorías de aparatos o herramientas a la venta.

Jornada especial de reciclaje este domingo
(Venezuela)

EcoClick es un grupo de **ciudadanos conscientes** que buscan **promover** el cuidado y la conservación de nuestro planeta a través de acciones **claves** y la promoción de las 3R: Reducir, Reutilizar y Reciclar.

Esta **jornada** de reciclaje, entre otras, se realizó en ocasión del Día Mundial de la Tierra. Recibieron, entre otros objetos, **residuos** de papel, **cartón**, **pilas**, **bombillos**, **aluminios**, **latas**, **cajas**, **cartuchos de impresión** y **artefactos electrodomésticos**.

¿Estamos listos?

1. ¿Cuándo se celebra el Día Mundial de la Tierra? ¿Cuándo y dónde comenzó? ¿Quiénes lo iniciaron? ¿Cuáles fueren los resultados?

   El Día Mundial de la Tierra se celebra el 22 de abril. La primera manifestación tuvo lugar el 22 de abril de 1970. Fue promovido por el senador demócrata por el Estado de Wisconsin Gaylord Nelson. Participaron 2000 universidades, 10 000 escuelas y centenares de comunidades. El gobierno de los EE.UU. creó la Agencia de Protección Ambiental (*EPA*) y una serie de leyes protectoras.

2. ¿Qué hacemos El Día Mundial de la Tierra?

   Pasamos el día al aire libre; plantamos un jardín, una huerta (*vegetable garden*), arbustos o árboles; hacemos trabajo voluntario en la comunidad; recogemos basura en el vecindario; participamos en programas de reciclaje; vamos de excursión; arreglamos pistas y senderos en el parque; les hablamos a los niños de la ecología; utilizamos transporte alternativo...

3. ¿Qué artículos se reciclan en su comunidad?

   Se reciclan... papel, plástico, cartón, latas, botellas, frascos de vidrio, chatarra (*scrap*) metálica, aparatos electrónicos, pilas (*batteries*) y bombillos (*lightbulbs*)...

4. ¿Qué puede hacerse durante todo el año para conservar o producir energía, agua, alimentos...?

   Tome duchas cortas; reutilice agua cuando sea posible; recolecte agua de lluvia en un barril; plante arbustos, árboles e hierbas nativas; lave cargas completas de ropa y vajilla; establezca una pila de abono (*compost*); plante una huerta; prepare cantidades mayores de comida de una vez; no desperdicie comida; maneje (*drive*) menos; comparta (*share*) el auto; use transporte público; ande a pie o en bicicleta; compre artículos usados; done artículos usados; instale placas solares...

¡Leamos!

El Universal, miércoles 18 de abril de 2012, Caracas. Este domingo 22 de abril la **ONG** *Eco-Click* celebrará **en grande** el Día Mundial de La Tierra, **por lo que**, en conjunto con la **emisora** Hot 94 y la **Alcaldía de Sucre**, organizaron una jornada especial de reciclaje, de 3:00 pm a 6:00 pm en la Plaza Miranda del Centro Comercial Millenium.

Lista de residuos que estarán recibiendo

Papel, cartón, aluminio, plástico, pilas, bombillos **ahorradores**, **artefactos electrónicos** y electrónicos, **chatarra ferrosa** y no ferrosa (pequeña y **mediana**), **aceite comestible**, cartuchos de impresión y toners.

Condiciones de los residuos

Papel y cartón: se puede reciclar **periódicos**, papel blanco, **recibos**, **revistas**, cartones de alimentos, cartón en general, **embalaje**, **folletos** y **sobres**. Deben estar **limpios**, secos y libres de grasas.

Para ayudar con la logística se está solicitando a los **donantes** separar estos residuos en tres grupos: revistas y papel bond; periódicos; cartón.

No se reciclará: cartón de huevos, papeles **sucios** o contaminados, papel **glasé**, **plastificado**, aluminio y **encerados**.

Se estará recibiendo cualquier tipo de plástico (**recordar aplastarlos**). En caso de estar contaminados con comida, debe **enjuagarse** el **envase**.

Aluminio: latas previamente aplastadas y enjuagadas.

Pilas **gastadas**: se recibirán contenedores de la **campaña** "Recolecta Tus Pilas". Si se llevan pilas individuales, ponerle **teipe** al polo positivo de la pila cilíndrica (**bastón**).

A los interesados en crear un punto de recolección de pilas, **se estará entregando** el **aviso** para **pegarlo** en el envase. Si se llevan **potes** de cinco litros, guardarlos para la campaña.

Bombillos ahorradores. Son residuos **peligrosos** y contienen mercurio; por eso es muy delicada su manipulación. No se recibirán bombillos **rotos** y deben estar bien **envueltos** o **sellados** en **bolsa** plástica.

Vitaambiente entregará un Manual de **manipulación** así como información sobre bombillos ahorradores/pilas para ser entregados en la jornada.

Chatarra electrónica: se recibirán **celulares** viejos y artículos electrónicos pequeños y medianos. Proponen que con teipe indiquen las **fallas** que tiene el artefacto para que en caso de que alguien desee **arreglarlo** se lo pueda llevar.

Aceite vegetal: se recibirá el aceite en contenedor de plástico con **tapa de rosca**.

Cartuchos de impresión y toner: se recibirá cualquier tipo de cartucho de impresión y toners.

Importante

Todos los residuos serán reciclados y **aprovechados de acuerdo a** su condición.

Se podrá **disfrutar** gratis de **toques** acústicos de Gustavo Casas, el iPod shuffle humano, de Rawayana y del grupo Majarete Sound Machine.

From *El Universal Venezuela*, http://www.eluniversal.com/caracas. Used with the permission of *El Universal Venezuela*. Many thanks to Elides Rojas.

Declaración de misión de Vitaambiente

Vitaambiente nace de la **inquietud** de un grupo de **empresarios** venezolanos que decidimos asumir la responsabilidad de **desarrollar** e implementar un Modelo Integrado de **Gestión** (M.I.G.), para el correcto **acopio**, recolección y reciclaje de **desechos** peligrosos, **brindándole** a la sociedad, la alternativa de darle un destino final **seguro** y económico a todo desecho peligroso que su **entorno** produce.

El mundo cambia minuto a minuto, y entendemos que el hombre quiere disfrutar de los avances de la tecnología, pero debemos ser conscientes de la obligación que tenemos de respetar el Medio Ambiente, para no alterar el tan frágil equilibrio de la naturaleza, es por ello que en *Vitaambiente* asumimos la responsabilidad y el **compromiso** de contribuir con nuestro **granito de arena** a la preservación de nuestro entorno para las generaciones **venideras**.

From *Vitaambiente*, www.vitaambiente.com. Used with the permission of Vitali Ojalvo and *Vitaambiente*. Many thanks to Vitali Ojalvo.

VOCABULARIO

ciudadanos	citizens	revistas	magazines
conscientes	aware, sensitive	(el) embalaje	packaging material
promover	to promote	folletos	brochures
claves	essential, key	(los) sobres	envelopes
jornada	(special) day	limpios	clean
residuos	waste	(los) donantes	donors
(el) cartón	cardboard	sucios	dirty
pilas	batteries	glasé	glazed
bombillos	lightbulbs	plastificado	laminated
aluminios	aluminum	encerados	wax-coated
latas	cans	recordar	remember, don't forget
cajas	boxes, cartons	aplastarlos	to crush/flatten them
cartuchos de impresión	printer cartridges	enjuagarse	rinse out
artefactos electrodomésticos	small kitchen appliances	(el) envase	container
		gastadas	used, worn-out
(la) ONG (organización no gubernamental)	NGO (non-governmental organization)	campaña	campaign
		(el) teipe	electrical tape
en grande	in a big way	bastón	cylindrical (battery)
por lo que	thus, so, therefore	se estará entregando [entregar]	will be distributed
emisora	radio station		
Alcaldía de Sucre	municipality of Sucre (Caracas)	aviso	notice, warning
		pegarlo	to glue/attach it
ahorradores	energy-saving	(los) potes	containers, tubs
artefactos electrónicos	electronic devices	peligrosos	dangerous
chatarra	scrap	rotos	broken
ferrosa	iron	envueltos [envolver]	wrapped (up)
mediana	medium-size	sellados [sellar]	sealed
(el) aceite	oil	bolsa	bag, sack
comestible	edible, food-grade	(la) manipulación	handling
periódicos	newspapers	(los) celulares	cell phones
recibos	receipts, bills	fallas	defects, flaws

arreglarlo	*to repair it*	(la) gestión	*management*
tapa de rosca	*screw cap*	acopio	*gathering, storing*
aprovechados	*used, maximized*	desechos	*waste, rubbish*
de acuerdo a	*according to*	brindándole [brindar]	*giving/offering (to it)*
disfrutar	*enjoy*	seguro	*safe, secure*
(los) toques	*numbers, songs*	entorno	*environment, milieu*
(la) inquietud	*concern, worry*	compromiso	*commitment*
empresarios	*entrepreneurs*	granito de arena	*bit, part (LIT., grain of sand)*
desarrollar	*to develop, design*	venideras	*coming, future*

EJERCICIO
15·1

¿De qué se trata? *Read the following statements, then suggest items from the following list that each person should recycle.*

artefactos electrónicos	cartuchos de impresión	periódicos	botellas de plástico
embalaje	revistas	botellas de vidrio	folletos
sobres	cajas	papel blanco	cartón
papel de color			

1. "Leemos *El Mundo* y *El País* todos los días."

   _____

2. "Acabo de comprarme una nueva computadora; la vieja no funcionaba."

   _____

3. "En la oficina recibimos una gran cantidad de paquetes y cartas por correo."

   _____

4. "Mis alumnos usan todavía cuadernos y papel rayado."

   _____

5. "Los jugadores de mi equipo toman muchos refrescos durante y después del partido."

   _____

6. "¡Nos envían tantos panfletos, volantes y correo basura!"

   _____

7. "Acaban de hacer recargar la impresora."

   _____

Opciones *Choose the logical completion for each sentence. There may be more than one.*

1. En la categoría papel y cartón, se puede reciclar

   a. periódicos.   b. embalaje.   c. latas.

2. Observe que todos los bombillos ahorradores

   a. son rotos.   b. son peligrosos.   c. contienen mercurio.

3. Los artículos no reciclados incluyen

   a. papel blanco.   b. papel encerado.   c. cartón de huevos.

4. Para señalarle a alguien que desee arreglar un artefacto electrónico, se usa el teipe para indicar

   a. las fallas.   b. la chatarra.   c. los folletos.

5. Para el reciclaje, el artículo que necesita un envase con tapa de rosca es

   a. los recibos.   b. el aceite vegetal.   c. un bombillo.

6. Los envases de plástico y las latas deben estar previamente

   a. aplastados.   b. enjuagados.   c. entregados.

7. La asociación *Vitaambiente* tiene como objetivo

   a. la reutilización de toners.   b. el acopio de desechos.   c. la preservación del entorno.

8. Durante la jornada de reciclaje *Vitaambiente* entregará

   a. unas instrucciones de uso.   b. unos celulares.   c. un manual.

¿Cierto o falso? *Indicate whether each statement is true or false, using **C** for **cierto** (true) or **F** for **falso** (false). If a statement is false, provide a corrected statement in Spanish.*

1. C   F   La ONG *EcoClick* se compone únicamente de empresarios.

   _____

2. C   F   El Día Mundial de la Tierra se celebra en el mes de junio.

   _____

3. C   F   Todos los contenedores deben ser enjuagados y aplastados, si es posible.

   _____

4. C   F   Se estará recibiendo cualquier tipo de plástico.

   _____

5. C F En este evento no habrá entretenimiento.

    _____

6. C F Para esta recolección puede mezclarse papel de todo tipo.

    _____

7. C F *Vitaambiente* se compone únicamente de ciudadanos conscientes.

    _____

8. C F Esta jornada es el único día de reciclaje que organizará *EcoClick*.

    _____

EJERCICIO
15·4

Reflexiones *Consider the following themes and questions, and discuss them in Spanish.*

1. ¿Pertenece usted a grupos ecologistas? ¿A qué organizaciones pertenece?

    _____

    _____

    _____

2. ¿Piensa participar en actividades para conmemorar el Día Mundial de la Tierra, o en otros esfuerzos ecológicos? Descríbalos.

    _____

    _____

    _____

3. ¿Se siente usted optimista o pesimista sobre el porvenir de nuestro planeta? ¿Por qué? ¿Por qué no?

    _____

    _____

    _____

4. En su opinión, ¿por qué se asocia la ecología casi siempre con la política? ¿Se asocia también con la economía?

    _____

    _____

    _____

Mi vocabulario *Select the word or phrase that does not belong in each group.*

1. a. emisora	b. estación	c. transmisor	d. estadía
2. a. residuos	b. desechos	c. bolsas	d. chatarra
3. a. folletos	b. panfletos	c. impresos	d. impresoras
4. a. leche	b. botella	c. lata	d. envase
5. a. roto	b. envuelto	c. sellado	d. cubierto
6. a. de acuerdo a	b. según	c. por lo que	d. conforme a
7. a. enjuagar	b. aplastar	c. limpiar	d. lavar
8. a. clave	b. crucial	c. clavel	d. decisivo
9. a. recuerdo	b. acopio	c. recolección	d. almacenamiento
10. a. compromiso	b. pacto	c. falta	d. responsabilidad

Contrarios *Match each word with its opposite.*

1. _____ arreglado   a. tranquilidad

2. _____ sucio   b. separar

3. _____ ahorrador   c. limpio

4. _____ comestible   d. seguro

5. _____ recordarse   e. confiscando

6. _____ pegar   f. roto

7. _____ disfrutar   g. olvidarse

8. _____ inquietud   h. incomible

9. _____ brindando   i. aburrirse

10. _____ peligroso   j. gastador

Equivalentes *Complete each sentence by substituting words or phrases from the following list for the words or phrases in small type.*

aceptar	futuras	pequeño esfuerzo	ambiente
gozar	perturbar	camino	hombres de negocios
preocupación	carga	iniciar	residuo
comprender	nocivo	sabemos	deber [N.]
ofreciéndole	se transforma		

1. *Vitaambiente* nace de la _____ de un grupo de
   <small>inquietud</small>

   _____ venezolanos que decidimos _____
   <small>empresarios</small>   <small>asumir</small>

   la responsabilidad de _____ e implementar un Modelo Integrado
   <small>desarrollar</small>

   de Gestión.

2. _____ a la sociedad, la alternativa de darle un
   <small>Brindándole</small>

   _____ final seguro y económico a todo _____
   <small>destino</small>   <small>desecho</small>

   _____.
   <small>peligroso</small>

3. El mundo _____ minuto a minuto, y _____
   <small>cambia</small>   <small>entendemos</small>

   que el hombre quiere _____ de los avances de la tecnología.
   <small>disfrutar</small>

4. Pero debemos _____ la _____ que tenemos
   <small>ser conscientes de</small>   <small>obligación</small>

   de respetar el Medio Ambiente, para no _____ el tan frágil equilibrio
   <small>alterar</small>

   de la naturaleza.

5. Es por ello que en *Vitaambiente* asumimos [...] el _____ de
   <small>compromiso</small>

   contribuir con nuestro _____ a la preservación de nuestro
   <small>granito de arena</small>

   _____ para las generaciones _____.
   <small>entorno</small>   <small>venideras</small>

¡No se olvide! Lo impersonal

In English, the impersonal is expressed by using a neuter, singular subject *it* (*it rained*), the passive voice (*mail is answered*), or *they, people, you,* or *one* (*they eat, people eat, you eat, one eats*). Spanish expresses the impersonal in several ways, as follows.

- With verbs (usually referring to the weather) that are always impersonal.

Llueve.	*It's raining.*
Nevaba. } **Estaba nevando.** }	*It was snowing.*
Hace frío.	*It's cold.*

- With forms of **ser** + adjective + infinitive or **ser** + adjective + **que** to express an opinion, a judgment, or a generality.

Es importante reciclar.	*It's important to recycle.*
Es necesario que aplastemos las latas.	*It's necessary that we flatten the cans.*

Note that with **ser** + adjective + **que**, the verb that follows is usually in the subjunctive. However, the verb after **que** can be in the indicative, if one is stating an obvious fact.

Es cierto que mi amigo **vendrá.**	*It's certain (that) my friend will come.*

- **Se** + third-person verb form (singular or plural) expresses a generality. (See Chapters 13, 22, and 25.)

Se puede reciclar periódicos.	*Newspapers can be recycled.*
No se reciclará cartón de huevos.	*Egg cartons are not recycled.*

- Verb forms with **se** are also used in the progressive construction (**estar** + present participle) in all tenses. (See Chapter 6.)

Se está solicitando a los donantes separar estos residuos.	*Donors are being asked to separate these waste items.*
Se estará recibiendo cualquier tipo de plástico.	*All types of plastic are being accepted.*

- Simple third-person plural verb forms (without **se**) can also express the impersonal.

Beben vino en España.	{ *They drink wine in Spain.* { *People drink wine in Spain.* { *One drinks wine in Spain.*
Recibirán todo tipo de papel.	*They will accept all types of paper.*
Estarán recibiendo todo tipo de papel.	*They will be accepting all types of paper.*

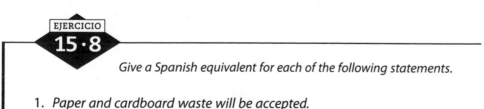

EJERCICIO
15·8

Give a Spanish equivalent for each of the following statements.

1. *Paper and cardboard waste will be accepted.*

   _____

2. *They organized a special recycling day.*

   _____

3. *They'll also be accepting lightbulbs and batteries.*

_____

4. *Donors are being asked to separate their waste paper into three groups.*

_____

_____

5. *It is important to take on (asumir) the responsibility to preserve the environment.*

_____

_____

¡Vaya más lejos!

♦ Busque **EcoClick Venezuela** para obtener información sobre este programa venezolano de reciclaje.

♦ Busque **Vitaambiente Venezuela** para obtener información sobre las actividades de este grupo empresarial.

♦ Busque las organizaciones ecológicas que le interesan a usted (Greenpeace, World Wildlife Fund, Friends of the Earth, 350.org...) para ver si operan en países hispanohablantes. ¿Hay también otras organizaciones ecológicas en esos países o regiones?

♦ Busque las normas de los programas de reciclaje en una ciudad hispanohablante. ¿Son distintas de las suyas?

El olinguito, nuevo carnívoro descubierto
(Colombia/Ecuador)

Jueves, 15 de agosto 2013. Washington. (EFE). Los científicos del Instituto Smithsonian han identificado al olinguito como la primera especie de carnívoro descubierta en las Américas en los últimos treinta y cinco años.

¿Estamos listos?

1. De visita a un zoológico, ¿qué animales busca usted primero?

   Voy a ver a los/las... mamíferos; pájaros, aves [м.], aves de rapiña, loros (*parrots*); insectos; reptiles [м.], anfibios; grandes gatos, leones [м.], tigres [м.], leopardos; canes [м.], lobos (*wolves*), zorros (*foxes*), coyotes [м.], hienas; elefantes [м.], rinocerontes [м.], hipopótamos; antílopes [м.], jirafas y cebras; monos (*monkeys*), gorilas [м.], chimpancés [м.], primates; canguros, koalas [м.], marsupiales [м.]; osos, pandas [м.], mapaches [м.] (*raccoons*), olingos; roedores [м.] (*rodents*)...

2. ¿Qué comen los herbívoros, los carnívoros y los omnívoros?

   Comen... frutas, verduras, hierbas, hojas (*leaves*), hongos (*mushrooms*), semillas (*seeds*), bulbos; presa (*prey*), animales pequeños o grandes, aves, peces, insectos...

3. Cuando anda usted por el campo o por el bosque y desea divisar (*spot*) pájaros o animales, ¿qué usa?

   Uso mi(s)... ojos, orejas, nariz, manos, gafas (*eyeglasses*), binoculares, telescopio, teléfono inteligente, libros, guías...

4. Para divisar a animales salvajes, ¿qué busca usted? ¿Qué escucha?

   Busco/Escucho su(s)... forma, contorno, talla (*size*), color; nidos (*nests*), guaridas (*dens*); huellas o rastros (*footprints*); hierbas o ramajes [м.] (*foliage*) consumidos; excrementos, residuos característicos; sonidos, cantos, movimientos...

5. En el campo, ¿usan los científicos los mismos medios para buscar a animales?

   Utilizan los científicos... cámaras o videocámaras, fotografía infraroja, grabadores [м.] muy sensibles...

6. En el laboratorio, ¿cómo se clasifican las especies?

   Se clasifican por... análisis [м.] de ADN (*DNA*)...

¡Leamos!

El olinguito (*Bassaricyon neblina*) se ha observado en la jungla, hay especímenes en museos y se le ha exhibido en **zoológicos** de todo el mundo, pero por más de cien años ha sido víctima de una identidad falsa, **ya que** hasta ahora se le creía herbívoro.

El animal **luce** como una **mezcla** de gato doméstico y **osito de peluche**, y según los científicos debe **ubicarse** en la familia de los *Proyonidae* que **comparte** con los **mapaches, coatíes, kinkajúes** y olingos.

El olinguito pesa alrededor de un kilogramo, tiene ojos enormes y un denso **pelaje** de color **ocre**, y es nativo de las junglas de Colombia y Ecuador **envueltas** en las **brumas**, de dónde le proviene su **apellido** "neblina".

Además de ser el último miembro identificado en su familia, el olinguito tiene otra distinción: es la especie más nueva en el orden de los carnívoros [...]

"El descubrimiento del olinguito **nos recuerda** que todavía no se ha explorado todo el mundo y algunos de sus secretos más básicos todavía no se han revelado", **señaló** Kristofer Helgen, curador de mamíferos en el Museo Nacional de Historia Natural del Instituto Smithsonian en Washington.

"Si aún podemos encontrar nuevos carnívoros, ¿qué otras sorpresas **nos aguardan?**" comentó Helgen, quien dirigió el **equipo** científico. "Hay tantas especies en el mundo que la ciencia todavía no conoce. El **documentarlas** es un primer paso para comprender **plenamente** la riqueza y diversidad de la vida en la Tierra".

Este descubrimiento requirió diez años de trabajo y **ni siquiera** fue la **meta** original del proyecto que buscaba completar el primer estudio **integral** de los olingos, un **conjunto** de especies de carnívoros que viven en los árboles y **pertenecen** al **género** *Bassaricyon*. El equipo de Helgen, que **calificó** hoy durante su presentación a este mamífero como su "más excitante descubrimiento", quería determinar cuántas especies de olingos había, y cómo están distribuidas.

Inesperadamente un examen detallado de más del 95 por ciento de los especímenes de olingos en los museos de todo el mundo, junto con análisis de **ácido desoxirribonucleico (ADN)** y la **revisión** de **datos de campo** históricos reveló la existencia del olinguito, una especie antes no descrita.

La primera **pista provino** de los dientes y el cráneo de olinguito, que eran más pequeños y tienen forma diferente que los de olingos. El examen de **pieles** en los museos mostró que esta especie nueva era también más pequeña y tenía un pelaje más **largo** y denso.

Los **registros de campo** mostraron que el olinguito vivía en un área única del norte de los Andes a elevaciones de 1.500 a 2.700 metros sobre el **nivel** del mar, mucho más altas que el hábitat de las especies de olingo conocidas.

Todos estos datos provienen de especímenes recolectados **a comienzos del** siglo pasado, y el paso siguiente para Helgen y su equipo fue determinar si los olinguitos todavía viven en la jungla.

El zoólogo Miguel Pinto, en Ecuador, **proporcionó** la primera prueba de la existencia del olinguito con unos pocos segundos de imágenes captadas con una cámara de video. Esto **motivó** una expedición a las **laderas occidentales** de los Andes que, durante tres semanas, observó a los animales, activos **mayormente** durante la noche, y documentó aspectos de su vida como que comen principalmente frutas, rara vez bajan de los árboles y tienen una **cría por vez**.

Los científicos determinaron, **asimismo**, que el 42 por ciento del hábitat histórico de los olinguitos ya se ha convertido para uso agrícola o urbano.

From *La Vanguardia,* http://www.lavanguardia.com. Used with the permission of Agencia EFE America. Many thanks to Edgar Luna.

VOCABULARIO			
zoológicos	*zoos*	meta	*goal, objective*
ya que	*since, considering*	integral	*comprehensive*
luce [lucir]	*looks, appears*	conjunto	*group*
mezcla	*mixture*	pertenecen [pertenecer]	*belong*
osito de peluche	*teddy bear, plush bear*	género	*genus*
ubicarse	*be situated/placed*	calificó [calificar]	*described, called*
comparte [compartir]	*(it) shares*	inesperadamente	*unexpectedly*
(los) mapaches	*raccoons*	ácido desoxirribo-	*deoxyribonucleic*
(los) coatíes	*coatis (raccoon family, the Americas)*	nucleico (ADN)	*acid (DNA)*
(los) kinkajúes	*kinkajous (rainforest mammal, raccoon family, Central and South America)*	(la) revisión	*review, study*
		datos de campo	*field notes*
		pista	*clue*
		provino [provenir]	*came (from)*
		(las) pieles	*skins, pelts*
(el) pelaje	*coat, pelt*	largo	*long*
(el) ocre	*ochre, dark yellow*	registros del campo	*field logs*
envueltas	*enveloped, wrapped*	(el) nivel	*level*
brumas	*mists, fogs*	a comienzos del	*early in the*
apellido	*last name, surname*	proporcionó [proporcionar]	*provided, supplied*
neblina	*mist, haze*		
nos recuerda [recordar]	*reminds us*	motivó [motivar]	*prompted, inspired*
señaló [señalar]	*noted, observed*	laderas	*slopes*
nos aguardan [aguardar]	*are waiting for us*	occidentales	*western*
equipo	*team*	mayormente	*mainly, principally*
(el) documentarlas	*studying/documenting them*	(la) cría	*cub, kit*
		por vez	*at a time*
plenamente	*fully*	asimismo	*additionally, also*
ni siquiera	*not even*		

EJERCICIO
16·1

¿De qué se trata? *Who might ask or say the following? Choose* **Z** *for* **un zoólogo** (a zoologist), **N** *for* **un niño** (a child), *or* **O** *for* **un olinguito** (an olinguito). *Include all correct responses.*

	Z	N	O
1. "¿Qué es un olinguito?"	☐	☐	☐
2. "Es la primera especie de carnívoro descubierta en las Américas en los últimos treinta y cinco años."	☐	☐	☐
3. "De hecho, no soy herbívoro; como muchas frutas y nueces, pero también insectos, gusanos (*worms*), huevos, pájaros."	☐	☐	☐
4. "Originalmente completábamos nuestro estudio de los olingos."	☐	☐	☐
5. "Paso casi todo el tiempo en los árboles."	☐	☐	☐
6. "¿Por qué no puedo ver a los olinguitos durante el día?"	☐	☐	☐
7. "Utilizamos los datos de campo históricos y el análisis de ADN."	☐	☐	☐
8. "¿Qué? ¿Me han filmado? ¿Cuándo? ¡Estaba demasiado oscuro!"	☐	☐	☐

EJERCICIO
16·2

Opciones *Choose the phrase or phrases that correctly complete each sentence. Include all correct responses.*

1. Los zoólogos comenzaron por estudiar
   a. los olinguitos domésticos.
   b. la familia de los olingos.
   c. los especímenes en los museos.

2. Terminaron su investigación por
   a. los análisis ADN.
   b. un entrenamiento de olinguitos.
   c. una expedición en los Andes.

3. En la naturaleza se encuentran los olinguitos en
   a. Ecuador.
   b. Nuevo México.
   c. Colombia.

4. Los olinguitos difieren de los olingos porque
   a. los dientes tienen forma diferente.
   b. son más pequeños.
   c. su pelaje es más largo y denso.

5. Es difícil observar a los olinguitos porque
   a. su hábitat es limitado.
   b. son nocturnos.
   c. se quedan en los árboles.

6. En Ecuador se ha probado la existencia de los olinguitos
   a. escuchándolos.
   b. captando unas imágenes.
   c. alimentándolos.

7. El hábitat de los olinguitos es muy
   a. húmedo.
   b. bajo.
   c. alto.

8. Los olingos y los olinguitos son de la misma familia que un animal familiar; es
   a. el oso.
   b. el mapache.
   c. la rata.

EJERCICIO

16·3

¿Cierto o falso? *Indicate whether each statement is true or false, using* **C** *for* **cierto** (true) *or* **F** *for* **falso** (false). *If a statement is false, provide a corrected statement in Spanish.*

1. C F El olinguito no existía antes.

   _____

2. C F Los olinguitos nunca se ven en los museos ni en los zoológicos.

   _____

3. C F Los olinguitos comen solamente carne.

   _____

4. C F Los científicos trabajaron más de diez años antes de descubrirlo.

   _____

5. C F El estudio estaba limitado a un examen físico de los especímenes.

   _____

6. C F El olinguito tiene una camada de entre dos y cuatro crías.

   _____

7. C F Casi la mitad de su hábitat se ha convertido para usos humanos.

   _____

Reflexiones *Consider the following themes and questions, and discuss them in Spanish.*

1. ¿Por qué poseen los museos tantos especímenes y tantas pieles de animales? En los siglos XVIII y XIX, ¿cómo estudiaban los naturalistas a los animales y las plantas?

_____

_____

_____

_____

2. En la época actual, ¿qué técnicas e instrumentos se han añadido a la práctica de los zoológicos?

_____

_____

_____

_____

3. ¿Conoce usted otros ejemplos de la destrucción de hábitats? Nombre algunos animales amenazados o en peligro de extinción.

_____

_____

_____

_____

_____

4. ¿Es importante buscar y verificar la existencia de especies desconocidas? ¿Por qué?

_____

_____

_____

_____

Mi vocabulario *Select the word or phrase that does not belong in each group.*

1. a. pajarera   b. acuario   c. zoológico   d. zoólogo

2. a. nieve   b. neblina   c. niebla   d. bruma

3. a. aguardar   b. permanecer   c. esperar   d. pertenecer

4. a. amarillo   b. ocre   c. verdoso   d. dulce

5. a. número   b. apellido   c. nombre   d. apelativo

6. a. parecer   b. sembrar   c. lucir como   d. semejarse a

7. a. guapo   b. equipo   c. grupo   d. conjunto

8. a. vertiente   b. ladrido   c. ladera   d. cerro

9. a. objetivo   b. meta   c. objeción   d. propósito

10. a. pista   b. huella   c. traza   d. huelga

Contrarios *Match each word with its opposite.*

1. _____ mezcla   a. previsiblemente

2. _____ integral   b. parcialmente

3. _____ envuelto   c. incompleto

4. _____ señalar   d. oriental

5. _____ inesperadamente   e. quitar

6. _____ proporcionar   f. separación

7. _____ occidental   g. descubierto

8. _____ plenamente   h. ignorar

Equivalentes *Complete each sentence by substituting words or phrases from the following list for the words or phrases in small type.*

a principios del	derivan	principalmente	un cachorro
estas evidencias	recogidos	casi nunca	nos recuerda a
registró	colocarse	pendientes	suscitó
combinación			

1. El animal _____ una _____ de gato doméstico y osito
   <small>luce como</small>   <small>mezcla</small>

   de peluche, y según los científicos debe _____ en la familia de los
                                            <small>ubicarse</small>

   Proyonidae.

2. _____ _____ de especímenes _____
   <small>Estos datos</small>   <small>provienen</small>   <small>recolectados</small>

   _____ siglo pasado.
   <small>a comienzos del</small>

3. Esto _____ una expedición a las _____ occidentales
        <small>motivó</small>   <small>laderas</small>

   de los Andes que, durante tres semanas, observó a los animales, activos

   _____ durante la noche, y _____ aspectos de su
   <small>mayormente</small>   <small>documentó</small>

   vida como que comen principalmente frutas, _____ bajan de los árboles
                                              <small>rara vez</small>

   y tienen _____ por vez.
            <small>una cría</small>

¡No se olvide! El presente perfecto y el **se** impersonal
The present perfect

The present perfect expresses a past action or actions that may influence the present or that started in the past and continue into the present: **He visto el futuro.** *I have seen the future.* The past event described can be relatively recent. As in English, the present perfect tense can often be replaced by a form of the preterit tense, with very similar meaning: **he comido** = **comí** *I have eaten* = *I ate.*

Like other perfect tenses in Spanish, the present perfect is made up of a conjugated form of **haber** + the past participle. To form the past participle of regular verbs, drop the infinitive ending, and add **-ado** to **-ar** verbs and **-ido** to **-er** and **-ir** verbs: **hablar** > **hablado**, **entender** > **entendido**, **partir** > **partido**.

For **-er** and **-ir** verbs where the stem ends in a vowel, add an accent mark over the **i** in the past participle: **caer** > **caído**, **creer** > **creído**, **leer** > **leído**. (See also Chapter 8.)

Give the infinitive of each of the following irregular past participles.

1. abierto _____

2. cubierto _____

3. dicho _____

4. escrito _____

5. hecho _____

6. ido _____

7. muerto _____

8. puesto _____

9. roto _____

10. sido _____

11. visto _____

12. vuelto _____

Impersonal se

The use of **se**—the third-person singular or plural reflexive pronoun—creates the equivalent of the passive voice in English.

El olinguito se ha observado.	*The olinguito has been observed.*
No se ha explorado todo el mundo.	*The whole world has not been studied.*

¡Ojo!

In Spanish, there is a verb construction that contains the double pronoun **se le**.

se le ha exhibido	$\left\{\begin{array}{l}\textit{it has been exhibited} \\ \textit{they have exhibited it}\end{array}\right.$
se le creía herbívoro	$\left\{\begin{array}{l}\textit{it was believed to be a herbivore} \\ \textit{they believed it to be a herbivore}\end{array}\right.$

Le (or **les**) in these examples is a direct object pronoun referring to **el olinguito**. The pronoun would normally be written as **lo** or **los**, but Spanish usage sometimes replaces **lo(s)** with **le(s)**. This is another case of regional style or **leísmo**.

Give (a) the English equivalent, (b) the Spanish infinitive, and (c) the preterit of the verb forms in bold, which appear in the reading.

1. Los científicos... **han identificado** al olinguito como la primera especie de carnívoro descubierta en las Américas en los últimos treinta y cinco años.

   a. _____ b. _____ c. _____

2. El olinguito... **se ha observado** en la jungla.

   a. _____ b. _____ c. _____

3. Hay especímenes en museos y **se le ha exhibido** en zoológicos de todo el mundo.

   a. _____ b. _____ c. _____

4. Por más de cien años **ha sido** víctima de una identidad falsa, ya que hasta ahora se le creía herbívoro.

   a. _____ b. _____ c. _____

5. El descubrimiento del olinguito nos recuerda que todavía **no se ha explorado** todo el mundo.

   a. _____ b. _____ c. _____

6. Algunos de sus secretos más básicos todavía **no se han revelado**.

   a. _____ b. _____ c. _____

7. El 42 por ciento del hábitat histórico de los olinguitos ya **se ha convertido** para uso agrícola o urbano.

   a. _____ b. _____ c. _____

¡Vaya más lejos!

- Busque fotos del **olinguito** en línea. ¿Ve allí también olingos? ¿Hay una obvia diferencia entre estas especies?

- Busque en línea otros miembros de la familia de los *Proyonidae*. ¿Hay algunos que viven cerca de o en su región?

- Busque artículos en español sobre **animales amenazados** o **animales en peligro de extinción**.

FRAGMENTOS LITERARIOS

Diálogo entre Babieca y Rocinante

Miguel de Cervantes (España)

Hay novelas que incluyen también poemas, tanto serios como humorísticos. *Don Quijote*, la clásica novela de Miguel de Cervantes, tiene poemas al principio, al final y en mitad de la obra.

¿Estamos listos?

1. ¿Le gusta a usted leer? ¿Cuáles son sus lecturas favoritas?

   Me gusta(n)... la ficción, las novelas, los cuentos, la historia, la poesía, las obras de teatro, los artículos, los periódicos, las revistas, los ensayos, las historietas, las novelas gráficas, los cómics...

2. ¿Qué medios de lectura prefiere?

   Prefiero leer (en)... libros, revistas, periódicos, diarios, mi lector de libros electrónicos, mi tableta, mi iPad, mi teléfono inteligente, mi computadora...

3. Enumere algunos autores que prefiere.

4. ¿Qué sabe sobre la obra *El ingenioso hidalgo don Quijote de la Mancha*?

5. ¿Cómo es don Quijote? ¿Qué representa?

   Es... ávido lector de aventuras de caballeros andantes, ingenuo, crédulo, enamorado, iluso, sincero, optimista, romántico, valiente, atrevido, confundido...

6. ¿Ya ha visto un retrato (*portrait*) o una escultura de don Quijote? Si es así, ¿dónde lo ha visto?

¡Leamos!

Cervantes empieza la primera parte del *Quijote* con unos poemas humorísticos y laudatorios. El "Diálogo entre Babieca y Rocinante" representa una conversación entre Babieca (caballo del héroe medieval el Cid) y Rocinante (caballo y compañero del "antihéroe" don Quijote).

BABIECA	**¿Cómo estáis**, Rocinante, tan **delgado**?
ROCINANTE	Porque **nunca se come, y se trabaja**.
BABIECA	Pues **¿qué es de** la **cebada** y de la **paja**?
ROCINANTE	No me deja mi **amo** ni un **bocado**.
BABIECA	**Anda**, señor que estáis muy **mal criado**,
	pues vuestra lengua de **asno** al amo **ultraja**.
ROCINANTE	Asno se es de la **cuna** a la **mortaja**.
	¿Queréislo ver? Miradlo enamorado.
BABIECA	**¿Es necedad** amar?
ROCINANTE	**No es gran prudencia.**
BABIECA	**Metafísico** estáis.
ROCINANTE	Es que no como.
BABIECA	**Quejaos** del **escudero**.
ROCINANTE	No es **bastante**.
	¿Cómo me he de quejar, en mi **dolencia**,
	si el amo y escudero o **mayordomo**
	son tan **rocines** como Rocinante?

Miguel de Cervantes Saavedra, from *El ingenioso hidalgo don Quijote de la Mancha* (Madrid: Imprenta de Juan de la Cuesta, 1605).

VOCABULARIO

¿Cómo estáis...? [estar]	*How (is it that) you are . . . ?*	¿Queréislo [querer] ver? [ARCHAIC]	*Do you want to see (him)?*
delgado	*thin, slim*	Miradlo [mirar] enamorado.	*Take a look at him, lovestruck.*
nunca se come, y se trabaja	*never eating, and (only) working*	¿Es necedad...?	*Is it foolishness . . . ?*
¿qué es de...?	*what about . . . ? / how about . . . ?*	No es gran prudencia.	*It's not very smart/wise.*
cebada	*barley, grain*	metafísico	*philosopher, metaphysician*
paja	*straw, hay*	quejaos [quejarse] [IMP.]	*(you) complain*
amo	*master*	escudero	*squire (Sancho Panza, don Quijote's squire)*
bocado	*mouthful*		
anda [andar]	*come on, go on*	bastante	*enough*
mal criado	*badly raised, ill-mannered*	¿Cómo me he de...?	*How can I . . . ?*
		dolencia	*malady, trouble*
asno	*donkey, ass*	mayordomo	*head servant, majordomo*
ultraja [ultrajar]	*offends, insults*		
cuna	*cradle*	rocines	*skinny (like a nag, work horse), ignorant*
mortaja	*shroud*		

The sonnet as a poetic form

A sonnet has the following characteristics:

◆ The sonnet is a poem composed of 14 lines, each with 12 syllables. A sonnet in dialogue form is one in which two or more voices carry on a converstion.

◆ The sonnet consists of an introduction, an expansion on a theme, and a conclusion that gives meaning to the rest of the poem.

◆ The lines of a sonnet are often organized into four stanzas: two stanzas of four lines each and two stanzas of three lines each. The first four-line stanza presents the theme of the sonnet, and the second four-line stanza expands on it. The first three-line stanza reflects on the main idea, and the final three-line stanza concludes with a philosophical thought.

Reread the poem with this description in mind.

EJERCICIO 17·1

¿De qué se trata? *Who is speaking? Choose **B** for **Babieca** or **R** for **Rocinante**.*

	B	R
1. "¡Tú me pareces demasiado delgado!"	☐	☐
2. "¿Por qué tienes hambre?"	☐	☐
3. "Es que no dejo de trabajar y mi amo no me da de comer."	☐	☐
4. "Debo llamarlo asno porque se enamora estúpidamente."	☐	☐
5. "Mi amo don Quijote y su escudero Sancho Panza se parecen mucho a mí."	☐	☐
6. "Ayudé al Cid campeador a ganar batallas."	☐	☐

EJERCICIO 17·2

Opciones *Choose the phrase or phrases that correctly complete each sentence. Include all correct responses.*

1. Babieca se pregunta por qué Rocinante

   a. come cebada.　　　b. está tan delgado.　　　c. trabaja tanto.

2. La cebada y la paja son

   a. granos.　　　b. lo que le falta a Rocinante.　　　c. alimentos para caballos.

3. Su amo le parece a Rocinante

   a. mezquino.　　　b. enamorado.　　　c. tonto.

4. Babieca le acusa a Rocinante de

   a. estar mal criado.   b. ultrajar a su amo.   c. comportarse amablemente.

5. Babieca le llama metafísico a Rocinante porque

   a. no come.   b. es irónico.   c. le parece sabio.

6. El amo de Rocinante

   a. tiene hambre también.   b. es mayordomo.   c. conoce a Babieca de sus lecturas.

¿Cierto o falso? *Indicate whether each statement is true or false, using* **C** *for* **cierto** *(true) or* **F** *for* **falso** *(false). If a statement is false, provide a corrected statement in Spanish.*

1. C   F   Los dos caballos pertenecen a la misma época.

   _____

2. C   F   Rocinante está tan delgado porque pasa hambre.

   _____

3. C   F   Babieca le llama asno a su amo el Cid.

   _____

4. C   F   Rocinante cree en la fuerza del amor.

   _____

5. C   F   En su propia opinión, Rocinante no se queja suficientemente del escudero.

   _____

   _____

6. C   F   Con todo, Rocinante, su amo y el escudero se parecen mucho.

   _____

   _____

Reflexiones *Consider the following themes and questions, and discuss them in Spanish.*

1. ¿Por qué es obra importante el *Quijote*?

   _____

   _____

   _____

2. Alonso Quijano (don Quijote) leyó muchas aventuras (¿demasiadas?) de caballeros andantes. Para usted, ¿son factores de cambio personal lo que ha leído o lo que ha visto en la televisión o en el cine? Dé algunos ejemplos.

   _____

   _____

   _____

3. ¿Por qué a veces hacen el ridículo los enamorados o las enamoradas? ¿En qué se concentran? ¿Qué olvidan?

   _____

   _____

   _____

4. ¿Qué (o a quiénes) representan los caballos? ¿Son más o menos razonados que las personas? ¿Qué efecto produce esta técnica literaria? ¿Conoce otras obras que la utilizan?

   _____

   _____

   _____

Mi vocabulario *Select the word that does not belong in each group.*

1. a. criado   b. criticado   c. cultivado   d. educado

2. a. almohada   b. cuna   c. futón   d. cama

3. a. reclamar   b. divertirse   c. gemir   d. quejarse

4. a. mula   b. asno   c. burro   d. conejo

5. a. puñado   b. bocado   c. demasiado   d. cucharada

6. a. sabiduría   b. absurdidad   c. tontería   d. necedad

7. a. maíz   b. trigo   c. cebada   d. verduras

Contrarios *Match each word with its opposite.*

1. _____ gordito   a. trabajar

2. _____ indiferente   b. dolencia

3. _____ amo   c. delgado

4. _____ descansar   d. ultrajar

5. _____ felicitar   e. sirviente

6. _____ necedad   f. enamorado

7. _____ salud   g. prudencia

Equivalentes *Complete each sentence by substituting words or phrases from the following list for the words or phrases in small type.*

educado	insulta	patrón	filósofo
juicioso	suficientemente	flaco	lamentar
sufrimiento	ignorantes	del nacimiento a la muerte	tontería

1. ¿Cómo estáis, Rocinante, tan _____?
   <small>delgado</small>

2. No me deja mi _____ ni un bocado.
   <small>amo</small>

3. Anda, señor que estáis muy mal _____.
   <small>criado</small>

4. Pues vuestra lengua de asno al amo _____.
   <small>ultraja</small>

5. Asno se es _____.
   <small>de la cuna a la mortaja</small>

6. ¿Es _____ amar? —No es _____.
   <small>necedad</small>   <small>gran prudencia</small>

7. _____ estáis.
   <small>Metafísico</small>

8. Quejaos del escudero. —No _____.
   <small>es bastante</small>

9. ¿Cómo me he de _____, en mi

   _____?
   <small>dolencia</small>

   <small>quejar</small>

10. ¿Son tan _____ como Rocinante?
    <small>rocines</small>

¡No se olvide! El voseo

The use of **vos** as the second-person singular pronoun, along with its verb conjugations (recognizable as today's **vosotros** forms), was disappearing in Spain as early as the eighteenth century. Here you will learn the **vos** forms for recognition only. Early texts, such as *Don Quijote*, make frequent use of it in dialogue.

Note that the **voseo** form is heard today throughout Central America, in conversation as well as in the media—either instead of **tú** and its forms or alongside **tú**. It is also widely used in Argentina, Uruguay, Bolivia, Paraguay, and locally in other Spanish-speaking regions. Thus, in your reading, you may come across it in transcribed interviews and dialogues.

The possessive adjective in the **voseo** form is **vuestro(s)/vuestra(s)**: **vuestra lengua de asno** *your ass's tongue*. The reflexive pronoun is **os**.

os quejáis	*you complain*
quejaos	*complain!*
no os quejéis	*don't complain!*

¡Ojo!

The affirmative imperative of the **voseo** form ends in **-d** (**¡Hablad!**). In reflexive forms, the final **-d** drops before the attached reflexive pronoun **os**. Here are some examples of **vos** forms.

	llamar	dormir	estar	ser
PRESENT INDICATIVE	(vos) llamáis	dormís	estáis	sois
IMPERFECT	(vos) llamabais	dormíais	estabais	erais
PRETERIT	(vos) llamasteis	dormisteis	estuvisteis	fuisteis
FUTURE	(vos) llamaréis	dormiréis	estaréis	seréis
PRESENT CONDITIONAL	(vos) llamaríais	dormiríais	estaríais	seríais
PRESENT SUBJUNCTIVE	(vos) llaméis	durmáis	estéis	seáis
IMPERFECT SUBJUNCTIVE	(vos) llamarais	durmierais	estuvierais	fuerais
IMPERATIVE	llamad	dormid	estad	sed
NEGATIVE IMPERATIVE	no llaméis	no durmáis	no estéis	no seáis

EJERCICIO
17·8

*Provide both the familiar **tú** and the formal **usted** verb forms for the verb in bold in each of the following sentences.*

	tú	usted

1. ¿Cómo **estáis**, Rocinante, tan delgado? _____ _____

2. Anda, señor que **decís** tonterías. _____ _____

3. ¿**Queréislo ver**? _____ _____

4. Metafísico **parecéis**. _____ _____

5. **Miradlo** enamorado. _____ _____

6. **Quejaos** del escudero. _____ _____

¡Vaya más lejos!

♦ Busque información sobre la vida y las obras de **Miguel de Cervantes**.

♦ Busque versiones contemporáneas (películas, obras teatrales, óperas, ballet) del *Quijote*. Por ejemplo, en el cine, *Adventures of Don Quixote* (1933), *Don Quixote de la Mancha* (1947), *Don Quixote* (1957), *Man of La Mancha* (1972), *Don Quijote cabalga de nuevo* (1973), *Don Quixote* (2000), *Lost in La Mancha* (2002), *Donkey Xote* (2007), *Don Quixote* (2010); dos obras de ópera, *Don Quixote* (Kienzl), *Don Quichotte* (Massenet); un ballet, *Don Quixote* (Petipa/Minkus); una comedia musical, *Man of La Mancha* (Wasserman/ Leigh/Darion).

♦ Busque la **historia del Cid campeador** y su caballo Babieca.

♦ Busque en línea otros sonetos en español, por ejemplo, los de **Lope de Vega**, **Sor Juana Inés de la Cruz**, **Garcilaso de la Vega** o **Luis de Góngora**.

Llegada a Barcelona
Carmen Laforet (España)

La narradora, Andrea, llegó a Barcelona para estudiar, a los dieciocho años, poco después de la Guerra Civil española (1936–1939). Como creció en un pueblo pequeño, Andrea **se asombra** al ver la gran ciudad.

¿Estamos listos?

1. ¿A qué edad fue solo/a de viaje por primera vez? ¿Adónde fue? ¿Por qué razón viajó?

   Viajé para... visitar a parientes, visitar a amigos, tomarme vacaciones, ir a un campamento de verano, hacer un viaje escolar, hacer deportes, hacer música, estudiar, trabajar, trabajar como voluntario/a...

2. Piense en su último viaje. ¿Qué medios de transporte usó?

   Anduve... en coche, en moto, en autobús, en taxi, en tren, en avión, en tranvía (*tram, trolley*), en metro (*subway*), en bicicleta, en patines sobre ruedas (*rollerblades*), a caballo, en esquís, en bote, en barco...

3. ¿Adónde fue? ¿Por qué viajó ese día?

4. ¿Cómo prefiere viajar, generalmente? ¿Por qué?

   Me gusta(n)... la independencia, la velocidad, el relajamiento, el estímulo, los transportes públicos, la comodidad (*comfort*), mi moto, mi bicicleta, mi coche, mi avión, mi bote, el aire libre, el ejercicio, economizar, conducir, volar (*to fly*), navegar...

5. De viaje, ¿tuvo dificultades o problemas?

   Sí, tuve problemas con... los billetes, las reservaciones, el equipaje, los retrasos (*delays*), el tiempo (*weather*), una avería (*breakdown*) de coche (de tren, de tranvía), el hotel o el alojamiento, los precios...

6. Identifique la última ciudad o el último pueblo que vio por primera vez. ¿Cuál fue su primera impresión de ese lugar?

   Me pareció... grande, animado/a, lleno/a de gente, congestionado/a, agradable, hermoso/a, bello/a, próspero/a, pequeño/a, tranquilo/a, vacío/a, feo/a, pobre...

¡Leamos!

Por dificultades en el último momento para adquirir billetes, llegué a Barcelona a medianoche, en un tren **distinto** del que había anunciado, y no me esperaba nadie.

Era la primera noche que viajaba sola, pero no estaba **asustada**; por el contrario, me parecía una aventura agradable y excitante aquella profunda libertad en la noche. La sangre, después del viaje largo y **cansado**, me empezaba a circular en las piernas **entumecidas** y con una sonrisa de **asombro** miraba la gran Estación de Francia y los grupos que estaban **aguardando** el expreso y los que llegábamos con tres horas **de retraso**.

El **olor** especial, el gran **rumor** de la gente, las luces siempre tristes, tenían para mí un gran encanto, **ya que envolvía** todas mis impresiones en la maravilla de haber llegado por fin a una ciudad grande, adorada en mis **ensueños** por **desconocida**.

Empecé a seguir—una **gota** entre la corriente—el **rumbo** de la masa humana que, **cargada** de **maletas**, **se voleaba** en la salida. Mi **equipaje** era un **maletón** muy **pesado**—porque estaba casi lleno de libros—y lo llevaba yo misma con toda la fuerza de mi juventud y de mi ansiosa expectación.

Un aire marino, pesado y fresco, entró en mis **pulmones** con la primera sensación confusa de la ciudad: una masa de casas dormidas; de establecimientos cerrados; de **faroles** como **centinelas borrachos** de **soledad**. Una respiración grande, dificultosa, venía con el **cuchicheo** de la **madrugada**. Muy cerca, a mi espalda, enfrente de las **callejuelas** misteriosas que conducen al **Borne**, sobre mi corazón excitado, estaba el mar.

Debía parecer una figura **extraña** con mi aspecto **risueño** y mi viejo **abrigo** que, a impulsos de la brisa me **azotaba** las piernas, defendiendo mi maleta, **desconfiada** de los obsequiosos "**camálics**".

Recuerdo que, en pocos minutos, me quedé sola en la gran **acera**, porque la gente corría a **coger** los **escasos** taxis o **luchaba** por **arracimarse** en el tranvía.

Uno de esos viejos coches de caballos que **han vuelto a surgir** después de la guerra **se detuvo** delante de mí y lo tomé sin **titubear**, causando la envidia de un señor que **se lanzaba** detrás de él desesperado, agitando el sombrero.

Corrí aquella noche, en el **desvencijado** vehículo, por **anchas** calles **vacías** y **atravesé** el corazón de la ciudad lleno de luz a toda hora, como yo quería que estuviese, en un viaje que me pareció corto y que para mí se cargaba de belleza.

El coche **dio la vuelta** a la plaza de la Universidad y recuerdo que el bello edificio me **conmovió** como un grave saludo de bienvenida.

Enfilamos la calle de Aribau, donde vivían mis **parientes**, con sus **plátanos** llenos aquel octubre de **espeso** verdor y su silencio vívido de la respiración de mil **almas** detrás de los balcones **apagados**. Las ruedas del coche levantaban una **estela de ruido**, que **repercutía** en mi **cerebro**. **De improviso** sentí **crujir** y **balancearse** todo el **armatoste**. Luego quedó inmóvil.

—Aquí es —dijo el **cochero**.

Carmen Laforet, excerpt from *Nada* (Barcelona: Ediciones Destino, 1945/1960). Reprinted with the permission of Agencia Literaria Carmen Balcells, Barcelona. Many thanks to Ana Paz.

se asombra [asombrarse]	*is amazed*	abrigo	*overcoat*
distinto	*different*	azotaba [azotar]	*was whipping around*
asustada	*frightened*	desconfiada	*distrustful*
cansado	*tiring*	camálics [CATALAN]	*porters*
entumecidas	*numb, asleep*	acera	*sidewalk*
asombro	*astonishment*	coger	*catch, grab*
aguardando [aguardar]	*waiting*	escasos	*scarce*
de retraso	*late*	luchaba [luchar]	*struggled*
(el) olor	*odor*	arracimarse	*pack themselves in*
(el) rumor	*buzz, rumble*	han vuelto [volver]	*have reappeared*
ya que	*since*	a surgir	
envolvía [envolver]	*combined*	se detuvo [detenerse]	*stopped*
ensueños	*daydreams*	titubear	*hesitating*
desconocida	*strange, unknown*	se lanzaba [lanzarse]	*threw himself*
gota	*drop*	desvencijado	*rattletrap*
rumbo	*direction, path*	anchas	*wide, broad*
cargada	*loaded*	vacías	*empty*
maletas	*suitcases*	atravesé [atravesar]	*crossed*
se voleaba [volearse]	*thrust itself*	dio [dar] la vuelta	*circled*
(el) equipaje	*luggage*	conmovió [conmover]	*touched, moved*
(el) maletón	*big bag*	enfilamos [enfilar]	*we went down*
pesado	*heavy*	(los) parientes	*relatives*
(los) pulmones	*lungs*	plátanos	*plane trees*
(los) faroles	*streetlights*	espeso	*dense*
(los) centinelas	*guards, sentinels*	(las) almas [el alma]	*souls, beings*
borrachos	*drunk(en)*	apagados	*darkened, extinguished*
(la) soledad	*solitude*	estela de ruido	*trail of noise*
cuchicheo	*whisper*	repercutía [repercutir]	*reverberated*
madrugada	*dawn*	cerebro	*brain*
callejuelas	*side streets*	de improviso	*suddenly*
(el) Borne	*port district of Barcelona*	crujir	*creak*
		balancearse	*rock, sway*
extraña	*strange, odd*	(el) armatoste	*old contraption*
risueño	*smiling*	cochero	*coachman*

EJERCICIO 18·1

¿De qué se trata? *Who is speaking? Choose* **N** *for* **la narradora** *(the narrator),* **P** *for* **su pariente en Barcelona** *(her relative in Barcelona), or* **C** *for* **el cochero** *(the coachman).*

	N	P	C
1. "Llegué a Barcelona a medianoche, mucho más tarde que había anunciado."	☐	☐	☐
2. "Yo no tenía miedo, sino que estaba excitada y curiosa."	☐	☐	☐
3. "¡Fui a la Estación de Francia a las nueve de la mañana pero ella no estaba!"	☐	☐	☐
4. "¿Quién es esta chica? ¿La llevo? ¿Puede pagar el pasaje?"	☐	☐	☐
5. "Ya voy a acostarme. Esa hija de mi hermano se arreglará sola."	☐	☐	☐
6. "Esta ciudad bella y misteriosa encerrará mi futuro."	☐	☐	☐

EJERCICIO 18·2

Opciones *Choose the phrase or phrases that correctly complete each sentence. Include all correct responses.*

1. Andrea (la narradora) llegó a Barcelona

   a. a tiempo. b. muy tarde. c. muy temprano.

2. Ella se sentía

   a. excitada. b. libre. c. asustada.

3. Su viaje estuvo

   a. cansado. b. entumecido. c. largo.

4. En la Estación de Francia, ella tomó

   a. un coche de caballos. b. el tranvía. c. un taxi.

5. En la ciudad Andrea estaba atenta a la naturaleza. Percibía

   a. las hojas de los árboles. b. los pájaros nocturnos. c. el olor del mar.

6. El equipaje de la narradora estaba pesado por

   a. los libros. b. su gran tamaño. c. su ropa y sus zapatos.

7. Antes de llegar a la casa de los parientes, el cochero dio la vuelta

   a. detrás de la Estación. b. delante de la Universidad. c. a lo largo del mar.

EJERCICIO

18·3

¿Cierto o falso? *Indicate whether each statement is true or false, using* **C** *for* **cierto** (true) *or* **F** *for* **falso** (false). *If a statement is false, provide a corrected statement in Spanish.*

1. C F Andrea creció en un pueblo lejos de Barcelona.

   _____

2. C F En la Estación ella iba a tomar el expreso a medianoche.

   _____

3. C F Llegó a Barcelona para comenzar los estudios universitarios.

   _____

4. C F A primera vista a Andrea no le gusta la ciudad.

   _____

5. C F La narradora está muy atenta a su entorno.

   _____

EJERCICIO

18·4

Reflexiones *Consider the following themes and questions, and discuss them in Spanish.*

1. "Esos viejos coches de caballos que han vuelto a surgir después de la guerra." ¿A qué guerra se refiere? ¿Cuándo pasó esa guerra? ¿Quiénes fueron los antagonistas?

   _____

   _____

   _____

2. Este viaje tiene gran importancia para la narradora, Andrea. ¿Cómo lo sabemos?

   _____

   _____

   _____

3. ¿Por qué dice Andrea, "el bello edificio [de la Universidad] me conmovió como un grave saludo de bienvenida"?

   _____

   _____

   _____

Mi vocabulario *Select the word or phrase that does not belong in each group.*

1. a. farro   b. farol   c. lámpara   d. linterna

2. a. insuficientes   b. escasos   c. abundantes   d. raros

3. a. diferente   b. otro   c. igual   d. distinto

4. a. rumbo   b. sentido   c. dirección   d. salsa

5. a. detenerse   b. marcharse   c. pararse   d. quedarse

6. a. aguardando   b. yéndose   c. esperando   d. haciendo cola

7. a. equipaje   b. maleta   c. malestar   d. maletón

8. a. rumor   b. rugido   c. ruido   d. rueda

Contrarios *Match each word or phrase with its opposite.*

1. _____ de anticipación   a. se puso en marcha

2. _____ madrugada   b. borrachos

3. _____ ligero   c. de retraso

4. _____ abstemios   d. pesado

5. _____ risueño   e. atardecer

6. _____ adquirir   f. triste

7. _____ silencio   g. vender

8. _____ se detuvo   h. rumor

Equivalentes *Complete each sentence by substituting words or phrases from the following list for the words or phrases in small type.*

carruajes	dudar	puerta	el resentimiento
equipaje	paró	comencé	obtener
han reaparecido	la dirección	problemas	se tiraba

1. Por _____ en el último momento para _____
   dificultades   adquirir

   billetes, llegué a Barcelona a medianoche.

2. _____ a seguir—una gota entre la corriente—
   Empecé

   _____ de la masa humana que, cargada de
   el rumbo

   _____, se voleaba en la _____.
   maletas   salida

3. Uno de esos viejos _____ de caballos que _____
   coches   han vuelto a surgir

   después de la guerra _____ delante de mí y lo tomé sin
   se detuvo

   _____, causando _____ de un señor que
   titubear   la envidia

   _____ detrás de él.
   se lanzaba

¡No se olvide! Por vs. para

Both **por** and **para** are often the equivalent of English *for*. However, they are not at all interchangeable in Spanish. Even in reading, you'll need to understand how they are used, so that the meaning is clear. Both **por** and **para** also appear in numerous fixed expressions.

Por is used

- To talk about unspecified movement (*through, around, this/that way*)

   Mire **por esta ventana**.
   Viajaba **por el campo**.
   Venga **por aquí**.

- To indicate the cause or reason (*due to, because of*)

   Por su promoción puede mudarse.

- To express duration or an indefinite moment in time

   Estudié **por muchos años**.
   Me voy mañana **por la mañana**.

- To express *to pay for* or an exchange or substitution (*instead of, in place of*)

   No pago mucho **por este vestido**.
   Voy al banco **por mi madre**.

Para is used

- To indicate a target, a destination, or a recipient

  El libro es **para ti**.
  Tomo el autobús **para Madrid**.

- Preceding an infinitive, as the equivalent of *in order to*, *so that*, indicating a goal or an objective

  Estudio **para aprender**.
  Trabajamos **para vivir**.

- With expressions of time when a deadline looms

  Lo termino **para el viernes**.

- To indicate someone's opinion or perspective

  Para mí, es normal.
  Para Andrea todo se cargaba de belleza.

EJERCICIO
18·8

*For each of the following phrases or sentences, give the correct English equivalent for **por** or **para**, using one of the expressions from the list that follows.*

due to, because (of)	on the contrary	finally
in my opinion, from (my) perspective	in (order to)	through, around

1. **por** dificultades en el último momento **para** adquirir billetes

   _____

   _____

2. **Por el contrario** me parecía una aventura agradable y excitante.

   _____

3. El olor especial... [tenía] **para mí** un gran encanto.

   _____

4. en la maravilla de haber llegado **por fin** a una ciudad grande, adorada en mis ensueños **por** desconocida

   _____

   _____

5. Corrí aquella noche... **por** anchas calles vacías.

   _____

El/un con un sustantivo femenino singular

Feminine nouns that begin with a stressed **a-** or **ha-** use **el** instead of **la** (and **un** instead of **una**) in the singular. (If we say **la agua** or **una agua**, one of the **a** sounds is lost.) The plural form (**las aguas**) is regular.

> **el** agua, **el** alma, **el** asma, **un** hada (*fairy*)
>
> BUT   **las** aguas, **las** almas, **las** asmas, **unas** hadas

¡Vaya más lejos!

- ◆ Busque información sobre la vida y las obras de **Carmen Laforet**.
- ◆ Lea la novela completa *Nada* (1945) por Carmen Laforet.
- ◆ Busque información sobre la geografía y la historia de la ciudad de **Barcelona**.
- ◆ Busque información sobre la **Guerra Civil Española** (1936–1939) y su significado.

Yo soy un hombre sincero • Guajira Guantanamera

José Martí (Cuba)

José Martí (1853–1895) fue político y héroe militar así como periodista, filósofo y poeta cubano. Fundador del Partido Revolucionario Cubano desde su exilio en los Estados Unidos, Martí organizó la Guerra del 95—es decir, 1895, la última guerra de la independencia de Cuba contra España—en la que murió en combate. Sus obras literarias se consideran precursores del modernismo.

Algunas estrofas de los *Versos sencillos*—colección escrita y publicada por José Martí en Nueva York en 1891—fueron adaptadas a la canción de amor cubana, "Guajira Guantanamera". Ha llegado a ser la canción patriótica definitiva de Cuba. Cada estrofa viene de un poema diferente de la colección.

¿Estamos listos?

1. ¿Conoce a otros poetas, escritores o artistas que son/eran también pensadores y filósofos políticos, activistas políticos, revolucionarios o políticos en su país? ¿De dónde vienen?

2. En su opinión, ¿por qué podrían combinarse la poesía y la política en la misma persona? ¿Qué tienen en común esas actividades?

3. Estas personas de la poesía y la política, ¿cómo podrían calificarse?

   Podrían calificarse como... pensadores/as creativos/as, viajeros/as, forasteros/as (*outsiders*), rebeldes, visionarios/as, oradores/as elocuentes, líderes convincentes, carismáticos/as, idealistas, utopistas, optimistas, soñadores/as (*dreamers*), progresivos/as, disidentes, inconformistas, osados/as (*bold*), bien preparados/as, formados/as, instruidos/as, eruditos/as...

4. ¿A cuáles actividades se dedican estas personas?

   Estas personas... asumen riesgos, tienen una sensibilidad humanitaria, tienen una visión global, actúan fuera de la corriente dominante...

¡Leamos!

Yo soy un hombre sincero

Yo soy un hombre sincero
De donde **crece** la palma,
Y antes de morirme quiero
Echar mis versos del **alma**.

Yo vengo de todas partes,
Y **hacia** todas partes voy:
Arte soy entre las artes,
En los montes, monte soy.

Yo sé los nombres **extraños**
De las **yerbas** y las flores,
Y de **mortales engaños**,
Y de sublimes **dolores**.

Yo he visto en la noche oscura
Llover sobre mi cabeza
Los rayos de **lumbre** pura
De la divina **belleza**.

Alas nacer vi en los **hombros**
De las mujeres hermosas:
Y salir de los **escombros**,
Volando las mariposas.

He visto vivir a un hombre
Con el **puñal al costado**,
Sin decir jamás el nombre
De aquella que **lo ha matado**.

Rápida, como un **reflejo**,
Dos veces vi el alma, dos:
Cuando murió el **pobre viejo**,
Cuando ella me dijo adiós.

Temblé una vez —**en la reja**,
A la entrada de la **viña**,—
Cuando la **bárbara abeja**
Picó en la **frente** a mi niña.

Gocé una vez, **de tal suerte**
Que gocé **cual nunca**: —cuando
La sentencia de mi muerte
Leyó el **alcaide** llorando.

Oigo un **suspiro**, **a través**
De las tierras y la mar,
Y no es un suspiro, —es
Que mi hijo va a despertar.

Si dicen que del **joyero**
Tome la **joya** mejor,
Tomo a un amigo sincero
Y **pongo a un lado** el amor.

Yo he visto al **águila herida**
Volar **al azul** sereno,
Y morir en su **guarida**
La **víbora del veneno**.

Yo sé bien que cuando el mundo
Cede, **lívido**, al **descanso**,
Sobre el silencio profundo
Murmura el **arroyo manso**.

Yo he puesto la mano **osada**,
De horror y **júbilo yerta**,
Sobre la **estrella apagada**
Que cayó frente a mi puerta.

Oculto en mi **pecho** bravo
La **pena** que me lo **hiere**:
El hijo de un **pueblo esclavo**
Vive por él, **calla** y muere.

Todo es hermoso y constante,
Todo es música y razón,
Y todo, como el diamante,
Antes que luz es **carbón**.

Yo sé que el **necio se entierra**
Con gran **lujo** y con gran **llanto**.
Y que no hay fruta en la tierra
Como la del **camposanto**.

Callo, y entiendo, y **me quito**
La **pompa** del **rimador**:
Cuelgo de un árbol **marchito**
Mi **muceta de doctor**.

José Martí, from *Versos sencillos* (New York: Louis Weiss & Co., 1891).

crece [crecer]	*grows*	pongo [poner] a un lado	*I will set aside*
echar	*to release, pour*	(el) águila [F.]	*eagle*
(el) alma [F.]	*soul*	herida	*wounded*
hacia	*toward, to, into*	al azul	*into the blue sky*
extraños	*exotic, foreign*	guarida	*nest*
yerbas	*grasses, herbs*	víbora	*viper*
mortales	*fatal*	del veneno	*from its venom*
engaños	*tricks, ruses*	cede [ceder]	*yields, gives way*
(los) dolores	*sorrows, grief*	lívido	*(deathly) pale*
(la) lumbre	*light, fire*	descanso	*(eternal) sleep/rest*
belleza	*beauty*	arroyo	*stream, brook*
alas	*wings*	manso	*peaceful, calm*
nacer	*sprouting, being born*	osada	*bold, audacious*
hombros	*shoulders*	júbilo	*joy, jubilation*
escombros	*debris, rubble*	(la mano) yerta	*stiff and cold (hand)*
(el) puñal	*dagger, knife*	estrella	*star*
al costado	*in his ribs/side*	apagada	*extinguished*
lo ha matado [matar]	*has killed him*	oculto [ocultar]	*I am hiding*
reflejo	*fleeting image*	pecho	*heart, breast*
(el) pobre viejo	*poor old man (the poet's father)*	pena	*sorrow*
		hiere [herir]	*wounds, hurts*
temblé [temblar]	*trembled, shuddered*	pueblo esclavo	*enslaved nation/people*
en la reja	*at the gate*	calla [callar]	*falls silent*
viña	*vineyard*	(el) carbón	*coal*
bárbara	*savage*	necio	*fool*
abeja	*bee*	se entierra [enterrarse]	*is buried*
(la) frente	*forehead, brow*	lujo	*luxury, opulence*
gocé [gozar]	*I enjoyed*	llanto	*weeping, mourning*
de tal suerte	*in such a way/manner*	camposanto	*cemetery*
cual nunca	*as never before*	me quito [quitarse]	*I rid myself of*
(el) alcaide	*(prison) warden*	pompa	*pretentiousness*
suspiro	*sigh*	(el) rimador [PEJ.]	*inferior poet*
a través de	*across*	cuelgo [colgar]	*I hang*
joyero	*jeweler*	marchito	*withered*
joya	*jewel*	muceta de doctor	*doctoral hood*

¿De qué se trata? *Match the beginning of each sentence with the phrase that correctly completes it to reconstruct the lines of the poem.*

1. _____ Yo soy un hombre sincero
2. _____ Y antes de morirme quiero
3. _____ Yo vengo de todas partes
4. _____ Arte soy entre las artes
5. _____ Yo sé los nombres extraños
6. _____ Y de mortales engaños
7. _____ Yo he visto en la noche oscura
8. _____ Los rayos de lumbre pura

a. echar mis versos del alma.
b. en los montes, monte soy.
c. de las yerbas y las flores.
d. de donde crece la palma.
e. llover sobre mi cabeza.
f. de la divina belleza.
g. y de sublimes dolores.
h. y hacia todas partes voy.

Opciones *Choose the phrase or phrases that correctly complete each sentence. Include all correct responses.*

1. En el poema vemos que el poeta es un hombre

   a. observador.　　　　b. sensible.　　　　c. sincero.

2. Tiene mucha experiencia en las cosas de(l)

   a. la tecnología.　　　b. la naturaleza.　　c. alma.

3. ¿Sabemos quién ha herido al hombre con "el puñal al costado"? —Sí/No,

   a. no lo sabemos.　　b. sabemos su nombre.　　c. una mujer.

4. ¿Cuándo el poeta vio el alma? —Cuando

   a. se fue su enamorada.　b. se murió su padre.　c. la abeja picó a su niña.

5. ¿Cuándo tembló el poeta? —Cuando

   a. la mariposa salió.　　b. su niño se despertó.　　c. la abeja picó a su niña.

6. ¿Cómo leyó el alcaide la sentencia de la muerte del poeta? —La leyó

   a. riendo.　　　　b. llorando.　　　　c. gozando.

7. Lo que el poeta valora sobre el amor es

   a. el silencio profundo.　b. la joya mejor.　c. la amistad verdadera.

8. Lo que se oculta en el pecho del poeta es

   a. una estrella apagada.　b. el dolor de su pueblo.　c. la pena que le hiere al pecho.

¿Cierto o falso? *Indicate whether each statement is true or false, using* **C** *for* **cierto** (true) *or* **F** *for* **falso** (false). *If a statement is false, provide a corrected statement in Spanish.*

1. C   F   El poeta viene de donde nieva mucho.

_____

2. C   F   Tiene visiones maravillosas derivadas de la naturaleza.

_____

3. C   F   El poeta no tiene hijos.

_____

4. C   F   Durante su vida ha tenido problemas con la justicia.

_____

5. C   F   El hombre con el puñal al costado no se murió.

_____

6. C   F   El poeta se ve como el hijo humilde de un pueblo que sufre.

_____

7. C   F   Al final de su vida, el poeta pide ser enterrado con gran lujo y con gran llanto.

_____

8. C   F   Al final del poema, el poeta dice que está orgulloso por ser rimador.

_____

Reflexiones *Consider the following themes and questions, and discuss them in Spanish.*

1. Primero, lea este poema silenciosamente. Después, léalo en voz alta y note el esquema de rima. Cuando oye el poema, ¿le parece a usted diferente? ¿En qué se diferencia?

_____

_____

_____

_____

2. ¿El poeta tiene razón en clasificar este poema entre sus *Versos sencillos*? En su opinión, ¿éste es un poema sencillo?

_____

_____

_____

_____

3. ¿Qué elementos líricos ve usted en este poema? ¿Hay también elementos de la política o del pensamiento revolucionario? En su opinión, ¿los dos aspectos podrían coexistir en la misma obra?

_____

_____

_____

_____

¡Leamos!

Guajira Guantanamera

Yo soy un hombre sincero
De donde crece la palma,
Y antes de morirme quiero
Echar mis versos del alma. (I:1)

Mi verso es de un verde **claro**
Y de un **carmín encendido**:
Mi verso es un **ciervo** herido
Que busca en el monte **amparo**. (V:3)

Cultivo una rosa blanca
En julio como enero,
Para el amigo sincero
Que me da su mano **franca**. (XXXIX:1)

Con los pobres de la tierra
Quiero yo **mi suerte echar**:
El arroyo de la **sierra**
Me complace más que el mar. (III:2)

"Guajira Guantanamera" is adapted from poems in José Martí's *Versos sencillos* (New York: Louis Weiss & Co., 1891).

VOCABULARIO

claro	*light, bright*	franca	*open, sincere*
(el) carmín	*crimson*	mi suerte echar	*to throw in my lot*
encendido	*burning, flaming*	sierra	*mountains*
ciervo	*deer*	me complace [complacer]	*pleases me*
amparo	*refuge, shelter*		

Mi vocabulario *Select the word that does not belong in each group.*

1. a. sierra   b. guarida   c. monte   d. cordillera

2. a. mal   b. dolor   c. gozo   d. pena

3. a. herida   b. belleza   c. gracia   d. hermosura

4. a. carmín   b. verde   c. reja   d. azul

5. a. engaño   b. inepto   c. necio   d. tonto

6. a. amparo   b. claridad   c. fuego   d. lumbre

7. a. costados   b. hombros   c. brazos   d. escombros

8. a. quitar   b. colgar   c. coger   d. tomar

9. a. seco   b. marchito   c. extraño   d. lívido

10. a. halcón   b. abeja   c. águila   d. canario

Contrarios *Match each word with its opposite.*

1. _____ manso   a. llanto

2. _____ sencillez   b. apagado

3. _____ ocultar   c. lujo

4. _____ encendido   d. complacer

5. _____ osado   e. bárbaro

6. _____ pobreza   f. yerto

7. _____ callar   g. pompa

8. _____ júbilo   h. tímido

9. _____ caliente   i. echar

10. _____ molestar   j. hablar

Equivalentes *Complete each sentence by substituting words or phrases from the following list for the words or phrases in small type.*

se abandona	entiendo	rígida	audaz
extinguida	río	bajó	felicidad
rojo	brillante	las montañas	la tierra
contenta	pálido	tocado	destino
refugio	tranquilo	enfrente de	reposo
unir			

1. Yo ____{sé}___ bien que cuando ____{el mundo}___ / ____{Cede}___

   ____{lívido}___ al ____{descanso}___ / Sobre el silencio profundo / Murmura el

   ____{arroyo}___ ____{manso}___ .

2. Yo he puesto la mano ____{osada}___ / De horror y ____{júbilo}___

   ____{yerta}___ / Sobre la estrella ____{apagada}___ / Que ____{cayó}___

   ____{frente a}___ mi puerta.

3. Mi verso es de un verde ____{claro}___ / Y de un ____{carmín}___

   encendido: / Mi verso es un ciervo ____{herido}___ / Que busca en el monte

   ____{amparo}___ .

4. Con los pobres de la tierra / Quiero yo mi ____{suerte}___ ____{echar}___ /

   El arroyo de ____{la sierra}___ / Me ____{complace}___ más que el mar.

¡No se olvide! Verbo conjugado + infinitivo

Spanish uses many linked verbs, where the infinitive completes the meaning of a conjugated verb or a preceding infinitive: **Quisiera comer.** *I want to eat.* (See also Chapter 7.)

A number of Spanish verbs are followed directly by the infinitive, with no intervening preposition. Here are some of the most common.

caber *to fit, be possible*	**necesitar** *to need to*
deber *should, ought to*	**olvidar** *to forget to*
decidir *to decide to*	**pensar** *to intend to*
dejar *to let, allow, permit to*	**poder** *can, to be able to*
decidir *to decide to*	**preferir** *to prefer to*
desear *to want to*	**prometer** *to promise to*
esperar *to hope to, wait to*	**querer** *to want to*
hacer *to make*	**recordar** *to remember to*
intentar *to try to*	**saber** *to know how to*
lograr *to succeed in*	**soler** *to be in the habit of, be used to*

Yo **debería aprender** a cocinar.	*I should learn to cook.*
¿Qué les **hace pensar** eso?	*What makes you think that?*
¿**Podrían identificar**lo?	*Would they be able to identify it?*
Los autorretratos **solían ser** los objetos favoritos de los artistas jóvenes.	*Self-portraits used to be young artists' favorite projects.*

Other verbs are followed by the prepositions **con**, **de**, **en**, **por**, or **a** + infinitive. These combinations are best memorized from context or by study of a comprehensive grammar.

- ◆ Verb + **con** + infinitive

  contar con *to count on, to rely on*
  contentarse con *to be satisfied with*
  soñar con *to dream of*

Cuento con verla a menudo.	*I count on seeing her often.*

- ◆ Verb + **de** + infinitive

acabar de *to have just*	**encargarse de** *to take charge of*
alegrarse de *to be glad to*	**ocuparse de** *to be busy with, attend to*
cesar de *to cease, stop*	**olvidarse de** *to forget to*
dejar de *to stop, fail to*	**tratar de** *to try to*

Acabamos de comer, ¿y tú?	*We just finished eating. How about you?*
Trataron de completar la tarea.	*They tried to finish the homework.*

- ◆ Verb + **en** + infinitive

consentir en *to consent to*	**pensar en** *to consider (doing something)*
consistir en *to consist of*	**quedar en** *to agree to/on*
convenir en *to agree to/on*	**tardar en** *to be late, delay in*
insistir en *to insist on*	

Piensa en tomar vacaciones.	*She's considering taking a vacation.*

- ◆ Verb + **por** + infinitive

  acabar por *to end up by (doing something)*
  estar por *to be in favor of (doing something)*
  terminar por *to end up by (doing something)*

Están por salir inmediatamente.	*They're in favor of leaving immediately.*

- ◆ Verb + **a** + infinitive

aprender a *to learn how to*	**ir a** *to go to, be going to*
ayudar a *to help to*	**llegar a** *to come to*
comenzar a *to begin to*	**prepararse a** *to prepare to*
decidirse a *to make up one's mind to*	**salir a** *to go out, leave to*
empezar a *to begin to*	**venir a** *to come to*
enseñar a *to teach how to*	**volver a** *to do something again*
invitar a *to invite to*	

Jorge me **ayudó a construir** esta cerca.	*Jorge helped me build this fence.*
Estamos **aprendiendo a nadar**.	*We're learning to swim.*

Use the given elements to create complete and correct sentences in Spanish, using the present tense.

1. ¿ / usted / saber / preparar / el / almuerzo / ?

_____

2. nosotros / pensar / ir / de / vacaciones / en / verano

_____

3. Bárbara / olvidarse de / llevar / su / paraguas

_____

4. ellos / no / poder / llegar / a / tiempo

_____

5. yo / contentarse con / ir / a / la / playa

_____

6. ustedes / dejar de / comer / carnes / rojas

_____

7. tú / acabar de / plantar / los / bulbos

_____

8. él / insistir en / adoptar / a / este / perro

_____

9. nosotros / estar por / salir / a / cenar / esta / noche

_____

10. ellas / prepararse a / presentarse / al / examen

_____

11. usted / ayudar a / transportar / al / enfermo

_____

12. ¿ / tú / aprender a / hablar / portugués / ?

_____

Give (a) the English equivalent of the expression created by the word combination in bold in the following excerpts from the reading, then provide (b) the infinitive of the conjugated verb.

1. Y antes de morirme **quiero / Echar** mis versos del alma.

   a. _____   b. _____

2. Yo **he visto** en la noche oscura / **Llover** sobre mi cabeza / Los rayos de lumbre pura / De la divina belleza.

   a. _____   b. _____

3. Alas **nacer vi** en los hombros / De las mujeres hermosas:

   a. _____   b. _____

4. **He visto vivir** a un hombre / Con el puñal al costado

   a. _____   b. _____

5. Yo **he visto** al águila herida / **Volar** al azul sereno,

   a. _____   b. _____

6. Con los pobres de la tierra / **Quiero** yo mi suerte **echar**:

   a. _____   b. _____

¡Vaya más lejos!

◆ Busque en internet otros poemas de los *Versos sencillos* (1891) de **José Martí**.

◆ Busque en YouTube algunas versiones cantadas de "**Guajira Guantanamera**". ¿Conoce a los artistas?

◆ Busque información sobre el papel de **José Martí** en la liberación de Cuba.

◆ Busque información sobre otros políticos-poetas hispanohablantes. Por ejemplo, **Gioconda Belli**, **Ernesto Cardenal**, **Roque Dalton**, **Luis Muñoz Marín**, **Pablo Neruda** y **Mario Vargas Llosa**.

El alma de la máquina
Baldomero Lillo (Chile)

·20·

Los cuentos de Baldomero Lillo (1867–1923) se consideran los mejores ejemplos del realismo social en Chile. El autor pasó su adolescencia trabajando como empleado en la tienda de la **empresa** minera de su comuna de Lota (Chile). Así conocía íntimamente la vida y el trabajo de los mineros.

¿Estamos listos?

1. ¿Qué trabajo hace (o ha hecho) usted? ¿Es un trabajo de cuello blanco? ¿o de obrero (de cuello azul)?

   Trabajo/Trabajaba como... abogado/a, banquero/a, comerciante, publicista, contador(a), empresario/a, hombre/mujer de negocios; bibliotecario/a, editor(a), escritor(a), guía [M., F.] (*guide*), maestro/a (*schoolteacher*); periodista, traductor(a), profesor(a) de...; ingeniero/a, analista de sistemas, especialista en IT, programador(a), consultor(a) (independiente), científico/a, químico/a, físico/a, biólogo/a, técnico/a...; administrador(a), director(a), secretario/a...; dentista, enfermero/a, médico/a, sicólogo/a, trabajador(a) social, veterinario/a...; cajero/a (*cashier*), vendedor(a), cocinero/a, peluquero/a (*hair stylist*), empleado/a doméstico/a, niñero/a (*nanny*)...; actor/actriz, arquitecto/a, artista, atleta, cineasta, compositor(a), fotógrafo/a, músico/a...; agricultor(a), camionero/a, carpintero/a, conductor(a), constructor(a), electricista, jardinero/a, mecánico/a, minero, obrero/a, pintor(a) de brocha gorda (*housepainter*), plomero/a, techador(a) (*roofer*)...; (agente de) policía / mujer policía, bombero/a (*firefighter*), cartero/a (*mail carrier*), marinero, piloto/a, soldado / mujer soldado...

2. Para usted, ¿qué tareas le resultan más fáciles? ¿Cuáles le resultan más difíciles?

   Para mí, es (el/la)... administración, codificación, corrección; dirección, marketing [M.], organización, programación, publicidad [F.], venta; carpintería, conducción, construcción, jardinería, limpieza, reparación; ayudar a los otros, consejo, terapia, curación; dibujo, diseño, edición, enseñanza, escritura, hacer música, hacer películas, lectura, montaje [M.] (*edit, as movies*), pintura, traducción...

3. ¿Hay ciertas tareas que hace usted automáticamente? ¿Piensa cuando hace esas tareas? ¿o son totalmente automáticas?

4. ¿Sabe usted concentrarse? ¿Qué tareas o actividades puede hacer en la "zona"? Es decir, ¿qué hace usted muy bien sin pensar?

¡Leamos!

El alma de la máquina (I)

La silueta del **maquinista** con su **traje de dril** azul **se destaca** desde el **amanecer** hasta la noche en lo alto de la plataforma de la máquina. Su **turno** es de doce horas consecutivas.

Los obreros que extraen de los **ascensores** los carros de **carbón** lo miran con envidia **no exenta de encono**. Envidia, porque mientras ellos **abrasados** por el sol en el verano y **calados** por las lluvias en el invierno **forcejean sin tregua** desde el **brocal del pique** hasta la **cancha de depósito**, **empujando** las pesadas vagonetas, él, bajo la **techumbre** de zinc no da un paso ni **gasta** más energía que la indispensable para manejar la **rienda** de la máquina.

Y cuando, **vaciado** el mineral, los **tumbadores** corren y **jadean** con la vaga esperanza de obtener algunos segundos de **respiro**, a la envidia se añade el encono, viendo cómo el ascensor los **aguarda** ya con una nueva carga de **repletas carretillas**, mientras el maquinista, desde lo alto de su puesto, parece decirles con su severa **mirada**:

—¡**Más a prisa**, **holgazanes**, más a prisa!

Esta **decepción** que se repite en cada viaje, les hace pensar que si la **tarea** les **aniquila**, **culpa es de** aquel que para **abrumarles** la fatiga no necesita sino **alargar** y **encoger** el brazo.

Jamás podrán comprender que esa labor que les parece tan insignificante, es más **agobiadora** que la del **galeote atado** a su banco. El maquinista, **al asir** con la **diestra** el **mango** de **acero** del **gobierno** de la máquina, pasa instantáneamente a formar parte del enorme y complicado organismo de **hierro**. Su ser pensante se convierte en autómata. Su cerebro se paraliza. A la vista del **cuadrante** pintado de blanco, donde se mueve la **aguja** indicadora, el presente, el pasado y el **porvenir** son reemplazados por la idea fija. Sus nervios en tensión, su pensamiento todo se reconcentra en las **cifras** que en el cuadrante representan las **vueltas** de la gigantesca **bobina** que enrolla dieciséis metros de cable en cada revolución.

Como las catorce vueltas necesarias para que el ascensor **recorra** su **trayecto** vertical se efectúan en menos de veinte segundos, un segundo de distracción significa una revolución más, y una revolución más, demasiado lo sabe el maquinista, es: el ascensor **estrellándose**, arriba, contra las **poleas**; la bobina, **arrancada** de su centro, precipitándose como un **alud** que nada detiene, mientras los **émbolos**, locos, rompen las **bielas** y hacen saltar las **tapas** de los cilindros. Todo esto puede ser la consecuencia de la más pequeña distracción de su parte, de un segundo de olvido.

Por eso sus **pupilas**, su **rostro**, su pensamiento se inmovilizan. Nada ve, nada **oye** de lo que pasa **a su rededor**, sino la aguja que gira y el **martillo de señales** que **golpea** encima de su cabeza. Y esa atención no tiene tregua. Apenas **asoma** por el brocal del pique uno de los ascensores, cuando un doble **campanillazo** le avisa que, abajo, el otro espera ya con su carga completa. **Estira** el brazo, el vapor empuja los émbolos y **silba** al escaparse por las **empaquetaduras**, la bobina enrolla acelerada el **hilo** del metal y la aguja del cuadrante **gira aproximándose** velozmente a la **flecha de parada**. Antes que la **cruce**, atrae hacia sí la **manivela** y la máquina se detiene **sin ruido**, **sin sacudidas**, como un **caballo blando de boca**.

Baldomero Lillo, from *Sub sole* (Santiago: Editorial A. Bello, 1907).

empresa	*concern, business*	mango	*handle*
(el) maquinista	*operator*	acero	*steel*
(el) traje de dril	*drill (a strong cotton*	gobierno	*governor (speed regulator)*
	cloth) coveralls	hierro	*iron*
se destaca [destacarse]	*stands out*	(el) cuadrante	*dial*
(el) amanecer	*dawn*	aguja	*needle, clock hand*
turno	*(work) shift*	(el) porvenir	*future*
(los) ascensores	*elevators*	cifras	*numbers, digits*
(el) carbón	*coal*	vueltas	*turns, revolutions*
no exenta de	*not devoid of*	bobina	*spool, reel*
encono	*ill-will, bitterness*	recorra [recorrer]	*goes through, completes*
abrasados	*(sun)burned*	trayecto	*journey, trajectory*
calados	*soaked*	estrellándose	*crashing*
forcejean [forcejear]	*struggle (along)*	[estrellarse]	
sin tregua	*without respite*	poleas	*pulleys, tackles*
(el) brocal del pique	*mouth of the coal pit*	arrancada de	*dragged out of*
cancha de depósito	*collection floor*	(el) alud	*rockslide, avalanche*
empujando [empujar]	*pushing*	émbolos	*pistons*
(la) techumbre	*ceiling, roof*	bielas	*connecting rods*
gasta [gastar]	*uses, spends*	tapas	*lids, caps*
rienda	*rein*	pupilas	*pupils (of eyes)*
vaciado	*emptied (out)*	rostro	*face*
(los) tumbadores	*coal cart handlers*	oye [oír]	*he hears*
jadean [jadear]	*are gasping*	a su rededor	*around him*
respiro	*respite*	martillo de señales	*signal hammer*
aguarda [aguardar]	*waits, is waiting*	golpea [golpear]	*strikes, is striking*
repletas	*filled, full*	asoma [asomar]	*appears*
carretillas	*handcarts*	campanillazo	*loud ring*
mirada	*look, glance*	estira [estirar]	*he stretches out*
más a prisa	*faster*	silba [silbar]	*hisses, whistles*
(los) holgazanes	*idlers, loafers*	empaquetaduras	*gaskets*
(la) decepción	*disappointment*	hilo	*cable, wire*
tarea	*work, task*	gira [girar]	*spins, rotates*
aniquila [aniquilar]	*crushes, annihilates*	aproximándose	*approaching*
culpa es de	*the guilt lies with*	[aproximarse]	
abrumarles	*overwhelm them*	flecha de parada	*stop arrow*
alargar	*extend, stretch out*	cruce [cruzar]	*it crosses/passes*
encoger	*draw back, flex*	manivela	*handle, crank*
agobiadora	*taxing, oppressive*	sin ruido	*noiselessly*
(el) galeote	*galley slave*	sin sacudidas	*smoothly, jolt-free*
atado	*tied, bound*	caballo blando	*horse with a soft mouth*
al asir	*(upon) grasping*	de boca	*(easy-to-handle)*
diestra	*right hand*		

¡Leamos!

El alma de la máquina (II)

Y cuando aún vibra en la **placa** metálica el **tañido** de la **última** señal, el martillo la **hiere** de nuevo con un golpe seco, **estridente** a la vez. A su **mandato** imperioso el brazo del maquinista se alarga, los **engranajes rechinan**, los cables oscilan y la bobina **voltea** con **vertiginosa** rapidez. Y las horas suceden a las horas, el sol sube al **cénit**, desciende; la tarde llega, declina, y el **crepúsculo**, surgiendo **al ras del** horizonte, **alza** y extiende cada vez más a prisa su **penumbra** inmensa.

De pronto un **silbido ensordecedor** llena el espacio. Los tumbadores **sueltan** las carretillas y **se yerguen briosos**. La tarea del día ha terminado. De las distintas secciones anexas a la mina salen los obreros en **confuso tropel**. En su prisa por abandonar los **talleres se chocan** y **se estrujan**, mas no se levanta una voz de **queja** o de protesta: los rostros están radiantes. Poco a poco el rumor de sus pasos sonoros **se aleja** y **desvanece** en la **calzada sumida** en las **sombras**. La mina ha quedado desierta.

Sólo en el departamento de la máquina se distingue una **confusa** silueta humana. Es el maquinista. Sentado en su alto **sitial**, con la diestra **apoyada** en la manivela, permanece inmóvil en la semioscuridad que lo rodea. Al concluir la tarea, cesando bruscamente la tensión de sus nervios, **se ha desplomado** en el banco como una masa inerte.

Un proceso lento de reintegración al estado normal se opera en su cerebro **embotado**. **Recobra** penosamente sus facultades anuladas, atrofiadas por doce horas de obsesión, de idea fija. El autómata vuelve a ser otra vez una criatura de carne y hueso que ve, que oye, que piensa, que sufre.

El enorme mecanismo **yace** paralizado. Sus **miembros potentes**, **caldeados** por el movimiento, se enfrían produciendo **leves chasquidos**. Es el alma de la máquina que se escapa por los poros del metal, para encender en las **tinieblas** que cubren el alto sitial de hierro, las **fulguraciones** trágicas de una **aurora** toda roja desde el **orto** hasta el cénit.

VOCABULARIO

placa	(metal) plate/sheet	ensordecedor	deafening
tañido	tolling, ringing (bell)	sueltan [soltar]	drop, let go of
última	most recent, last	se yerguen [erguirse]	they straighten up
hiere [herir]	pounds (on), wounds	briosos	spirited, full of pep
estridente	raucous, unpleasant	confuso	disorderly
mandato	order, command	(el) tropel	mass, horde
(los) engranajes	gears, machinery	(los) talleres	work areas
rechinan [rechinar]	grind	se chocan [chocarse]	collide (with each other)
voltea [voltear]	turns, rotates	se estrujan [estrujarse]	crush (each other)
vertiginosa	dizzying	queja	complaint
(el) cénit	zenith, high point	se aleja [alejarse]	moves off
crepúsculo	twilight, dusk	desvanece [desvanecer]	fades away
al ras del	level with	calzada	road, avenue
alza [alzar]	rises (up)	sumida [sumir]	plunged, immersed
penumbra	darkness, shadow	sombras	shadows
silbido	whistle	confusa	vague, indistinct

(el) sitial	*seat, post*	potentes	*powerful*
apoyada en	*resting on*	caldeados	*heated up*
se ha desplomado	*he has collapsed*	leves	*slight, small*
[desplomarse]		chasquidos	*cracking sounds*
embotado	*dull, muddled*	tinieblas	*darkness, shadows*
recobra [recobrar]	*he recovers*	(las) fulguraciones	*flares, flames*
yace [yacer]	*lies*	aurora	*dawn*
miembros	*limbs*	orto	*(moment of) sunrise*

EJERCICIO
20·1

¿De qué se trata? *Who might say or think the following? Choose* **O** *for* **el obrero** (the worker) *or* **M** *for* **el maquinista** (the machine operator).

	O	M
1. "¿Por qué su tarea es tan fácil?"	☐	☐
2. "Después de doce horas podré volver a casa."	☐	☐
3. "¡Ay! Esta carretilla está pesada."	☐	☐
4. "¡Cuidado! ¡Llega otra!"	☐	☐
5. "Cuando los miro, piensan que les digo: —¡Más a prisa!"	☐	☐
6. "Él no necesita sino alargar y encoger el brazo."	☐	☐
7. "Finalmente la máquina se para y me suelta."	☐	☐

EJERCICIO
20·2

Opciones *Choose the phrase or phrases that correctly complete each sentence. Include all correct responses.*

1. El maquinista lleva un

   a. uniforme militar.   b. traje de dril.   c. calzado deportivo.

2. Los obreros sienten resentimiento hacia el maquinista porque

   a. él parece trabajar poco.   b. su trabajo es diferente.   c. ellos trabajan mucho.

3. Los tumbadores

   a. extraen un carro al día.   b. a veces descansan.   c. trabajan sin descanso.

4. Para manejar la rienda de la máquina se necesita

   a. movimientos regulares.   b. concentración.   c. encono.

5. El trabajo del maquinista es agobiador porque

   a. él forma parte de la máquina.   b. está a bordo de un barco.   c. la máquina nunca para.

6. El gran mecanismo se compone de

   a. acero.   b. alud.   c. hierro.

7. Un segundo de distracción significa

   a. una máquina fuera de control.   b. una catástrofe.   c. un descanso.

¿Cierto o falso? *Indicate whether each statement is true or false, using* **C** *for* **cierto** *(true) or* **F** *for* **falso** *(false). If a statement is false, provide a corrected statement in Spanish.*

1. C F   Este cuento describe la relación entre el obrero y su aparato.

_____

2. C F   El maquinista tiene una relación agradable y creativa con la máquina.

_____

3. C F   Los obreros arrancan y empujan continuamente las carretillas llenas.

_____

4. C F   El maquinista les dice a menudo a los obreros: —¡Más a prisa!

_____

5. C F   Nada ve, nada oye el maquinista de lo que pasa a su rededor.

_____

6. C F   La máquina controla la elevación y la bajada de los ascensores.

_____

7. C F   El aparato siempre se detiene ruidosamente y con sacudidas.

_____

Mi vocabulario *Select the word that does not belong in each group.*

1. a. revolución   b. giro   c. gira   d. vuelta
2. a. camión   b. viaje   c. trayecto   d. camino
3. a. cara   b. caro   c. fisonomía   d. rostro
4. a. aparecer   b. mostrarse   c. asombrar   d. asomar
5. a. alambre   b. cable   c. hilo   d. alameda
6. a. aguja   b. manecilla   c. mantequilla   d. flecha
7. a. palo   b. manga   c. manivela   d. mango
8. a. respiro   b. pavo   c. tregua   d. pausa
9. a. cruzar   b. atravesar   c. recordar   d. recorrer

Contrarios *Match each word or phrase with its opposite.*

1. _____ encoger   a. amistad
2. _____ diestra   b. empujado
3. _____ asomar   c. libre
4. _____ a prisa   d. lentamente
5. _____ encono   e. alargar
6. _____ porvenir   f. desaparecer
7. _____ atado   g. mano izquierda
8. _____ arrancado   h. pasado

Equivalentes *Complete each sentence by substituting words or phrases from the following list for the words or phrases in small type.*

alba	se distingue	quemados	arrancan
horario	sin interrupción	carretillas	mojados
luchan	celos	observan	moviendo
descanso			

1. La silueta del maquinista con su traje de dril azul _____ desde el

   _____ hasta la noche.
   <small>amanecer</small>   <small>se destaca</small>

2. Su _____ es de doce horas _____.
   <small>turno</small>   <small>consecutivas</small>

3. Los obreros que _____ de los ascensores los carros de carbón lo
   <small>extraen</small>

   _____ con _____.
   <small>miran</small>   <small>envidia</small>

4. Porque mientras ellos _____ por el sol en el verano y
   <small>abrasados</small>

   _____ por las lluvias en el invierno _____ sin
   <small>calados</small>   <small>forcejean</small>

   _____ ... _____ las pesadas _____.
   <small>tregua</small>   <small>empujando</small>   <small>vagonetas</small>

¿De qué se trata? *Arrange the following events, taken from the second section of the reading, in the order in which they appear in the reading.*

1. _____   a. Los engranajes continúan rechinando a las órdenes del martillo.

2. _____   b. El sol empieza a descender.

3. _____   c. Los obreros alegres se alejan de los talleres.

4. _____   d. Un silbido marca el fin del día laboral.

5. _____   e. El brazo del maquinista obedece a los movimientos de la máquina.

6. _____   f. El mecanismo yace paralizado.

7. _____   g. El crepúsculo extiende su penumbra inmensa.

8. _____   h. Se opera en el cerebro del maquinista la recuperación de sus facultades.

9. _____   i. Pero el maquinista se queda inmóvil, desplomado en el banco.

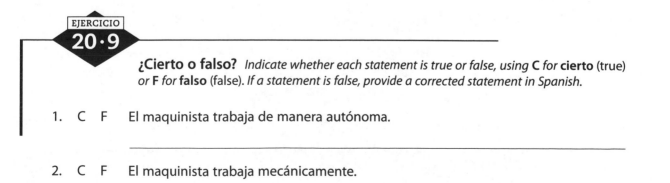

EJERCICIO
20·8

Opciones *Choose the phrase or phrases that correctly complete each sentence. Include all correct responses.*

1. El brazo del maquinista se alarga y encoge para
   a. limpiarse la frente.
   b. obedecer a la máquina.
   c. manejar el gobierno.

2. El silbido indica
   a. el fin del día laboral.
   b. la puesta en marcha.
   c. un obrero enfermo.

3. Al oír el silbido, los tumbadores
   a. sueltan las vagonetas.
   b. se alegran.
   c. abandonan la mina.

4. Al fin del día se siente el último sonido de(l)
   a. maquinista que suspira.
   b. los engranajes que rechinan.
   c. los pasos de los obreros.

5. El maquinista queda inmóvil porque
   a. sus facultades están suspendidas.
   b. su cerebro está embotado.
   c. no quiere volver a casa.

6. La criatura de carne y hueso es
   a. siempre un autómata.
   b. el maquinista de noche.
   c. la máquina paralizada.

7. Los últimos rayos de la puesta del sol iluminan
   a. el sitial de hierro.
   b. los ojos del maquinista.
   c. el camino de los mineros.

EJERCICIO
20·9

¿Cierto o falso? *Indicate whether each statement is true or false, using C for **cierto** (true) or F for **falso** (false). If a statement is false, provide a corrected statement in Spanish.*

1. C   F   El maquinista trabaja de manera autónoma.

_____

2. C   F   El maquinista trabaja mecánicamente.

_____

3. C F Los obreros se alegran al fin del día.

   _____

4. C F El turno de doce horas empieza al crepúsculo.

   _____

5. C F El maquinista parte en seguida, al lado de los obreros.

   _____

6. C F El maquinista recobra lentamente sus facultades humanas.

   _____

7. C F En este cuento, el alma de la máquina se escapa cada noche.

   _____

Mi vocabulario *Select the word that does not belong in each group.*

1. a. tañido   b. toque   c. campanillazo   d. tenedor

2. a. errar   b. alzar   c. erguir   d. levantar

3. a. tinieblas   b. penuria   c. sombra   d. penumbra

4. a. dañar   b. herir   c. heredar   d. golpear

5. a. asistir   b. asir   c. atar   d. agarrar

6. a. mandato   b. decreto   c. orden   d. mandarina

7. a. amanecer   b. aurora   c. amapola   d. orto

8. a. tropel   b. muchedumbre   c. horda   d. muchacho

9. a. vigoroso   b. enojoso   c. brioso   d. enérgico

EJERCICIO 20·11

Contrarios *Match each word with its opposite.*

1. _____ desvanecer
2. _____ soltar
3. _____ embotado
4. _____ erguirse
5. _____ leve
6. _____ vertiginoso
7. _____ queja
8. _____ ensordecedor
9. _____ estridente

a. inaudible
b. pesado
c. alegría
d. atar
e. aparecer
f. armonioso
g. lento
h. lúcido
i. desplomarse

EJERCICIO 20·12

Equivalentes *Complete each sentence by substituting words or phrases from the following list for the words or phrases in small type.*

a las órdenes · con dificultad · rápidamente · anochecer
enérgicos · recupera · aparato · muy fuerte
siguen · asciende · extiende · sube
baja · se levantan · súbitamente · dejan caer
oscuridad · tullidas

1. _____ del _____, el brazo del maquinista
   <small>Al mandato</small>   <small>mecanismo</small>

   _____.
   <small>se alarga</small>

2. Y las horas _____ las horas, el sol _____...,
   <small>suceden a</small>   <small>sube</small>

   _____; la tarde llega, declina, y el _____...,
   <small>desciende</small>   <small>crepúsculo</small>

   _____ y extiende cada vez más _____
   <small>alza</small>   <small>a prisa</small>

   su _____ inmensa.
   <small>penumbra</small>

3. _____ un silbido _____ llena el espacio. Los tumbadores
   <small>De pronto</small>   <small>ensordecedor</small>

   _____ las carretillas y _____ _____.
   <small>sueltan</small>   <small>se yerguen</small>   <small>briosos</small>

4. _____ _____ sus facultades anuladas,
   <small>Recobra</small>   <small>penosamente</small>

   _____ por doce horas de obsesión.
   <small>atrofiadas</small>

Reflexiones *Consider the following themes and questions, and discuss them in Spanish.*

1. Este cuento se narra completamente en tiempo presente. ¿Qué efecto tiene eso?

   _____

   _____

   _____

2. ¿En su opinión, el autor admira la industrialización? ¿En qué trabajos o industrias trabajan hoy día los obreros de esa manera?

   _____

   _____

   _____

3. ¿Por qué los obreros desconfían del maquinista? ¿El autor cree también que el trabajo del maquinista es más fácil? ¿Podemos comprender profesiones u ocupaciones muy distintas a la nuestra?

   _____

   _____

   _____

4. ¿Los obreros son seres humanos con emociones? ¿Y el maquinista? ¿Cómo se describe? "Su ser pensante se convierte en autómata." ¿Es verdad?

   _____

   _____

   _____

5. ¿Qué sucederá si el maquinista comete un error? ¿Cree usted que el autor admira su trabajo?

   _____

   _____

   _____

6. En su opinión, ¿la máquina se parece a un ser viviente? Si lo es, ¿dónde vive? ¿Cuándo vive?

   _____

   _____

   _____

7. ¿Quién (o qué) es el alma de la máquina? ¿Es una sola entidad o una entidad doble?

   _____

   _____

   _____

8. El cuento termina con una imagen: el alma de la máquina que se escapa ilumina la silla de hierro. ¿Qué significa esta imagen? En esta visión, ¿dónde se encuentra el mundo natural? ¿La naturaleza tiene aquí un papel?

_____

_____

_____

¡No se olvide! Los pronombres complementos directo e indirecto

Both direct and indirect object pronouns replace nouns that have already been mentioned or are understood.

♦ *Direct object pronouns* replace nouns that directly receive the action of a transitive verb. The original verb + noun has no preposition or implied preposition in Spanish.

Compra *un sándwich*. *Lo* compra.	*He buys a sandwich. He buys it.*
Veo a *Silvia*. *La* veo.	*I see Silvia. I see her.*

Direct object pronouns (**lo**, **la**) can replace a person, an animal, or an object.

¡Ojo!

Remember that the Spanish personal **a** (for example, **veo a Silvia**), which has no English equivalent, precedes a direct object person, pet, domestic animal, or an inanimate object for which the speaker has feeling (for example, **amo a mi país**). It is not considered a preposition.

♦ *Indirect object pronouns* replace the noun (always a person or animal) that follows the prepositions **a** or **para** in a prepositional phrase (**a** + noun, **para** + noun), or an implied prepositional phrase.

Hablo *a Silvia*. *Le* hablo.	*I speak to Silvia. I speak to her.*

All intransitive verbs, such as verbs of communication (for example, **hablar a**, **dar a**, **decir a**) take an indirect object noun or pronoun. Note that in Spanish, when an indirect object pronoun is used, the original noun or a stressed pronoun is often repeated after the verb for emphasis.

***Le* hablo *a Silvia*. *Le* hablo *a ella*.**	*I speak to Silvia. I speak to her.*

Here are the Spanish object pronouns.

	DIRECT OBJECT PRONOUNS		INDIRECT OBJECT PRONOUNS	
ENGLISH	WITH **ver** *to see*		WITH **dar a** *to give*	
me	me	**Me** ve.	me	**Me** da el libro.
you [FAM.]	te	**Te** ve.	te	**Te** da el libro.
him, her, it, you	lo [M.]	**Lo** ve.	le [M., F.]	**Le** da el libro.
[FORM. SING.]	la [F.]	**La** ve.		
us	nos	**Nos** ve.	nos	**Nos** da el libro.
you [FAM. PL.]	os	**Os** ve.	os	**Os** da el libro.
them, you	los [M. PL.]	**Los** ve.	les [M./F. PL.]	**Les** da el libro.
[FORM. SING.]	las [F. PL.]	**Las** ve.		

◆ *Stressed pronouns* are used after prepositions. Note that they are identical to Spanish subject pronouns, except for **mí** and **ti**: **mí, ti, él, ella, usted, ello** (*it*), **nosotros, vosotros, ellos, ellas, ustedes**.

With the preposition **con** *with*, **mí** and **ti** become **conmigo** and **contigo**.

Partí **sin ellos**.	*I left without them.*
Venga **conmigo**.	*Come with me.*

EJERCICIO
20·14

Direct object pronouns *In these excerpts from the reading, the direct object pronoun is shown in bold. First (a) determine its noun antecedent, re-reading if necessary, then (b) re-create the phrase or sentence using the noun instead of the direct object pronoun.*

1. Los obreros... **lo** miran con envidia.

   a. _____

   b. _____

2. viendo cómo el ascensor **los** aguarda ya con una nueva carga

   a. _____

   b. _____

3. y una revolución más, demasiado **lo** sabe el maquinista, es: el ascensor estrellándose

   a. _____

   b. _____

4. Antes que **la** cruce, atrae hacia sí la manivela.

   a. _____

   b. _____

5. El martillo **la** hiere de nuevo con un golpe seco.

   a. _____

   b. _____

6. Permanece inmóvil en la semioscuridad que **lo** rodea.

a. _____

b. _____

EJERCICIO
20·15

Indirect object pronouns *In these excerpts from the reading, the indirect object pronoun is shown in bold. First (a) determine its noun antecedent, re-reading if necessary, then (b) re-create the phrase or sentence using both the noun and the indirect object pronoun.*

1. mientras el maquinista... parece decir**les** con su severa mirada: —¡Más a prisa, holgazanes...!

a. _____

b. _____

2. para abrumar**les** la fatiga no necesita sino alargar y encoger el brazo

a. _____

b. _____

3. jamás podrán comprender que esa labor que **les** parece tan insignificante

a. _____

b. _____

4. Un doble campanillazo **le** avisa que, abajo, el otro espera ya con su carga completa.

a. _____

b. _____

¡Vaya más lejos!

- Vea (en DVD o en YouTube) *Tiempos modernos* (*Modern Times*) (1936), la película de Charlie Chaplin, que representa al obrero víctima de la industrialización y la producción en cadena.

- Vea en DVD *Subterra* (2004), la película de Marcelo Ferrari, protagonizada por Francisco Reyes y Paulina Gálvez, basada en las obras de Baldomero Lillo.

- Busque en línea (www.google.es) artículos sobre el **derrumbe de la mina de San José** (Chile) en 2010 y el rescate de los 33 mineros.

- Lea otros cuentos de **Baldomero Lillo**. (Se encuentran en línea.) Sus libros son: *Subterra*, 1904; *Sub sole*, 1907; *Relatos populares*, 1947, *El hallazgo y otros cuentos del mar*, 1956; *Pesquisa trágica*, 1963.

BELLAS ARTES Y CINE

La música salva vidas en mi país: Entrevista a Gustavo Dudamel

Jesús Ruiz Mantilla (Venezuela)

Gustavo Dudamel, músico y director de orquestas, llegó a ser director de la Sinfónica de Los Ángeles en 2009, a los 28 años. Hasta ahora, es el más famoso de los alumnos educados en el "**Sistema**" de orquestas de su país, Venezuela. Habló con un reportero de *El País* en Madrid.

¿Estamos listos?

1. ¿Qué tipo de música prefiere usted? ¿Qué tipo de música escucha generalmente?

   Escucho... música pop, rock, rap, música clásica, música sacra/religiosa, música de cámara (*chamber*), música folclórica, música country, blues, jazz...

2. ¿Cómo prefiere escuchar música?

   Prefiero escuchar... en el radio, en el reproductor de MP3, en el teléfono inteligente, en el reproductor de CD, en el tocadiscos, en vivo, una banda, una orquesta, un cuarteto, un trío, un/a cantante, un coro...

3. ¿Toca un instrumento? ¿Qué instrumento toca?

   Toco... el piano, la guitarra, el banjo, la mandolina, la flauta, el violín, la viola, el violonchelo, el bajo eléctrico, el contrabajo, el saxofón, la trompeta, el trombón, el clarinete, el oboe, el bajón (*bassoon*), el corno francés, la flauta, el arpa, la armónica, la batería (*drums*), el tambor...

4. ¿Cuándo empezó a tocar? ¿Toca o ha tocado música en un grupo? ¿Dónde ha tocado?

   Toco... en la escuela, en la universidad, en una banda, en un club de música, en una orquesta, en un coro, en un cuarteto, en un trío, en la iglesia, con los amigos, en los bailes...

5. ¿En qué actividades participan los jóvenes alumnos que conoce?

   Participan en... deportes, música, videojuegos, baile, artes, fotografía, cine, trabajo a tiempo parcial, voluntariado, lectura, clubes de ciencia y otros clubes, mirar la televisión, enviar textos, hablar por teléfono...

6. ¿Cuáles son los campos más comunes de los niños prodigio?

   Es/Son... la música, las matemáticas, la física, la astronomía, la química, la medicina, la informática, las computadoras, las artes, el teatro, el cine, la pintura, la escultura, la literatura, la poesía, la filosofía, los deportes, la gimnasia, la natación, el golf, el tenis, el tenis de mesa, el ajedrez (*chess*)...

¡Leamos!

Desde que era un **mocoso** dirigía a las grandes orquestas. En su casa. **A su aire**. No es que el pequeño Gustavo Dudamel indicara con la **batuta**—"con el **palito**, que lo llamaba yo", dice—la música que salía de los discos que le ponía su padre como si fuera un juego. Es que **paraba** el **tocadiscos**, daba indicaciones a la orquesta y después **volvía a apretar la tecla** del play **confiado** en que **le iban a hacer caso**.

Quizá entonces no, pero ahora sí que se lo hacen. Este venezolano, que mañana **cumple 27 años**, está educado en el revolucionario sistema de orquestas de su país creado por el maestro José Antonio Abreu en 1974 y que hoy **forma** musicalmente a unos 300.000 niños. [Dudamel] dirige [...] a la Filarmónica de Berlín, a la Sinfónica de Chicago o a la Mahler Chamber... Y, a partir de 2009, **se estrenará** como **titular** de la Sinfónica de Los Ángeles.

Los grandes han visto en él a una **especie** de **Mesías** que viene a salvar la música clásica con un **impulso desconocido**, una energía **caribeña** tan alegre y tan contagiosa que pone la **carne de gallina**. Podrán **comprobarlo** quienes le vean estos días en su **gira** española [...], **junto a** sus músicos **del alma**, los que forman la Joven Orquesta Simón Bolívar de Venezuela, que él **lidera** desde hace nueve años. [...]

Pregunta. Ritmo, energía. ¿Es lo que **aportan** ustedes desde Venezuela a un mundo, el de la música clásica, demasiado **anquilosado**?

Respuesta. Nosotros venimos a demostrar que las utopías **se cumplen**. Lo nuestro parecía imposible, nadie esperaba que la música clásica fuese un arma de **cambio** social, pero lo que ha hecho el maestro Abreu con las orquestas, sacando a niños de la **marginación** por medio de la música, demuestra que es posible. Y a un muy alto **nivel**. La música salva hoy la vida de muchos jóvenes en mi país. No importa que no **se acaben** dedicando **a ello**, aunque muchos lo hacen. Formándose así, se han convertido en el público de mañana también.

P. Usted es el símbolo de todo ese sistema. ¿Le **pesa** tanto **éxito** a una edad tan joven? ¿No es demasiada responsabilidad?

R. No, al contrario. Es una responsabilidad hermosísima, algo muy importante. Me llena de mucho **orgullo**, pero hay que **recalcar** que no es cuestión de uno, sino de muchos. Yo soy una **libélula** en ese universo del sistema de orquestas.

Jesús Ruiz Mantilla, excerpts from *Diario El País-España*, http://elpais.com/diario. Used with the permission of Prisa Noticias on behalf of *Diario El País*. Many thanks to María Hervás and Carlos Laorden.

VOCABULARIO

(el) Sistema	*music education program in Venezuela*	volvía [volver] a apretar la tecla	*pressed the button again*
mocoso [FAM.]	*child, boy*	confiado	*confident*
a su aire	*in his own way*	le iban [ir] a hacer caso	*they were going to pay attention to him*
batuta	*baton*		
palito	*little stick*	quizá	*perhaps*
paraba [parar]	*stopped*	cumple [cumplir] 27 años	*turns 27*
(el) tocadiscos	*phonograph*	forma [formar]	*educates*

se estrenará [estrenarse]	*(he) will premiere*	aportan [aportar]	*bring*
		anquilosado	*antiquated*
(el) titular	*director*	se cumplen [cumplirse]	*come true, be fulfilled*
(la) especie	*type*	cambio	*change*
(el) Mesías	*Messiah*	(la) marginación	*underclass*
impulso	*drive*	(el) nivel	*level*
desconocido	*new (kind of)*	se acaben [acabarse]	*end up*
caribeña	*Caribbean*	a ello [NEUTER PRON.]	*to it (to music)*
(la) carne de gallina	*goose bumps, gooseflesh*	(a la música)	
comprobarlo	*confirm it*	pesa [pesar]	*weigh (heavily)*
(la) gira	*tour*	éxito	*success*
junto a	*along with*	orgullo	*pride*
del alma	*cherished*	recalcar	*repeat*
lidera [liderar]	*has been conducting*	libélula	*dragonfly*

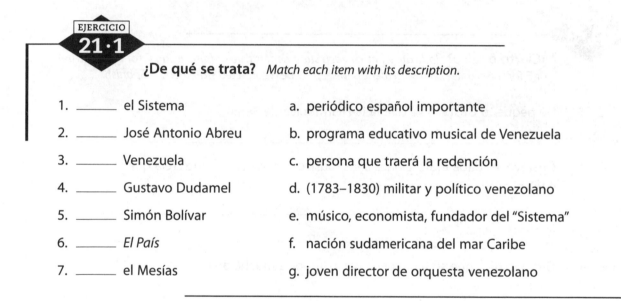

EJERCICIO 21·1

¿De qué se trata? *Match each item with its description.*

1. _____ el Sistema
2. _____ José Antonio Abreu
3. _____ Venezuela
4. _____ Gustavo Dudamel
5. _____ Simón Bolívar
6. _____ *El País*
7. _____ el Mesías

a. periódico español importante
b. programa educativo musical de Venezuela
c. persona que traerá la redención
d. (1783–1830) militar y político venezolano
e. músico, economista, fundador del "Sistema"
f. nación sudamericana del mar Caribe
g. joven director de orquesta venezolano

EJERCICIO 21·2

Opciones *Choose the phrase or phrases that correctly complete each sentence. Include all correct responses.*

1. El fundador del programa musical venezolano el "Sistema" es
   a. Dudamel.
   b. Abreu.
   c. Bolívar.

2. Esta entrevista tiene lugar
   a. en Los Ángeles.
   b. en Madrid.
   c. en Caracas.

3. Hoy en día Gustavo Dudamel dirige la
   a. Joven Orquesta Simón Bolívar.
   b. Sinfónica de Los Ángeles.
   c. Mahler Chamber.

4. La música clásica es un arma de cambio porque
   a. en Venezuela nadie apoya al Sistema.
   b. los niños aprenden a trabajar en equipo.
   c. las familias pobres venezolanas tienen nuevas posibilidades.

5. La libélula vive poco tiempo. Lo que quiere decir Gustavo por "Yo soy una libélula en ese universo del sistema de orquestas" es que
   a. él es un elemento permanente del sistema de orquestas.
   b. la libélula es muy hermosa.
   c. él formará parte del sistema de orquestas por relativamente poco tiempo.

EJERCICIO 21·3

¿Cierto o falso? *Indicate whether each statement is true or false, using* **C** *for* **cierto** *(true) or* **F** *for* **falso** *(false). If a statement is false, provide a corrected statement in Spanish.*

1. C F   De pequeño Gustavo ya dirigía la Filarmónica de Berlín.

   _____

2. C F   Gustavo les daba indicaciones a los músicos del disco porque creía que le iban a hacer caso.

   _____

   _____

3. C F   Gustavo dice que su fama personal le importa mucho a él.

   _____

4. C F   Los jóvenes del Sistema formarán el público de mañana.

   _____

5. C F   Todos los niños que participan en el Sistema vienen de familias ricas.

   _____

Reflexiones *Consider the following themes and questions, and discuss them in Spanish.*

1. De niño/a, ¿qué jugaba usted a ser? ¿Se han realizado o se realizan sus sueños?

_____

_____

_____

_____

2. ¿Piensa usted que le falta algo al sistema educativo de su país o de su ciudad? ¿Piensa que le ha faltado algo a usted durante los estudios?

_____

_____

_____

_____

3. ¿Piensa que la música clásica puede ser un arma de cambio? ¿Qué más puede servir como fuerza del cambio social?

_____

_____

_____

_____

EJERCICIO

21·5

Mi vocabulario *Select the word or phrase that does not belong in each group.*

1. a. reproductor de CD   b. tocadiscos   c. batuta   d. reproductor de MP3

2. a. vanidad   b. humildad   c. orgullo   d. satisfacción

3. a. celebridad   b. éxito   c. salida   d. fama

4. a. libélula   b. hormiga   c. mariposa   d. libelo

5. a. gira   b. viaje   c. girasol   d. excursión

Contrarios *Match each word or phrase with its opposite.*

1. _____ conocido   a. moderno

2. _____ marginación   b. acabarse

3. _____ anquilosado   c. orgullo

4. _____ utopía   d. ignorar

5. _____ hacer caso a   e. extraño

6. _____ empezar   f. integración

7. _____ humildad   g. realidad

Equivalentes *Complete each sentence by substituting words or phrases from the following list for the words or phrases in small type.*

del Caribe	interrumpía	nuevo	prestar atención
dirige	niño	presionar el botón	se realizan

1. Desde que era un _____ dirigía a las grandes orquestas.
   mocoso

2. Es que _____ el tocadiscos.
   paraba

3. Después volvía a _____ del play.
   apretar la tecla

4. Le iban a _____.
   hacer caso

5. Viene a salvar la música clásica con un impulso _____, una energía
   desconocido

   _____.
   caribeña

6. Nosotros venimos a demostrar que las utopías _____.
   se cumplen

7. Él _____ la Joven Orquesta desde hace nueve años.
   lidera

¡No se olvide! El superlativo

In English, the superlative of an adjective is formed with -est: *the richest neighbor*, *the reddest apple*. In addition, it can be expressed with *the most* and *the least* preceding the adjective: *the most interesting show*, *the least interesting show*.

Spanish typically uses **más** *the most* and **menos** *the least* in the construction article + noun + **más/menos** + adjective + **de** to indicate the superlative.

Es **la mujer más amable del** barrio.	*She is the kindest woman in the neighborhood.*

Spanish also uses **mejor** *best* and **peor** *worst* in superlative expressions, using the construction article + **mejor/peor** + noun + **de**.

¡Soy **la peor bailarina de** la clase!	*I am the worst dancer in the class!*

EJERCICIO 21·8

Give the Spanish equivalent for each of the following phrases.

1. the oldest university in the country _____

2. the worst restaurant in the neighborhood _____

3. the smartest professor [F.] (whom) we know _____

4. the least interesting movie (that) I've seen _____

5. the best musicians [M.] in the orchestra _____

6. the most important work (that) you do _____

An additional superlative construction attaches the suffix **-ísimo/a/os/as** to the adjective, for example, **importantísimo** *extremely important*, **hermosísimo** *extremely beautiful*.

Es una responsabilidad **hermosísima**...	*It's an extremely beautiful responsibility . . .*

The suffix **-ísimo/a/os/as** replaces the final vowel or is attached to the final consonant of an adjective. Note that in Spanish a word can have only one acute accent mark.

EJERCICIO 21·9

Give the masculine singular form of the single-word superlative for the following adjectives.

1. bello _____ 4. mucho _____

2. bueno _____ 5. grande _____

3. difícil _____ 6. fácil _____

¡No se olvide! Repaso del imperfecto de subjuntivo

The imperfect subjunctive in Spanish is most commonly indicated by a set of endings characterized by **-ra**. However, Spanish has a second, less common set of endings that is also used to conjugate the imperfect subjunctive. Instead of **-ra**, endings are characterized by **-se** (**-se, -ses, -se, -semos, -seis, -sen**), for example, **que (yo) hablase, que (tú) comieses, que (nosotros) dijésemos**. You may see the **-se** form in reading as well, especially in written material from Spain. In conversation, the forms **fuera** and **fuese** can be used interchangeably. (See also Chapters 9 and 11.)

EJERCICIO
21·10

Identify the verb form in bold as (a) present subjunctive or imperfect subjunctive, and provide (b) the infinitive of the subjunctive verb form.

1. No es que el pequeño Gustavo **indicara** con la batuta la música que salía de los discos.

   a. _____   b. _____

2. que le ponía su padre como si **fuera** un juego

   a. _____   b. _____

3. Podrán comprobarlo quienes le **vean** estos días en su gira.

   a. _____   b. _____

4. Nadie esperaba que la música clásica **fuese** un arma de cambio social.

   a. _____   b. _____

5. No importa que no **se acaben** dedicando a ello.

   a. _____   b. _____

¡Vaya más lejos!

- Busque en YouTube interpretaciones de **Gustavo Dudamel** frente a sus orquestas.
- Busque en YouTube **el Sistema** y **FESNOJIV** para ver y escuchar las orquestas jóvenes de Venezuela.
- ¿Conoce a algunos niños prodigio hispanohablantes? Busque por ejemplo (en el pasado) **Lope de Vega, Rubén Darío, Pablo Picasso** y (hoy día) **Raúl Chávez Sarmiento, Jorge Cori, Deysi Estela Cori Tello** y **Mireya Represa**. ¿De dónde vienen? ¿Cuáles eran o son sus especializaciones?
- Busque artículos (por ejemplo, en *Noticias24, El Universal* o *Globovisión*) sobre los acontecimientos actuales en Venezuela.

Les dejo de herencia mi libertad: Entrevista a Chavela Vargas

Eduardo Vázquez Martín
(Costa Rica/México)

Isabel Vargas Lizano, conocida como Chavela Vargas (1919–2012), fue una cantante costarricense naturalizada mexicana. Se la considera una figura principal y **peculiar** de la **música ranchera**. Habla de su **herencia** en la entrevista siguiente, dirigida por Eduardo Vázquez Martín, que data de 2003.

¿Estamos listos?

1. ¿Qué espectáculos le gustan a usted? ¿A cuáles le gusta asistir?

   A mí me gusta(n)... el teatro, las obras de teatro, la comedia musical, el cine, los conciertos de jazz, los conciertos de música clásica, la ópera, el ballet, el baile, el club...

2. ¿Qué actores, vocalistas, músicos le gustan? ¿Cuáles son sus favoritos?

3. ¿Qué cantantes le gustan? ¿Tiene usted sus CD, sus canciones grabadas (*recorded*)?

4. ¿Qué es la música ranchera?

5. ¿Qué películas ha visto usted recientemente?

6. ¿Qué tipos de películas le gustan particularmente?

   A mí me gusta(n)... las comedias, documentales, películas de terror, películas de miedo, películas de aventuras, películas de acción, películas de época (*historical*), películas de amor, películas de dibujos animados, películas extranjeras, filmes de autor...

7. ¿Los artistas y los músicos representan a veces su vida en su arte? Dé algunos ejemplos.

¡Leamos!

Pregunta. Chavela Vargas no nació en México, sino en Costa Rica y, **sin embargo**, es una artista **imprescindible** de la cultura mexicana del siglo veinte. ¿Tú cómo te ves?

Respuesta. Como una vieja loca que ama su tierra, que ama México, que ama **lo hermoso**, que ama la verdad. ¿Que soy un **ser medio raro**? Sí. Creo que estoy bastante loca, pero hay locos lindos y locos **desgraciados**, y yo soy de los bonitos. Estoy muy **orgullosa**, he llevado un mensaje de México por el mundo, y muchos mexicanos **de verdad**, nacidos ahí, no lo hacen.

P. Cuando hablas de México lo haces con orgullo, pero también con nostalgia y amor a un México que ya no existe. ¿Cuál es el México de entonces y cuál es el de hoy?

R. El México de antes era un México para enamorarse de él, de su gente, de sus noches, de sus cosas. El de hoy es un gigante inmenso que está dormido, está **quieto**. El día que despierte que **se encomienden** todos, yo no sé a quién, pero **van a volar patadas que pa' qué describo**. Y ése es el México que estoy esperando que despierte. [...]

P. Esos **amaneceres** en el **Tenampa**, ¿eran parte de la música, del corazón interpretativo de la música mexicana?

R. Eran parte de México. El México con el que la gente **se quedaba deslumbrada**. El México de Frida Kahlo, el México de Diego Rivera y Guadalupe [Pita] Amor, el de los cantantes. Estaba entonces el movimiento de los pintores jóvenes, a los que les gustaba tocar la guitarra. Un día fui a una fiesta en casa de Diego Rivera. Estaban tocando los jóvenes pintores, y Diego les dijo: "Así me gusta verlos, **de mariachis**, porque **de ahí no pasarán**".

P. ¿En esa misma fiesta estaba Frida Kahlo?

R. Sí, ahí estaba. Esa misma noche la bajaron en su **camilla**; venía vestida **de tehuana**, muy hermosa. **Presidió** la fiesta y todo era en honor de Frida, todo: Diego mismo, todo **giraba** alrededor de ella, porque era una mujer excepcional. Como ser humano y como artista **dejó de ser** ella para **engrandecer a** Diego, a mí **me consta**, lo viví muy de cerca. **Se negó** su propia genialidad. Pero era una mujer excepcional como artista, como esposa, como compañera, como revolucionaria, como todo. Y a veces le inventan romances, como con Trotski. Yo me divertía mucho con Trotski, y, como no les creía nada, le preguntaba a Frida: "¿Ustedes son comunistas o no?", y me decía: "**Pues ya ni sé**, es tanto el **enredo** que ya no sé si somos comunistas o qué somos". Ésa era Frida Kahlo.

P. ¿Qué fue para ti participar en la **película** *Frida*?

R. Salma Hayek estaba en México **de visita** en una casa y preguntó quién le podía cantar en la película *Frida* una canción. La **dueña** de la casa me conoce y le dijo que Chavela Vargas. Salma preguntó si **me podían localizar** y nos reunimos al día siguiente a comer. **Estando yo** en la casa de visita llamó a la directora de la película, Julie Taymor, y le dijo: "Conocí a Chavela, está aquí y pienso que es **la indicada** para cantar en la película". Julie, pues fascinada. Luego me preguntaron qué quería cantar y, como desde hace mucho tiempo **traigo** a "La Llorona" detrás de mí, en todas partes la veo, pues esa canté.

Eduardo Vázquez Martín, excerpts from *Letras Libres,* http://www.letraslibres.com/revista/artes-y-medios. Used with the permission of *Revista Letras Libres.* Many thanks to Ana José Martín.

peculiar	*original, unusual*	de mariachis	*(playing at) being*
música ranchera	*traditional style of*		*mariachis (musicians)*
	popular Mexican	de ahí no pasarán	*they won't go any further*
	music		*(in art)*
herencia	*legacy*	camilla	*stretcher, litter*
sin embargo	*nevertheless*	de tehuana	*dressed as a Tehuana*
imprescindible	*essential*		*(woman of*
lo hermoso	*the beautiful, what is*		*Tehuantepec, Zapotec*
	beautiful		*culture, southern*
(el) ser	*being*		*Mexico)*
medio raro	*a little strange*	presidió [presidir]	*presided over*
desgraciados	*unfortunate*	giraba [girar]	*revolved*
orgullosa	*proud*	dejó [dejar] de ser	*stopped being*
de verdad	*real*	engrandecer a	*strengthen, ennoble*
quieto	*calm*	me consta [constar]	*I'm sure*
se encomienden	*commend themselves,*	se negó [negarse]	*she denied herself*
[encomendarse]	*prepare for the worst*	pues ya ni sé [saber]	*well, I don't even know*
van a volar patadas	*kicks will fly, battles*	enredo	*mess*
[FAM.]	*will rage*	película	*film, movie*
que pa' qué describo	*there's no use my*	de visita	*visiting*
[FAM.]	*describing*	dueña	*hostess*
(los) amaneceres	*dawn, wee hours*	me podían localizar	*they could find me*
(el Salón) Tenampa	*famous nightclub in*	estando yo	*while I was*
	Mexico City	la indicada	*the suitable one, the best*
se quedaba [quedarse]	*were dazzled*		*bet*
deslumbrada		traigo [traer]	*I'm carrying around*

EJERCICIO

22·1

¿De qué se trata? *Match each item with its description.*

1. _____ Chavela Vargas

2. _____ Frida Kahlo

3. _____ Julie Taymor

4. _____ Salma Hayek

5. _____ Diego Rivera

6. _____ "La Llorona"

7. _____ El Tenampa

8. _____ Pita Amor

9. _____ León Trotski

a. pintora mexicana, esposa de Diego Rivera

b. canción tradicional mexicana

c. poeta y escritora mexicana

d. cantante legendaria costarricense-mexicana

e. político y revolucionario ruso, muerto en México

f. actriz y productora mexicana-estadounidense

g. directora estadounidense de teatro (musicales) y de cine

h. pintor y muralista, esposo de Frida Kahlo

i. club nocturno famoso en México, D.F.

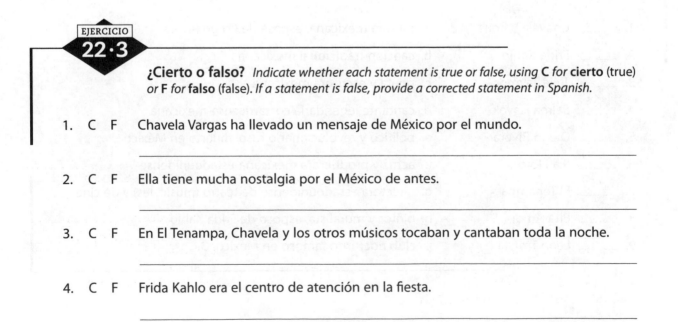

Opciones *Choose the phrase or phrases that correctly complete each sentence. Include all correct responses.*

1. Chavela Vargas nació en

   a. México.   b. el Tenampa.   c. Costa Rica.   d. Madrid.

2. Chavela se considera

   a. loca.   b. medio rara.   c. desgraciada.   d. de los bonitos.

3. Es también una persona

   a. nostálgica.   b. orgullosa.   c. tímida.   d. desafortunada.

4. Ella espera que el México de hoy

   a. duerma.   b. se enamore.   c. despierte.   d. no cambie.

5. Lo espera porque los mexicanos necesitan

   a. reposo.   b. poder.   c. energía.   d. entusiasmo.

6. Chavela amó y vivió muchos años en

   a. México.   b. el Tenampa.   c. las montañas de Veracruz.   d. Estados Unidos.

7. En la ciudad de México conocía a

   a. pintores.   b. mariachis.   c. políticos.   d. poetas.

8. Cantó "La Llorona"

   a. para ella sola.   b. por todas partes.   c. en la película *Frida*.   d. en la entrevista.

¿Cierto o falso? *Indicate whether each statement is true or false, using* **C** *for* **cierto** *(true) or* **F** *for* **falso** *(false). If a statement is false, provide a corrected statement in Spanish.*

1. C F   Chavela Vargas ha llevado un mensaje de México por el mundo.

   _____

2. C F   Ella tiene mucha nostalgia por el México de antes.

   _____

3. C F   En El Tenampa, Chavela y los otros músicos tocaban y cantaban toda la noche.

   _____

4. C F   Frida Kahlo era el centro de atención en la fiesta.

   _____

5. C F Frida Kahlo afirmó que Diego y ella eran comunistas.

_____

6. C F Según Chavela, Frida expresó totalmente su propia genialidad.

_____

7. C F Diego Rivera admiraba el arte de los pintores que tocaban la guitarra.

_____

8. C F Chavela seleccionó una canción tradicional para cantarla en la película *Frida*.

_____

La Llorona fue la esposa y madre legendaria que mató a sus hijos ahogándolos en un río para vengarse de su esposo infiel. Su fantasma camina a lo largo de los ríos en busca de sus hijos.

He aquí la letra de la canción que cantó Chavela en la película *Frida*.

¡Leamos!

La Llorona

Todos **me dicen** el negro, Llorona
Negro pero **cariñoso**.
Todos me dicen el negro, Llorona
Negro pero cariñoso.
Yo soy como el chile verde, Llorona
Picante pero **sabroso**.
Yo soy como el chile verde, Llorona
Picante pero sabroso.

Ay de mí, Llorona Llorona,
Llorona, llévame al río
Tápame con tu **rebozo**, Llorona
Porque me muero de frío

Si porque te quiero quieres, Llorona
Quieres que te quiera más
Si ya te he dado la vida, Llorona
¿Qué más quieres?
¿Quieres más?

VOCABULARIO			
me dicen [decir]	*they call me*	ay de mí	*alas, poor me*
cariñoso	*loving, affectionate*	tápame [tapar]	*wrap me (up)*
picante	*spicy*	rebozo	*woman's traditional shawl*
sabroso	*flavorful, delicious*		

Opciones *Choose the phrase or phrases that correctly complete each sentence. Include all correct responses.*

1. La persona que canta es
   a. la Llorona.
   b. un chile verde.
   c. un hombre que quiere a la Llorona.

2. Él se considera
   a. sabroso.
   b. cariñoso.
   c. picante.

3. Él
   a. está enamorado.
   b. es jefe de cocina.
   c. es ingenioso.

4. En el río, el cantante dice que quiere
   a. nadar.
   b. calentarse.
   c. que ella lo tape con su rebozo.

5. El cantante
   a. no tiene nada más que ofrecerle.
   b. está obsesionado con ella.
   c. se muere de frío.

Provide an English equivalent of the last five lines of the song.

1. _____

2. _____

3. _____

4. _____

5. _____

EJERCICIO
22·6

Reflexiones *Consider the following themes and questions, and discuss them in Spanish.*

1. ¿Dónde nació usted? ¿En qué país, ciudad o pueblo?

_____

_____

_____

2. ¿Se marchó usted de su lugar de nacimiento? ¿A qué edad se marchó? ¿Por qué?

_____

_____

_____

3. ¿Extraña su lugar de nacimiento? ¿Va de visita a veces? ¿Por qué motivos?

_____

_____

_____

4. ¿Por qué lugares tiene usted nostalgia? ¿Por qué? ¿Extraña usted a la gente, a los amigos y la familia, el clima, el paisaje, la belleza, la energía, los monumentos y museos, las actividades...?

_____

_____

_____

_____

EJERCICIO
22·7

Mi vocabulario *Select the word that does not belong in each group.*

1. a. lindo   b. bonito   c. feo   d. hermoso

2. a. indispensable   b. vital   c. imprescindible   d. inútil

3. a. desorden   b. confusión   c. claridad   d. enredo

4. a. puntapiés   b. abrazos   c. patadas   d. golpes

5. a. aburrido   b. estupefacto   c. deslumbrado   d. asombrado

6. a. madrugada   b. anochecer   c. alba   d. amanecer

Contrarios *Match each word with its opposite.*

1. _____ reducir   a. negarse

2. _____ indicado   b. llevarse

3. _____ traer   c. invitado

4. _____ confirmar   d. desgraciado

5. _____ dueña   e. engrandecer

6. _____ sabroso   f. insípido

7. _____ afortunado   g. inapropiado

Equivalentes *Complete each sentence by substituting words or phrases from the following list for the words or phrases in small type.*

ame	cúbreme	llaman	rico
encontrar	ofrecido	encontramos	

1. Todos me _____ el negro, Llorona.
   <small>dicen</small>

2. picante pero _____
   <small>sabroso</small>

3. _____ con tu rebozo, Llorona.
   <small>Tápame</small>

4. Quieres que te _____ más.
   <small>quiera</small>

5. Ya te he _____ la vida, Llorona.
   <small>dado</small>

6. Salma preguntó si me podían _____ y nos _____ al día
   <small>localizar</small>   <small>reunimos</small>

   siguiente a comer.

¡No se olvide! Tú vs. usted

The interview with Chavela Vargas is conducted in the **tú** form instead of in the **usted** form that we might have expected, given that Chavela is older than the interviewer and they might not be close friends. Indeed, they may be friends, but it's more likely that the interviewer is following custom in Spain, where **tú** is fast replacing **usted** in conversations between any two individuals. In most Latin American countries, speakers would retain **usted** in formal settings such as an interview. As a nonnative speaker—especially since you may visit different Spanish-speaking regions—it's best to use **usted** at first. Switch to **tú** if and when you're invited to do so.

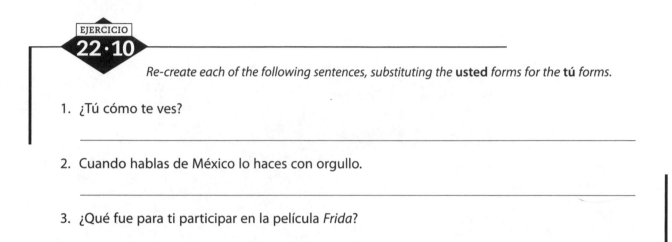

EJERCICIO 22·10

*Re-create each of the following sentences, substituting the **usted** forms for the **tú** forms.*

1. ¿Tú cómo te ves?

   _____

2. Cuando hablas de México lo haces con orgullo.

   _____

3. ¿Qué fue para ti participar en la película *Frida*?

   _____

¡No se olvide! Se para expresar la voz pasiva

The pronoun **se** is used in a common Spanish construction that expresses the passive voice. (See also Chapters 13, 15, 16, and 25.)

Se venden manzanas en este mercado.	*Apples are sold in this market.*
Se la **considera** una figura principal y peculiar de la música ranchera.	*She is considered an important and original exponent of música ranchera.*

A verb in the passive voice has no identifiable subject. The focus is on the object. In the first example given, **manzanas** is the direct object, and in the second, the direct object is **la** (meaning Chavela Vargas), expressed as *she* in English. Note that Spanish uses an active verb in the third-person singular or plural with **se**, while English uses the verb *to be* + a past participle.

¡Vaya más lejos!

- Busque (en YouTube) **Chavela Vargas** para escuchar su música (por ejemplo, "La Llorona") y ver entrevistas filmadas.
- Vea (en DVD o streaming) *Frida* (2002), dirigida por Julie Taymor y protagonizada por Salma Hayek.

Diego Rivera: Arte y revolución
Lelia Driben (México)

Marzo 2000. La obra de un pintor clásico como Diego Rivera trasciende los **caprichos** de la persona y su **maniquea** visión de la historia, el arte y la política. La exposición que presenta el Museo de Arte Moderno de México es una buena oportunidad de **constatarlo**, con **óleos** y **etapas** artísticas **desconocidas** fuera de los **ámbitos** académicos o eruditos. A medida que lea este artículo, siéntase libre de buscar en internet imágenes de las obras mencionadas.

¿Estamos listos?

1. ¿Hay museos y otras instituciones culturales en o cerca de su ciudad?

   Sí, hay... museos, galerías, obras de arte (al aire libre), esculturas, teatros, cines, auditorios, salas de concierto, locales de jazz, conciertos al aire libre...

2. ¿Aprovecha usted a menudo (a veces) esas oportunidades? ¿Cuáles prefiere?

3. ¿Conoce usted al pintor Diego Rivera (1886–1957)? ¿Dónde conoció sus obras? ¿En qué contexto? ¿Qué sabe de su arte?

   Rivera hizo... pinturas, retratos (*portraits*), autorretratos, cuadros, murales, frescos, dibujos (*drawings*) y bocetos (*sketches*)...

4. ¿Conoce a otros artistas mexicanos del siglo XX?

   Conozco la obra de... José Clemente Orozco, Frida Kahlo, Rufino Tamayo, David Alfaro Siqueiros, Manuel Álvarez Bravo, Leonora Carrington, Remedios Varo...

5. ¿Hay arte público en su ciudad? ¿De qué tipo?

   Hay... esculturas y estatuas, instalaciones, murales, grafitis artísticos, azulejos (*tile work*), videos, fotografías, jardines, edificios, arquitectura histórica, arquitectura moderna, puentes (*bridges*)...

6. ¿Dónde se encuentran las obras de arte públicas?

   Se encuentran en los/las... calles y carreteras (*roads*), paredes (*walls*) de los barrios, edificios públicos, bibliotecas, correos (*post offices*), escuelas y universidades, plazas, parques y jardines, comercios y empresas...

¡Leamos!

La exposición de Diego Rivera, que se presenta hasta el 19 de marzo en el Museo de Arte Moderno de México, **posee** especial relevancia porque permite **actualizar** la lectura **en torno a** su obra, sin **canonizaciones** ni **descalificaciones** estériles. Siguiendo un **recorrido** cronológico, entre los primeros cuadros **se destaca** el magnífico **autorretrato** elaborado en 1906 [*Autorretrato*], un año antes de su partida a Europa. La imagen reproduce, obviamente, a un Diego joven, capaz de **aprehender** con maestría las **leyes** del autorretrato, modulado por una **armónica** gradación tonal que combina azules y grises.

El pintor nacido en **Guanajuato** tenía entonces veinte años y ya en 1907 demostraba su talento en obras como "Retrato de Joaquín Ventura"—de vigorosa expresión **fisonómica**—y "La **casona** de **Vizcaya**" [1907]. Rivera se prueba en una pintura que circula entre el realismo de **corte** español y ciertos **rasgos** impresionistas. La lección del impresionismo está en el **juego** de **pinceladas** visibles, con cierto **espesor matérico**. Y hay en el **MAM** cuadros memorables de esta etapa **temprana**: "Nuestra Señora de París" [*Notre Dame de Paris*], "**Marché aux légumes**" y el espléndido **paisaje** de **Brujas denominado** "La casa sobre el **puente**", los tres de 1909.

Versátil y **sabio** en la **fragua** de sus pinturas, Diego **abarca** varias direcciones: vuelve a un realismo sutil en "El **molino** de Damme" (1909), y **acude** al **puntillismo** en "Tierras **quemadas** de **Cataluña**" (1911). Además, **maneja** con maestría la alternancia de colores en combinaciones cromáticas que, aun siendo intensas, están **atravesadas** por cierto **clima recogido**, de baja, silenciosa voz. Similar **sagacidad** exhiben sus gradaciones tonales, la **bruma** que **perfila** a Notre Dame sobre la **lejanía** del **plano de fondo** por ejemplo.

Estas mismas cualidades emergerán durante la segunda década del siglo, cuando el artista explora las investigaciones **cézannianas** hasta introducirse en el cubismo **sintético**. El "Retrato de Adolfo Best Maugard" (1913) recoge la lección de Paul Cézanne, mientras que "El arquitecto" (1915), "**Naturaleza muerta**" (1917), "**Ferrocarril** en Montparnasse" (1917) y "Plaza de toros en Madrid" (1915) son algunos de los cuadros cubistas más **logrados** dentro de esta exposición. Otra **tela** cubista sabiamente **conjugada** es el retrato del pintor Zinoviev (1913) [*Retrato del pintor Zinoviev*], realizado en el reverso de una imagen realista con **suaves** rasgos geometrizantes ejecutada en 1917 y titulada "Retrato de un militar".

Diego Rivera **realizó** dos grandes **aportes** al arte mexicano. Uno de ellos, importante, fue la introducción de la modernidad en el país a través del cubismo. El otro, fundacional, fue la iniciación del muralismo. Y con el muralismo la **concreción** de un movimiento de **vanguardia** singularísimo, diferente y controversial respecto a la vanguardia europea. ¿Es pertinente atribuir al muralismo rasgos vanguardistas? Creo que sí, porque como ocurre con todas las vanguardias significó una profunda transformación formal y temática: en sus relatos visuales **jerarquizó** el lugar del **campesino**, del **indígena** y la historia de México. [...] El **surgimiento** del muralismo coincidió con el fin de la Revolución Mexicana y el comienzo de una reestructuración social en México. Reorganización, no **cambio** total de un sistema por otro. ¿Habría alguna relación entre estas renovaciones político-sociales y el **reencauce** en la representación narrativa que Diego Rivera **imprime** a sus pinturas sobre los muros? [...]

[El] mural "Represión" hecho para la exposición del Museo de Arte Moderno de Nueva York (1931) [...] **resulta** el **testimonio** de una **denuncia**. **Asimismo**, el otro mural pintado para la misma **muestra**, "Electric Welding", abre la denuncia a más de un **sentido**: las figuras de los obreros están **de espaldas resaltando** el lugar del cuerpo que concentra la **carga** de trabajo; están también anonimizados porque no se muestran sus **rostros**, y aprisionados entre los muros y **aceros** de la fábrica. Diego acepta la **consagración** del centro—Nueva York y uno de sus museos *top*—pero no renuncia a establecer sus posiciones. Es una época **exal-**

tativa del progreso industrial y Rivera **no se aparta** de ello—recuerde el lector la gran **hélice** que cruza la parte central del fresco pintado para el Palacio de Bellas Artes [*El Hombre en la encrucijada*, 1934]—pero, además, muestra al sector social **oprimido**.

Por otro lado, Rivera se mantiene leal a la composición clásica aprendida, sobre todo, en Europa: el predominio de horizontales y verticales que ordenan al **nutrido despliegue** de objetos y protagonistas. Y esas son sus obras más sólidas. [...]

Lelia Driben, excerpts from *Letras Libres*, http://www.letraslibres.com/revista/artes-y-medios. Used with the permission of *Revista Letras Libres*. Many thanks to Ana José Martín.

VOCABULARIO

caprichos	*whims, caprices*
maniquea	*Manichean, extremist, "black and white"*
constatarlo	*confirm/validate this*
óleos	*oil paintings*
etapas	*stages, phases*
desconocidas	*unfamiliar*
ámbitos	*spheres, fields*
posee [poseer]	*has, possesses*
actualizar	*update*
en torno a	*about, with respect to*
(las) canonizaciones	*canonizations, excessive praise*
(las) descalificaciones	*insults, criticisms*
recorrido	*itinerary, path*
se destaca [destacarse]	*stands out*
autorretrato	*self-portrait*
aprehender	*understanding, grasping*
(las) leyes	*rules, laws*
armónica	*harmonious*
Guanajuato	*historic city in central Mexico*
fisonómica	*facial*
casona	*big house*
Vizcaya	*a Basque province of Spain*
(la) corte	*(royal) court*
rasgos	*traits, characteristics*
juego	*play*
pinceladas	*brushstrokes*
(el) espesor	*thickness*
matérico	*"Matierist" (painting defined by texture)*
(el) MAM (Museo de Arte Moderno de México)	*Museum of Modern Art of Mexico*
temprana	*early*

marché aux légumes	*(French) produce market*
(el) paisaje	*landscape*
Brujas	*Bruges (Belgian city)*
denominado	*called, named*
(el) puente	*bridge*
sabio	*wise, intelligent*
fragua	*forging, creation*
abarca [abarcar]	*embraces, takes on,*
molino	*mill, windmill*
acude [acudir]	*turns to*
puntillismo	*pointillism (painting defined by tiny dots)*
quemadas	*burned*
Cataluña	*Catalonia (autonomous province of northeastern Spain)*
maneja [manejar]	*handles, manipulates*
atravesadas	*permeated*
(el) clima	*atmosphere*
recogido	*cozy*
(la) sagacidad	*shrewdness*
bruma	*fog, mist*
perfila [perfilar]	*outlines*
lejanía	*distance*
plano de fondo	*background*
cézannianas	*in the style of Paul Cézanne, French post-impressionist*
sintético	*merged, unified*
naturaleza muerta	*still life*
(el) ferrocarril	*train, railway*
logrados	*successful*
tela	*(painting) canvas*
conjugada	*mixed, blended*
suaves	*soft, light*
realizó [realizar]	*made*
(los) aportes	*contributions*

(la) concreción	*solidifying*	sentido	*sense, direction*
vanguardia	*avant-garde*	de espaldas	*from the back*
jerarquizó [jerarquizar]	*situated*	resaltando [resaltar]	*emphasizing*
campesino	*peasant*	carga	*burden*
(el) indígena	*native, indigenous person*	rostros	*faces*
		aceros	*steel framing*
surgimiento	*emergence*	(la) consagración	*recognition, accolade*
cambio	*change*	exaltativa	*thrilling, exhilarating*
(el) reencauce	*reorientation*	no se aparta [apartarse]	*does not distance himself*
imprime [imprimir]	*imprints, stamps*		
resulta [resultar]	*turns out to be*	(la) hélice	*propeller*
testimonio	*declaration*	oprimido	*oppressed*
denuncia	*indictment*	nutrido	*ample, considerable*
asimismo	*in addition*	(el) despliegue	*display*
(la) muestra	*show, exhibit*		

EJERCICIO 23·1

¿De qué se trata? *Match each item with its description.*

1. _____ Represión

2. _____ Pablo Picasso

3. _____ Guanajuato

4. _____ Ferrocarril en Montparnasse

5. _____ la Revolución Mexicana

6. _____ Diego Rivera

7. _____ Adolfo Best Maugard

8. _____ Paul Cézanne

a. periodo de guerra entre 1910 y 1920

b. sujeto de un retrato de 1913

c. famoso pintor mexicano del siglo XX

d. famoso artista español del siglo XX

e. gran mural hecho para la exposición de Nueva York

f. ciudad donde nació Diego Rivera

g. obra cubista de Diego Rivera

h. pintor francés postimpresionista

Opciones *Choose the phrase or phrases that correctly complete each sentence. Include all correct responses.*

1. Esta exhibición tiene lugar en
   a. Paris.
   b. Los Ángeles.
   c. México, D.F.

2. Los autorretratos son típicos de los artistas
   a. jóvenes.
   b. mexicanos.
   c. egoístas.

3. El movimiento moderno del cubismo fue introducido en Europa por
   a. Frida Kahlo.
   b. Pablo Picasso.
   c. Diego Rivera.

4. La crítica admira
   a. esta versión del cubismo.
   b. la alternancia de colores.
   c. las gradaciones tonales.

5. La sección de la exposición "Arte para las masas" trata lógicamente de
   a. las obras puramente estéticas.
   b. la cocina.
   c. los murales públicos.

6. Los murales mexicanos de esta época elogian
   a. al campesino.
   b. al indígena.
   c. la historia de México.

7. En fin, las obras de Rivera se consideran
   a. sociopolíticas.
   b. clásicas.
   c. vanguardistas.

¿Cierto o falso? *Indicate whether each statement is true or false, using **C** for **cierto** (true) or **F** for **falso** (false). If a statement is false, provide a corrected statement in Spanish.*

1. C F Le gusta a esta crítica la objetividad de la exposición sobre Diego Rivera.

_____

2. C F La exposición incluye únicamente ejemplos del muralismo de Rivera.

_____

3. C F "Electric Welding" fue pintado para el Palacio de Bellas Artes de México, D.F.

_____

4. C F El movimiento muralista mexicana se dirigía a la élite.

_____

5. C F La Revolución Mexicana inició un cambio total de un sistema por otro.

_____

6. C F La ideología de Rivera lo condujo a revelar la opresión de los obreros.

_____

7. C F Rivera no entendía la exaltación del progreso industrial.

_____

EJERCICIO
23·4

Reflexiones *Consider the following themes and questions, and discuss them in Spanish.*

1. Busque en línea una obra del joven Diego Rivera, *Autorretrato* (1906). En esta pintura él se muestra en su estudio. ¿En qué lugar se colocaría usted para hacerse un autorretrato?

_____

_____

_____

_____

2. Compare un cuadro cubista de Pablo Picasso (por ejemplo, su *Mujer con mandolina* (1913) o su *Guitarra y violín* (1913)) con *Paisaje zapatista* (1915) o *Retrato de Martín Luis Guzmán* (1915) de Diego Rivera. ¿Qué diferencias ve usted?

_____

_____

_____

_____

3. Busque *Maternidad* (1954) por Rivera: ¿Qué juguetes de niños ve usted? Mire el primer plano de la pintura donde hay una representación del mundo y una paloma. En su opinión, ¿qué estará diciendo el artista sobre el presente y el futuro?

_____

_____

_____

_____

4. En la opinión de la crítica, ¿por qué y cómo pertenece el muralismo a la vanguardia artística del siglo XX?

_____

_____

_____

_____

5. Según usted, ¿el arte puede jugar un papel político? Dé algunos ejemplos.

_____

_____

_____

_____

Mi vocabulario *Select the word or phrase that does not belong in each group.*

1. a. abarcar   b. excluir   c. incluir   d. comprender

2. a. características   b. rasgos   c. atributos   d. atrasos

3. a. denominar   b. llamar   c. enumerar   d. nombrar

4. a. naturaleza muerta b. paisaje   c. molino   d. retrato

5. a. nieve   b. niebla   c. bruma   d. vapor

6. a. avanzada   b. vanguardia   c. modernidad   d. avaricia

7. a. óleos   b. aguacates   c. frescos   d. acuarelas

8. a. fracasado   b. logrado   c. conseguido   d. exitoso

EJERCICIO 23·6

Contrarios *Match each word or phrase with its opposite.*

1. _____ descalificación
2. _____ sabio
3. _____ indígena
4. _____ desconocido
5. _____ delgadez
6. _____ plano de fondo
7. _____ tarde
8. _____ discordante
9. _____ proximidad

a. famoso
b. limitado
c. armónico
d. espesor
e. canonización
f. lejanía
g. temprano
h. frente
i. extranjero

EJERCICIO 23·7

Equivalentes *Complete each sentence by substituting words or phrases from the following list for the words or phrases in small type.*

abraza	astuto	inolvidables	alterna
se demuestra	pinturas	artista	elaboración
las predilecciones	aspectos	fase	supera

1. La obra de un _____ clásico como Diego Rivera _____
   pintor   *trasciende*

   _____ de la persona.
   los caprichos

2. Rivera _____ en una pintura que _____ entre el
   se prueba   *circula*

   realismo de corte español y ciertos _____ impresionistas.
   rasgos

3. Y hay en el MAM _____ _____ de esta
   cuadros   *memorables*

   _____ temprana.
   etapa

4. Versátil y _____ en la _____ de sus pinturas, Diego
   sabio   *fragua*

   _____ varias direcciones.
   abarca

¡No se olvide! La a personal

A direct object noun referring to a thing or object usually follows a transitive verb directly, with no preposition: **¿Viste la película?** *Did you see the movie?*

However, a direct object noun referring to a person or people is generally preceded by the personal **a** (or **al** for masculine singular nouns).

¿Viste *a* Silvia?	*Did you see Silvia?*
Llamo *al* estudiante.	*I'm calling the student.*
Llamo *a* los estudiantes.	*I'm calling the students.*

The personal **a** is also placed before indefinite pronouns that refer to people: **No veo *a* nadie.** *I don't see anyone.* It can precede the names of pets, other animals, or inanimate objects toward which the speaker or writer feels a special connection. (See also Chapter 20.)

¡Ojo!

In addition to its use before direct objects referring to people or animals, **a** before a direct object noun tells the reader that this noun is the direct object of the verb. Since in Spanish the subject may either precede or follow the verb, the presence of **a** prevents ambiguity.

EJERCICIO
23·8

*List the direct object nouns preceded by the personal **a** that appear in the following sentences. Include their modifiers. Note that nouns may be modified by adjectives that precede or follow the noun.*

1. Los pintores eran tan pobres que no podían contratar a sus modelos.

   _____

2. Diego Rivera conoció a muchos artistas famosos de su día.

   _____

3. *Maternidad* es una de las muchas pinturas donde Rivera incluye a madres e hijos.

   _____

4. La imagen reproduce, obviamente, a un Diego joven.

   _____

5. Similar sagacidad exhiben sus gradaciones tonales, la bruma que perfila a Notre Dame sobre la lejanía del plano de fondo.

   _____

6. Es una época exaltativa del progreso industrial y Rivera no se aparta de ello [...] pero, además, muestra al sector social oprimido.

   _____

7. El predominio de horizontales y verticales que ordenan al nutrido despliegue de objetos y protagonistas.

   _____

Use the given elements to create complete and correct sentences in Spanish, using the present tense.

1. yo / buscar / mi / hija

   _____

2. ellos / ver / mucho / amigos / el fin de semana

   _____

3. Frida / querer / Diego

   _____

4. ¿ / tu / conocer / bien / tu / vecinos / ?

   _____

5. nosotros / amar / la humanidad

   _____

¡Vaya más lejos!

- Busque **The Diego Rivera Foundation** para ver las obras de Diego Rivera.

- Busque **cubismo** para ver las obras del período cubista que incluyen artistas como Pablo Picasso, Georges Braque y Juan Gris.

- Busque información sobre el **muralismo mexicano** para ver ejemplos de las obras de Diego Rivera, José Clemente Orozco y David Alfaro Siqueiros.

- Busque información sobre la **Revolución Mexicana** (1910–1920).

El primer cine
Luis Buñuel (España)

Luis Buñuel nació en 1900 en Calanda (Teruel, Aragón, España), y pasó su infancia y adolescencia en Zaragoza. En la Residencia de Estudiantes de Madrid conoció a Federico García Lorca y a Salvador Dalí, entre otros. En 1925 se trasladó a París para colaborar como crítico. Pero desde la realización de *Un perro andaluz* (1929), se consagró únicamente al cine, pasando a ser el más célebre cineasta español del siglo. Salió de Europa durante la Guerra Civil española, y pasó siete años en Hollywood antes de establecerse definitivamente en México. Buñuel murió en la Ciudad de México en 1983.

¿Estamos listos?

1. ¿Cómo prefiere ver películas?

   Para ver películas, prefiero... ir al cine, ir a festivales de cine, ir al cineclub; utilizar mi reproductor de DVD, alquilar o comprar DVD; ver mis viejos videocasetes; el streaming; la televisión (por cable); Internet (por computadora, tableta o teléfono inteligente); una pantalla (*screen*) grande/pequeña, un buen sistema de sonido...

2. ¿Qué actores y actrices le gustan? ¿Sigue las obras de ciertos directores de cine?

3. ¿Qué películas o tipos de películas le gustan a usted?

   Me gusta(n) particularmente el/los/las... comedias, dramas [M.], documentales [M.], películas biográficas (*biopics*), filmes clásicos, relatos policiales, películas de terror (de miedo, de aventuras, de acción, de vaqueros (*cowboy*), de época (*historical*), de amor, de ciencia ficción), dibujos animados, filmes extranjeros, cine de autor, cine alternativo...

4. Para usted, ¿qué representa el cine?

   Para mí, es principalmente una forma de... evasión personal, cambio de ambiente (de situación, de punto de vista), arte, estética, belleza, cultura, fantasía, aventura, expresión emotiva y sentimental, descanso, esparcimiento, instrucción, estímulo...

5. Para usted, ¿por qué le gusta ir al cine?

   Además, el cine me da la ocasión de... descansar, escaparme, aprender, lanzarme a la literatura o la ficción, vivir mis fantasías o mis sueños, viajar por otras partes, olvidarme de mis dificultades y problemas, pasar tiempo con mis amigos, identificarme con la trama y los personajes, salir de las cuatro paredes...

¡Leamos!

En 1908, siendo todavía un niño, descubrí el cine.

El **local** se llamaba "Farrucini". **Fuera**, sobre una hermosa **fachada** de dos puertas, una de entrada y otra de salida, cinco **autómatas** de un **organillo**, **provistos de** instrumentos musicales, **atraían bulliciosamente** a los curiosos. En el interior de la **barraca**, cubierta por una simple **lona**, el público se sentaba en bancos. Conmigo iba siempre mi **nurse, desde luego**. Me acompañaba a todas partes, **incluso** a casa de mi amigo Pelayo, que vivía al otro lado del **paseo**.

Las primeras imágenes animadas que vi, y que me **llenaron** de admiración, fueron las de un **cerdo**. Era una película de **dibujos**. El cerdo, **envuelto** en una **bufanda** tricolor, cantaba. Un fonógrafo **colocado** detrás de la **pantalla** dejaba oír la canción. La película era en colores, lo **recuerdo** perfectamente, lo que significa que la habían pintado imagen a imagen.

En aquella época, el cine no era más que una atracción de **feria**, un simple descubrimiento de la técnica. En Zaragoza, **aparte** el tren y los **tranvías** que ya habían entrado en los hábitos de la población, la **llamada técnica** moderna **apenas** había empezado a aplicarse. Me parece que en 1908 no había en toda la ciudad más que un solo automóvil y funcionaba por electricidad. El cine significaba la **irrupción** de un elemento totalmente nuevo en nuestro universo en la **Edad Media**. [...]

En la calle de Los Estébanes había otro cine que no recuerdo cómo se llamaba. En aquella calle vivía una **prima** mía, y desde la ventana de la cocina veíamos la película. Luego, **tapiaron** la ventana y pusieron una **claraboya** en la cocina; pero nosotros hicimos un **agujero** en el **tabique** por el que mirábamos por turnos aquellas imágenes **mudas** que se movían allí abajo. [...] En los cines de Zaragoza, además del pianista tradicional, había un explicador que, **de pie** al lado de la pantalla, comentaba la acción. Por ejemplo:

—Entonces el conde Hugo ve a su esposa en brazos de otro hombre. Y ahora, señoras y señores, verán ustedes al conde **sacar del cajón** de su **escritorio** un revólver para asesinar a la **infiel**.

El cine constituía una forma narrativa tan nueva e **insólita** que la inmensa mayoría del público **no acertaba** a comprender lo que veía en la pantalla ni a establecer una relación entre los **hechos**. Nosotros nos hemos acostumbrado **insensiblemente** al lenguaje cinematográfico, al **montaje**, a la acción simultánea o sucesiva e incluso al **salto atrás**. Al público de aquella época, **le costaba descifrar** el nuevo lenguaje.

De ahí la presencia del explicador.

Nunca olvidaré cómo me impresionó, a mí y a toda la sala por cierto, el primer **travelling** que vi. En la pantalla, una **cara** avanzaba hacia nosotros, **cada vez** más grande, como si fuera a **tragársenos**. Era imposible imaginar ni un instante que la cámara **se acercase** a aquella cara—o que **ésta aumentase de tamaño** por efecto de **trucaje**, como en las películas de **Méliès**. Lo que nosotros veíamos era una cara que se nos venía **encima** y que **crecía desmesuradamente**. **Al igual que santo Tomás**, nosotros creíamos lo que veíamos. [...]

Durante los veinte o treinta primeros años de su existencia, el cine estuvo considerado como una diversión de feria, algo **bastante** vulgar, **propio de la plebe**, sin **porvenir** artístico. Ningún crítico se interesaba por él. En 1928 o 1929, cuando comuniqué a mi madre mi intención de **realizar** mi primera película, ella **se llevó un gran disgusto** y casi **lloró**, como si yo le hubiera dicho: "Mamá, quiero ser **payaso**." Fue necesario que interviniera un **notario**, amigo de la familia, quien le explicó muy **serio** que con el cine se podía ganar bastante dinero y hasta producir obras interesantes, como las grandes películas **rodadas** en Italia, sobre temas de la **Antigüedad**. Mi madre se dejó convencer, pero no fue a ver la película que ella había financiado.

Luis Buñuel, excerpts from *Mi último suspiro*. Trad. Ana María de la Fuente (Barcelona: Random House Mondadori, 1982; Debolsillo, 2012). Used with the permission of Penguin Random House Grupo Editorial. Many thanks to Sergio Gómez.

VOCABULARIO

(el) local	place, establishment	no acertaba [acertar]	couldn't (manage to)
fuera	outside	hechos	facts, incidents
fachada	façade	insensiblemente	imperceptibly, gradually
(los) autómatas	automatons (figures)	(el) montaje	montage, film editing
organillo	barrel organ, hurdy-gurdy	salto atrás	flashback
provistos de	equipped with	le costaba [costar]	it was hard for them
atraían [atraer]	attracted, drew	descifrar	to decode
bulliciosamente	noisily	de ahí	thus, hence
barraca	shack	(el) travelling	dolly or tracking shot (cinema)
lona	canvas, tarpaulin	cara	face
(la) nurse	nanny	cada vez	progressively
desde luego	naturally, of course	tragársenos [tragar]	swallow us up
incluso	even	se acercase [acercarse]	was approaching
paseo	promenade, street	ésta aumentase [aumentar] de tamaño	it (the face) was getting bigger
llenaron [llenar]	filled		
cerdo	pig	(el) trucaje	trick photography, special effect
dibujos	cartoons		
envuelto	wrapped	Méliès	Georges Méliès (1861–1938), French film pioneer
bufanda	scarf, muffler		
colocado	placed		
pantalla	(movie) screen	encima	on top of
recuerdo [recordar]	I remember	crecía [crecer]	was growing
feria	carnival, funfair	desmesuradamente	excessively
aparte	aside from	al igual que	(just) like
(los) tranvías	trolleys, streetcars	Santo Tomás	Thomas, the apostle who believed only what he could see
llamada	so-called		
técnica	technology		
apenas	hardly	bastante	rather
(la) irrupción	invasion, bursting in	propio de la plebe	good for the masses
(la) Edad Media	Middle Ages	(el) porvenir	future
prima	cousin	realizar	of producing/creating
tapiaron [tapiar]	they bricked up	se llevó [llevarse] un gran disgusto	became horribly upset
claraboya	skylight		
agujero	hole	lloró [llorar]	wept
(el) tabique	(brick) wall	payaso	clown
mudas	silent, mute	notario	notary (in Spain, practices civil law)
de pie	standing, on foot		
sacar del cajón	take out of the drawer	serio	seriously
escritorio	desk	rodadas	shot (as a movie)
(la) infiel	unfaithful (woman)	(la) Antigüedad	(Greek and Roman) antiquity
insólita	unusual, unheard of		

Adscrito al surrealismo, a principios de 1929, Luis Buñuel llamó a Salvador Dalí para colaborar en el **guión** que pasaría a ser *Un perro andaluz*. El film tuvo un gran **éxito** entre la **intelectualidad** europea y **dio pie a** que un rico **conocido le pagara** a Buñuel *La edad de oro* (1930), considerada otra obra maestra del cine de vanguardia y que provocaría también un gran escándalo.

¡Leamos!

Esta **locura** por los sueños, por el **placer** de **soñar**, que nunca he tratado de explicar, es una de las inclinaciones profundas que **me han acercado** al surrealismo. *Un chien andalou* (*Un perro andaluz*) [...] nació de la convergencia de uno de mis sueños con un sueño de Dalí. [...] Dalí me invitó a pasar unos días en su casa y, al llegar a **Figueras**, yo le **conté** un sueño que había tenido poco antes, en el que una **nube desflecada** cortaba la luna y una **cuchilla de afeitar hendía** un ojo. Él, **a su vez**, me dijo que la noche anterior había visto en sueños una mano **llena de hormigas**. Y añadió: "¿Y si, partiendo de esto, hiciéramos una película?"

En un principio, **me quedé** indeciso; pero pronto **pusimos mano a la obra**, en Figueras. Escribimos el guión en menos de una semana, siguiendo una regla muy simple, adoptada de común acuerdo: no aceptar idea ni imagen alguna que pudiera dar lugar a una explicación racional, psicológica o cultural. Abrir todas las puertas a lo irracional. No admitir más que las imágenes que nos impresionaran, sin tratar de **averiguar** por qué.

En ningún momento **se suscitó** entre nosotros ni la **menor discusión**. Fue una semana de **identificación** completa. Uno decía, por ejemplo: "El hombre saca un **contrabajo**." "No", respondía el otro. Y el que **había propuesto** la idea aceptaba **de inmediato** la negativa. Le parecía **justa**. Por el contrario, cuando la imagen que uno **proponía** era aceptada por el otro, inmediatamente nos parecía luminosa, **indiscutible** y al momento entraba en el guión.

Cuando éste estuvo terminado, **en seguida advertí** que la película sería totalmente insólita y provocativa y que ningún sistema normal de producción la aceptaría. Por eso pedí a mi madre una cantidad de dinero, para producirla yo mismo. [...]

Luis Buñuel, excerpts from *Mi último suspiro*. Trad. Ana María de la Fuente (Barcelona: Random House Mondadori, 1982; Debolsillo, 2012). Used with the permission of Penguin Random House Grupo Editorial. Many thanks to Sergio Gómez.

VOCABULARIO			
adscrito (a)	*affiliated (with)*	conté [contar]	*recounted*
(el) guión	*scenario, screenplay*	(la) nube	*cloud*
éxito	*success*	desflecada	*ragged, cut-up*
(la) intelectualidad	*intelligentsia*	cuchilla de afeitar	*(shaving) razor*
dio [dar] pie a	*inspired, resulted in*	hendía [hendir]	*slit open*
conocido	*acquaintance*	a su vez	*in turn*
le pagara [pagar]	*financed for him*	llena de hormigas	*covered with ants*
locura	*passion, madness*	en un principio	*initially, at the outset*
(el) placer	*pleasure*	me quedé [quedarse]	*I was*
soñar	*dreaming*	pusimos [poner]	*we got to work*
me han acercado	*drew me to*	mano a la obra	
[acercar]		averiguar	*(to) figure out*
Figueras	*town in Catalonia, in*	se suscitó [suscitar]	*arose, stirred up*
	northeastern Spain	(la) menor discusión	*least disagreement*

(la) identificación	empathy, compatibility	justa	(exactly) right
contrabajo	double bass (musical	proponía [proponer]	proposed
	instrument)	indiscutible	indisputable
había propuesto [proponer]	had proposed	en seguida	immediately
de inmediato	immediately	advertí [advertir]	saw, noticed

EJERCICIO 24·1

¿De qué se trata? *Match each item with its description.*

1. _____ Federico García Lorca
2. _____ el surrealismo
3. _____ Salvador Dalí
4. _____ el travelling
5. _____ *La edad de oro*
6. _____ Figueras
7. _____ Georges Méliès
8. _____ Zaragoza

a. ciudad catalana

b. ciudad aragonesa

c. efecto cinematográfico

d. poeta español del siglo XX

e. movimiento artístico de vanguardia del siglo XX

f. pionero francés del cine

g. pintor surrealista español muy conocido

h. segunda película surrealista de Buñuel

EJERCICIO 24·2

Opciones *Choose the phrase or phrases that correctly complete each sentence. Include all correct responses.*

1. Buñuel vio películas por primera vez en

   a. 1929. b. 1908. c. 2008.

2. Durante la proyección de las primeras películas, lo que ponía música de fondo era

   a. el pianista. b. el organillo. c. el fonógrafo.

3. Para seguir los eventos de la película, el público necesitaba la presencia del

   a. camarógrafo. b. notario. c. explicador.

4. El trucaje que hace avanzar la cámara hacia el sujeto se llama

   a. el salto atrás. b. el travelling. c. la acción sucesiva.

5. Buñuel y Dalí se conocieron por primera vez

   a. en Madrid. b. en Figueras. c. en la Residencia de Estudiantes.

6. El guión de *Un perro andaluz* nació de la convergencia de

   a. dos hormigas.   b. dos sueños.   c. ideas distintas.

7. Su locura por el placer de soñar ha acercado a Buñuel

   a. al surrealismo.   b. a las finanzas.   c. al cine.

8. La madre de Buñuel se dejó convencer de que

   a. ella debía ver la película.   b. el cine era respetable.   c. ella obtendría beneficios.

EJERCICIO 24·3

¿Cierto o falso? *Indicate whether each statement is true or false, using* **C** *for* **cierto** *(true) or* **F** *for* **falso** *(false). If a statement is false, provide a corrected statement in Spanish.*

1. C F   El primer cine se dirige a la élite.

2. C F   Buñuel describe aquí las diferencias entre la vida moderna y la vida cuando era niño.

3. C F   Las primeras imágenes que vio eran en tecnicolor.

4. C F   Desde la cocina Buñuel y su prima podían ver y escuchar películas sonoras.

5. C F   En el cine los primeros espectadores no comprendían bien lo que tenía lugar en la pantalla.

6. C F   Le interesaba mucho a la madre de Buñuel la carrera artística de su hijo.

7. C F   Durante su colaboración, Buñuel y Dalí acordaron evitar toda explicación racional.

8. C F   Buñuel y Dalí estaban seguros de que su película tendría éxito entre el gran público.

Reflexiones *Consider the following themes and questions, and discuss them in Spanish.*

1. ¿Puede explicar por qué los espectadores no comprendían lo que veían en las primeras películas? ¿Ha experimentado usted esto con un nuevo medio? ¿Cómo aprender el "lenguaje" de los nuevos medios?

_____

_____

_____

_____

2. En los años veinte, Buñuel y Dalí eran surrealistas. Se prometieron "no aceptar idea ni imagen alguna que pudiera dar lugar a una explicación racional, psicológica o cultural". En su opinión, ¿eso es posible? ¿Trata usted a veces de darles una explicación a sus sueños?

_____

_____

_____

_____

3. Durante su carrera, las películas de Buñuel escandalizaron al público. Hoy en día, ¿qué (en el cine o la televisión) consigue molestar o chocar al público? ¿El público de hoy es distinto del público anterior?

_____

_____

_____

_____

4. ¿Ya ha colaborado con otra(s) persona(s) en un proyecto? ¿Fueron ustedes tan compatibles como Buñuel y Dalí en su proyecto de *Un perro andaluz*?

_____

_____

_____

_____

5. ¿Cree usted que los artistas son distintos de los no artistas? Si es así, ¿de qué manera?

_____

_____

_____

_____

EJERCICIO
24·5

Mi vocabulario *Select the word or phrase that does not belong in each group.*

1. a. piso   b. paseo   c. avenida   d. calle
2. a. provisto   b. equipado   c. previsto   d. dotado
3. a. callado   b. mudo   c. silencioso   d. mudable
4. a. cerdo   b. vaca   c. cerebro   d. caballo
5. a. desde luego   b. de ahí   c. por supuesto   d. claro
6. a. inmediatamente b. pronto   c. en seguida   d. casi
7. a. cabaña   b. barraca   c. casete   d. caseta
8. a. tapir   b. tapiar   c. cubrir   d. cerrar
9. a. tabique   b. claraboya   c. pared   d. muro
10. a. observar   b. advertir   c. advenir   d. comprender

EJERCICIO
24·6

Contrarios *Match each word or phrase with its opposite.*

1. _____ fuera   a. carente de
2. _____ provisto de   b. envuelto
3. _____ porvenir   c. bulliciosamente
4. _____ atraer   d. de pie
5. _____ descubierto   e. pasado
6. _____ fracaso   f. llenar
7. _____ silenciosamente   g. adentro
8. _____ indiscutible   h. rechazar
9. _____ vaciar   i. dudoso
10. _____ acostado   j. éxito

Equivalentes *Complete each sentence by substituting words or phrases from the following list for the words or phrases in small type.*

crear	mediara	realizar	se enojó
formalmente	saltimbanqui	filmadas	pagado
suficiente	futuro	periodista	típico
masa	persuadir		

1. El cine estuvo considerado como una diversión de feria... _____
   _{propio}

   de la _____, sin _____ artístico.
   _{plebe} _{porvenir}

2. Ningún _____ se interesaba por él.
   _{crítico}

3. Cuando comuniqué a mi madre mi intención de _____ mi primera
   _{realizar}

   película, ella _____ y casi lloró, como si yo le hubiera dicho: "Mamá,
   _{se llevó un gran disgusto}

   quiero ser _____".
   _{payaso}

4. Fue necesario que _____ un notario... quien le explicó muy
   _{interviniera}

   _____ que con el cine se podía ganar _____
   _{serio} _{bastante}

   dinero y hasta _____ obras interesantes, como las grandes películas
   _{producir}

   _____ en Italia.
   _{rodadas}

5. Mi madre se dejó _____, pero no fue a ver la película que ella había
   _{convencer}

   _____.
   _{financiado}

¡No se olvide! Los adverbios

Adverbs are single words or multi-word phrases that modify an adjective, a verb, or another adverb in a sentence. They answer the questions *where? when? how? why? how much?* or *how little?* Spanish uses many single-word adverbs as well as many adverbial phrases. Adverbial phrases often begin with a preposition such as **a**, **con**, **de**, **en**, or **por**.

The following adverbs and adverbial phrases are found in the reading. Observe how they are used in a sentence, then give the English equivalent of the adverb or adverbial phrase.

1. todavía _____
2. fuera _____
3. siempre _____
4. desde luego _____
5. a todas partes _____
6. incluso _____
7. apenas _____
8. luego _____
9. por turnos _____
10. de pie _____

11. entonces _____
12. ahora _____
13. de ahí _____
14. nunca _____
15. por cierto _____
16. cada vez _____
17. encima _____
18. al igual que _____
19. bastante _____
20. casi _____

*The reading contains many single- or multi-word adverbs that do not end in -**mente**, in addition to those included in **Ejercicio 24-8**. Find and list 12 of them, and provide their English equivalents.*

1. _____ _____
2. _____ _____
3. _____ _____
4. _____ _____
5. _____ _____
6. _____ _____
7. _____ _____
8. _____ _____
9. _____ _____
10. _____ _____
11. _____ _____
12. _____ _____

Adverbs formed with -mente

Many single-word adverbs in Spanish are formed by adding **-mente** to the feminine form of the adjective: **lento** > **lentamente**, **rápido** > **rápidamente**. The English equivalent often ends in *-ly*.

If the adjective does not end in **-o**, add **-mente** to the singular form of the adjective: **fácil** > **fácilmente**, **triste** > **tristemente**.

¡Ojo!

When two adverbs modify a verb, you may see examples where only the second adverb carries the suffix **-mente**. The first adverb will be the feminine form of the adjective.

Trabaja lenta y cuidadosamente.　　*He works slowly and carefully.*

EJERCICIO 24·10

*The following excerpts from the reading contain adverbs ending in **-mente** in bold. First (a) give the Spanish adjective on which each adverb is based. Then (b) create new, short sentences using these adverbs.*

1. Se consagró **únicamente** al cine.

    a. _____

    b. _____

2. Pasó siete años en Hollywood antes de establecerse **definitivamente** en México.

    a. _____

    b. _____

3. Atraían **bulliciosamente** a los curiosos.

    a. _____

    b. _____

4. Lo recuerdo **perfectamente**.

    a. _____

    b. _____

5. Significó la irrupción de un elemento **totalmente** nuevo en nuestro universo.

    a. _____

    b. _____

6. Nosotros nos hemos acostumbrado **insensiblemente** al lenguaje cinematográfico.

    a. _____

    b. _____

7. Veíamos… una cara que se nos venía encima y que crecía **desmesuradamente**.

   a. _____

   b. _____

8. Cuando la imagen… era aceptada por el otro, **inmediatamente** nos parecía luminosa, indiscutible.

   a. _____

   b. _____

¡Vaya más lejos!

- Vea (en YouTube o en DVD) los filmes de vanguardia de **Luis Buñuel**, *Un perro andaluz* (*Un chien andalou*, 1929) y *La edad de oro* (*L'Âge d'or*, 1930).

- Busque (en DVD o en streaming) otras películas de Buñuel. En los años cincuenta destacan *Los olvidados* (1950), *Él* (1952), *Abismos de pasión* (1953), *La vida criminal de Archibaldo de la Cruz* (1955) y *Nazarín* (1958). En los años sesenta dirigió *Viridiana* (1961), *El ángel exterminador* (1962), *Diario de una camarera* (1964), *Simón del desierto* (1965), *Bella de día* (1966) y *La vía láctea* (1969). Cerca del fin de su carrera hizo *El discreto encanto de la burguesía* (1972), *El fantasma de la libertad* (1974) y *Ese oscuro objeto del deseo* (1977).

- Busque información sobre **Georges Méliès**, **los hermanos Lumière** y otros pioneros del cine. Vea en DVD la película *Hugo* (2011) donde se muestran extractos de las obras de Méliès.

- En España hubo los pioneros del cine **Eduardo Jimeno**, **Alexandre Promio**, **Fructuós Gelabert** y **Segundo de Chomón**. Busque en YouTube uno o varios de esos cineastas y sus películas.

ARQUEOLOGÍA Y ANTROPOLOGÍA

El mundo maya
(México/Guatemala/Belice/ El Salvador/Honduras)

·25·

Los mayas, una de las culturas precolombinas más importantes, ocupaban gran parte de Mesoamérica: los países contemporáneos de Guatemala, Belice, Honduras, El Salvador y cinco estados del sureste del México actual. Su historia **abarca** cerca de 3000 años. Los descendientes de los mayas viven hoy día en la región, y muchos hablan alguno de los **idiomas** llamados "antiguos".

¿Estamos listos?

1. ¿Qué es Mesoamérica?

   Es la región del continente americano que comprende... la mitad meridional de México, Guatemala, El Salvador, Belice y el occidente de Honduras, Nicaragua y Costa Rica...

2. ¿De qué culturas precolombinas ha oído hablar?

   Los principales pueblos mesoamericanos precolombinos (establecidos antes de la conquista española) son las civilizaciones... olmeca, zapoteca, totonaca, teotihuacana, maya, tolteca, mixteca y azteca (mexica)...

3. ¿Se asemejan esas culturas mesoamericanas?

   De hecho, comparten... conocimientos, estudios, logros (*accomplishments*), invenciones, creencias, prácticas y costumbres.

   Se encuentran entre ellos... la agricultura, las matemáticas, la astronomía, el calendario de 260 días, la medicina...; la escritura glífica, el juego de pelota...; la arquitectura y los edificios, templos y centros ceremoniales hechos de piedra y barro...; el politeísmo, el arte político-religioso...; un sistema dualista de pensamiento (el bien contra el mal), ofrendas a la tierra, sacrificios, el viaje al más allá (*afterlife*)...

4. ¿Ha oído hablar de la civilización maya? ¿Por qué es conocida? ¿En qué contexto la ha encontrado?

5. ¿Recuerda usted las profecías mayas sobre la fecha 21 de diciembre del 2012? ¿En qué consistieron? En su opinión, ¿por qué algunas personas las tomaron en serio?

¡Leamos!

Descubrimiento de un friso maya en Holmul

El Tiempo Latino, 11 de agosto 2013. El descubrimiento de un **friso** maya en el sitio arqueológico **Holmul** en el departamento de **Petén** al norte de Guatemala, que investigadores **catalogan** como extraordinario, revelaría información sobre qué pasó con la civilización maya de **Tikal**, **según** su descubridor el antropólogo Francisco Estrada-Belli.

"Yo espero que este descubrimiento **deje más claro** que los mayas no eran tan **extraños**, ni se los llevaron los extraterrestres, eran como otra cultura, tenían entre ellos **reyes poderosos** que **intentaron** dominar toda la región y que **llegaron a ser** un **imperio**", dijo Estrada-Belli, profesor en el departamento de antropología de la Universidad Tulane.

El friso de 8 metros **de largo** por 2 metros **de alto**, se encuentra en la parte superior de un edificio o pirámide rectangular de unos 10 metros. Está ricamente decorado con imágenes de dioses y **gobernantes** y una larga inscripción dedicatoria. Su composición incluye tres personajes principales **vistiendo** ricos **atavíos** de plumas de **quetzal** y **jade**, sentados sobre cabezas de monstruos llamados *witz*.

El personaje central del friso se identifica como Och Chan Yopaat, que significa "el rayo entró al cielo", según los signos **jeroglíficos** en su **tocado** y en el texto debajo de su imagen. En el centro hay un monstruo y desde su boca **se desprenden** serpientes **emplumadas** de las cuales emergen los ancestros y **cerros laterales**. Entre ellos están las figuras de dos dioses ancianos, **otorgándole** al personaje central un objeto identificado por un signo jeroglífico como 'primer **tamal**'. Arriba de los personajes corre una banda de símbolos **astrales** conocida como 'banda celestial' que indica que las figuras representadas se encuentran en el mundo celestial de dioses y ancestros.

Según el antropólogo, el friso es de la **época clásica** y es de los pocos lugares que se han encontrado que mencionan al **reino** de Tikal.

"Para el año 600, **d.C.**, se consideró una época **oscura** del reino de Tikal, porque entonces estos dejaron de erigir **estelas presuntamente** porque **habían sido derrotados** y su pueblo había sido casi conquistado", explicó el antropólogo.

Estrada-Belli **agregó** que "aquí se cierra un círculo sobre los enemigos del reino de Tikal. Esto nos explica la relación que hubo entre el rey de Holmul, el rey de Naranjo y el rey de Kan, este último era el que dominaba, estaban **ubicados** alrededor de Tikal, junto a otros que eran enemigos del reino y lo estaban **sofocando**", dice el arqueólogo, "en los últimos momentos del **reinado** de Tikal".

"Del edificio donde está el friso, solo se ha descubierto en la parte exterior, falta la parte interior donde hay cuartos, creemos que puede haber decoración pintada, algún **entierro** o tumba", explicó.

El arqueólogo aún no deja de **asombrarse** del descubrimiento que hizo, el cual considera una gran responsabilidad.

"Sentí mucha emoción cuando lo vi, primero entusiasmo, luego mucho miedo, porque **si algo le pasa va a caer sobre mí**, si no se preserva bien, si van y lo destruyen, **incluso** pensé en que **mejor lo hubiera dejado tapado** otros mil años", dijo el arqueólogo.

Para el experto en **epigrafía** maya de la Universidad de Texas en Austin, David Stuart, la lectura del texto maya es excelente. Pero **a pesar de que** las autoridades **han calificado de** extraordinario el descubrimiento, Stuart dice que hay otros que le pueden **hacer competencia**.

"Es muy impresionante", dijo Stuart, y agregó que "yo ciertamente no diría que es 'la más espectacular' **fachada** de un templo. Hay otros edificios mayas que son **igual de** magníficos, si no posiblemente más", dijo Stuart.

Una de las cosas que llamó la atención de los arqueólogos que trabajaron en el lugar fue la forma en la que estaba preservado el friso.

"El edificio los mayas lo **enterraron**, le pusieron piedras muy grandes **encima**, lo hicieron con mucho cuidado hasta se ven las **huellas digitales** de ellos **impregnadas** en el **lodo**, se ve que lo pintaron varias veces", dijo Estrada-Belli, que explicó que será hasta abril del 2014 cuando vuelvan al lugar a continuar con los trabajos de investigación, debido a la **temporada** de invierno en el país.

Sobre las condiciones de seguridad del área donde se encuentra el descubrimiento, el arqueólogo dijo que el lugar está cerrado al tráfico del público pues está en un área de reserva natural que por ley está protegida y que **tiene vigilancia** las 24 horas para evitar **saqueos**.

"Cualquier ser humano en frente de ese friso, se siente tan pequeño porque es una cosa tan magnífica", **añadió** su descubridor.

From *El Tiempo latino*, http://eltiempolatino.com. Used with permission of The Associated Press Copyright © 2014. All rights reserved. Many thanks to Jessica Stremmel.

VOCABULARIO

abarca [abarcar]	*encompasses*	laterales	*(on the) side*
(los) idiomas	*languages*	otorgándole [otorgar]	*bestowing upon him*
friso	*frieze (carved upper wall)*	(el) tamal	*meat in cornmeal, wrapped in husks*
Holmul	*Maya site in northeastern Guatemala*	astrales	*celestial, astrological*
Petén	*northeastern department of Guatemala*	época clásica	*Maya classical period (~250–900 CE)*
catalogan [catalogar]	*classify, define*	reino	*kingdom, realm*
Tikal	*Maya capital (~200–900 CE)*	d.C.	*AD, Common Era, CE*
		oscura	*dark, dismal*
según	*according to*	estelas	*steles, carved upright slabs*
deje [dejar] más claro	*clarifies*		
extraños	*strange, unusual*	presuntamente	*presumably*
(los) reyes	*kings*	habían sido derrotados [derrotar]	*had been defeated*
poderosos	*powerful*		
intentaron [intentar]	*tried to*		
llegaron [llegar] a ser	*became*	agregó [agregar]	*added*
imperio	*empire*	ubicados	*situated*
de largo... de alto	*long . . . high*	sofocando [sofocar]	*suffocating, smothering*
(los) gobernantes	*rulers*	reinado	*reign*
vistiendo [vestir]	*wearing, dressed in*	entierro	*burial*
atavíos	*attire, ornamentation*	asombrarse	*being astonished*
(el) quetzal	*colorful bird of Guatemala*	si algo le pasa [pasar]	*if something happens to it*
(el) jade	*jade(-colored)*		
(los) witz	*Maya mountain spirit*	va [ir] a caer sobre mí	*it will be my fault (LIT., it will fall upon me)*
jeroglíficos	*hieroglyphic, written in pictures*	incluso	*even*
tocado	*headdress, hairdo*	mejor lo hubiera dejado [dejar] tapado	*better (if) I had left it hidden*
se desprenden [desprenderse]	*come out, emerge*		
emplumadas	*feathered, plumed*	epigrafía	*epigraphy (study of inscriptions)*
cerros	*hills*		

a pesar de que	in spite of the fact that	huellas digitales	fingerprints
han calificado de [calificar]	have qualified as, have described as	impregnadas	molded
		lodo	mud
hacer competencia	compete (with it)	temporada	season
fachada	façade	tiene [tener] vigilancia	is guarded
igual de	equally	saqueos	looting, plundering
enterraron [enterrar]	buried	añadió [añadir]	added
encima	on top of (it)		

EJERCICIO
25·1

¿De qué se trata? *Match each item with its description.*

1. _____ Francisco Estrada-Belli   a. el rayo entró al cielo

2. _____ Holmul   b. sitio maya en Guatemala

3. _____ Tikal   c. país de América Central

4. _____ Maya   d. monarcas de Tikal

5. _____ Petén   e. poderoso reino maya (~200–900 CE)

6. _____ Och Chan Yopaat   f. descubridor del friso de Tikal

7. _____ Guatemala   g. departamento guatemalteco al noroeste

8. _____ reyes de Naranjo y de Kan   h. civilización precolombina de Mesoamérica

EJERCICIO
25·2

Opciones *Choose the phrase or phrases that correctly answer each question. Include all correct responses.*

1. ¿Dónde se sitúa el friso recientemente descubierto?
   a. en el departamento de Petén
   b. en Holmul
   c. en Guatemala

2. En el friso, ¿qué le ofrecen los dioses al personaje central?
   a. el primer tamal
   b. un signo jeroglífico
   c. un tocado

3. ¿Por qué el pueblo de Tikal dejó de erigir estelas hacia 600 d.C.?
   a. había sido conquistado
   b. había sido derrotado
   c. había sido elevado

4. Según este recuento, ¿quiénes eran los reyes de esa época?
   a. el rey de Naranjo
   b. el rey de Kan
   c. el rey de Holmul

5. ¿Qué rey dominaba finalmente?
   a. el rey de Holmul
   b. el rey de Naranjo
   c. el rey de Kan

6. Según el descubridor, ¿qué partes del edificio quedarían todavía escondidas?
   a. cuartos decorados
   b. otros frisos
   c. una tumba

7. ¿De qué tiene miedo el arqueólogo?
   a. de que lo destruyan
   b. de que otro científico lo encuentre
   c. de que no se preserve

8. ¿De qué manera escondieron los mayas el edificio?
   a. con lodo
   b. con pintura
   c. con piedras

9. ¿Cuándo los científicos podrán regresar al sitio?
   a. de inmediato
   b. en la primavera
   c. después del invierno

10. ¿Por qué no está abierto el sitio al tráfico del público?
    a. está en una reserva natural
    b. el público no se interesa
    c. esperan evitar saqueos

EJERCICIO 25·3

¿Cierto o falso? *Indicate whether each statement is true or false, using* **C** *for* **cierto** (true) *or* **F** *for* **falso** (false). *If a statement is false, provide a corrected statement in Spanish.*

1. C F   A los mayas se los llevaron los extraterrestres.

   _____

2. C F   Los reyes mayas intentaron dominar toda la región.

   _____

3. C F   Las inscripciones son más significativas que las esculturas.

   _____

4. C F Los símbolos astrales representan el mundo de dioses y ancestros.

_____

5. C F Hay muchos otros lugares en el mundo maya que mencionan el reino de Tikal.

_____

_____

6. C F Los científicos ya descubrieron todo el edificio.

_____

7. C F El arqueólogo está convencido de que su descubrimiento queda seguro y protegido.

_____

_____

8. C F Los mayas trataron de enterrar todo el edificio, colocando encima piedras y lodo.

_____

_____

Mi vocabulario *Select the word that does not belong in each group.*

1. a. hurto   b. roble   c. robo   d. saqueo

2. a. polvo   b. fango   c. lodo   d. barro

3. a. catalogar   b. clasificar   c. ordenar   d. clarear

4. a. colocado   b. ubicado   c. colmado   d. emplazado

5. a. portada   b. frente   c. fachada   d. fecha

6. a. presuntamente   b. inmediatamente   c. supuestamente   d. probablemente

7. a. juntar   b. desprender   c. soltar   d. separar

8. a. conquistar   b. vencer   c. derrotar   d. colaborar

9. a. época   b. temporada   c. templanza   d. estación

10. a. idioma   b. ídolo   c. lengua   d. habla

11. a. estelas   b. atavíos   c. vestidos   d. prendas

Contra Costa County Library
Walnut Creek
5/8/2023   7:47:06 PM

- Patron Receipt -

ID: 21901019686595

1:
Transaction Type: Lost
Title: The complete idiot's guide to learning La
Item #: 31901054707205
Call #: 475 HARWOOD
Charge/Request Date: 2/17/2022
Due/NNA Date: 3/12/2022
Return Date:
Amount Due: $19.95

2:
Transaction Type: Lost
Title: Barron's E-Z French /
Item #: 31901055461117
Call #: 448.2421 KENDRIS
Charge/Request Date: 4/18/2022
Due/NNA Date: 5/12/2022
Return Date:
Amount Due: $16.99

Account information, library hours,
and upcoming closures can be found
at https://ccclib.org/contact-us/,
or by calling 1-800-984-4636.

Contrarios *Match each word with its opposite.*

1. _____ abarcar   a. extraño

2. _____ añadir   b. asombrarse

3. _____ otorgar   c. cerros

4. _____ poderoso   d. excluir

5. _____ descuido   e. sustraer

6. _____ normal   f. débil

7. _____ llanos   g. vigilancia

8. _____ aburrirse   h. quitar

Equivalentes *Complete each sentence by substituting words or phrases from the following list for the words or phrases in small type.*

barro	esmero	monarcas	colocaron
explique	portaron	conservadas	fuertes
quisieron	la construcción	marcianos	someter
se convirtieron en	misteriosos	taparon	

1. Yo espero que este descubrimiento _____ que los mayas no eran

deje más claro

   tan _____, ni se los _____ los

extraños   llevaron

   _____.

extraterrestres

2. Eran como otra cultura, tenían entre ellos _____

reyes

   _____ que _____ _____

poderosos   intentaron   dominar

   toda la región y que _____ un imperio.

llegaron a ser

3. _____ los mayas lo _____,

El edificio   enterraron

   le _____ piedras muy grandes encima, lo hicieron con

pusieron

   mucho _____ hasta se ven las huellas digitales de ellos

cuidado

   _____ en el _____.

impregnadas   lodo

Mucho de lo que oímos **acerca de** los mayas **tiene que ver con** su calendario. Fue el centro de su vida social y religiosa y **quizás** su **logro** cultural más importante. Derivado de los **conocimientos** matemáticos y astronómicos de la **casta sacerdotal**, se basa en una **cuenta** continua de los días, **a partir de** un día **cero** inicial. Es cíclico, porque se repite cada 52 años mayas. El mismo calendario **se sigue utilizando** hoy día en ciertas comunidades **guatemaltecas** y mexicanas.

¡Leamos!

El calendario maya o "cuenta de los días"

Las civilizaciones antiguas de Meso América **desarrollaron** calendarios escritos precisos y **de estos** el calendario de los mayas es el más sofisticado. […] Su precisión deriva **del hecho de que** se basa en la cuenta continua e ininterrumpida de los días (llamados *Kin* en maya) a partir del día cero inicial. **A lo largo de** la historia los **pueblos** han sentido la necesidad de contar con un punto fijo donde **iniciar** sus cálculos del tiempo. Con **este fin**, generalmente se ha determinado el punto inicial **o bien** usando un evento histórico […] o por un evento **hipotético** […]. Los mayas también descubrieron la necesidad de **tal fecha** y así, probablemente usando un evento astronómico significativo, **ubicaron** ese día inicial el 13 de agosto de 3114 a.C.

El conocimiento **ancestral** del calendario **guiaba** la existencia de los mayas a partir del momento de **su nacimiento** y **era muy poco lo que** escapaba a la influencia calendárica. Sabemos que los mayas llevaban varias cuentas calendáricas independientes de los *Kin* que estaban sincronizadas, **siendo** las de 260 y 365 días las más importantes. Las cuentas mayas de los días se escriben combinando números con **glifos**.

EL CALENDARIO DE 260 DIAS—TZOLKIN. El calendario *Tzolkin* de 260 días es el más usado por los pueblos del mundo maya. Lo usaban para **regir** los tiempos de su **quehacer agrícola**, su ceremonial religioso y sus **costumbres familiares**, **pues** la vida del hombre maya estaba predestinada por el día del *Tzolkin* que correspondía a la fecha de su nacimiento. Esta cuenta **consta de** los números del 1 al 13 y 20 **nombres** para los días representados **asimismo** por glifos individuales. Al llegar al **decimocuarto** día, el número del día **regresa** al 1 continuando la sucesión del 1 al 13 **una y otra vez**. Al día 21 se repite la sucesión de los nombres de los días y así sucesivamente. **Ambos** ciclos continúan de esta manera hasta los 260 días **sin que** se repita la combinación de número y nombre pues 260 es el **mínimo común múltiplo** de 13 y 20. Después el ciclo de 260 días **a su vez** se repite.

EL CALENDARIO DE 365 DIAS—HAAB. El calendario llamado *Haab*—un calendario solar—se basa en el **recorrido** anual de la Tierra alrededor del Sol en 365 días. Los mayas dividieron el año de 365 días en 18 "meses" llamados *Winal* de 20 días cada uno y 5 días **sobrantes** que **se les denominaba** *Wayeb*. Cada día se escribe usando un número del 0 al 19 y un nombre del *Winal* representado por un glifo, con la excepción de los días del *Wayeb* que se acompañan de números del 0 al 4.

EL CICLO DE 18,980 DÍAS—LA RUEDA CALENDÁRICA. La combinación de los calendarios de 260 y 365 días crea un ciclo **mayor** de 18,980 días (el mínimo común múltiplo de 260 y 365), a esta combinación se le ha llamado la Rueda Calendárica. Sus cuatro elementos (número-glifo *Kin* y número-glifo *Winal*) **juntos** sólo se repiten cada 18,980 días. Una gran cantidad de monumentos mayas solamente **registran** la fecha de la Rueda Calendárica.

From *Centro de Estudios del Mundo Maya* (Mérida, Yucatán), http://www.mayacalendar.com.

acerca de	*about*	glifos	*glyphs, hieroglyphics*
tiene [tener] que ver con	*concerns, has to do with*	Tzolkin	*the 260-day Maya calendar*
quizás	*perhaps*	regir	*regulate, govern*
logro	*achievement*	(el) quehacer agrícola	*agricultural work*
conocimientos	*knowledge, science*	(las) costumbres familiares	*family customs*
casta sacerdotal	*priestly caste*		
(la) cuenta	*sum, calculation*	pues	*since, because*
a partir de cero	*starting with zero*	consta [constar] de	*consists of*
se sigue [seguir] utilizando	*continues to be used*	(los) nombres	*names*
		asimismo	*also, as well*
guatemaltecas	*Guatemalan*	decimocuarto	*fourteenth*
desarrollaron [desarrollar]	*developed*	regresa [regresar]	*returns*
		una y otra vez	*over and over again*
de estos	*among these*	ambos	*both*
del hecho de que	*from the fact that*	sin que	*without*
a lo largo de	*throughout*	mínimo común múltiplo	*least common multiple*
pueblos	*communities*		
iniciar	*to begin, initiate*	a su vez	*in turn*
este fin	*this objective*	Haab	*the 365-day Maya calendar*
o bien	*or (rather)*		
hipotético	*hypothetical, possible*	recorrido	*rotation, trajectory*
tal fecha	*such a date*	sobrantes	*extra, left over*
ubicaron [ubicar]	*(they) assigned, (they) set*	se les denominaba [denominar]	*were called*
ancestral	*age-old, ancestral*		
guiaba [guiar]	*guided, directed*	rueda	*wheel*
su nacimiento	*their birth*	mayor	*greater*
era muy poco lo que	*there was very little (in life) that*	juntos	*together*
		registran [registrar]	*show, display*
siendo [ser]	*being*		

EJERCICIO

25·7

¿De qué se trata? *Match the beginning of each sentence with the phrase that correctly completes it to describe the Maya calendar.*

1. _____ El calendario de 260 días   a. poseía conocimientos matemáticos y astronómicos.

2. _____ La casta sacerdotal   b. nacía bajo la influencia de un día en particular.

3. _____ Toda la vida de los mayas   c. el año en 18 meses de 20 días cada uno.

4. _____ El *Haab* dividía   d. se componía de dos ciclos de 260 y 365 días.

5. _____ Cada niño   e. se usaba en combinación con el calendario solar.

6. _____ La Rueda calendárica   f. era regida por sus calendarios.

Opciones *Choose the phrase or phrases that correctly answer each question. Include all correct responses.*

1. ¿Cuántos días hay en el calendario Tzolkin de los mayas?

   a. 18,980   b. 260   c. 365

2. ¿Quién rige el calendario y la vida del pueblo maya?

   a. agricultores   b. lingüistas   c. sacerdotes

3. Para los mayas, ¿cuánta importancia tenían las matemáticas y la astronomía?

   a. escasa importancia   b. poder divino   c. reglas para vivir

4. ¿Qué día de un niño maya predestinaba el curso de su vida?

   a. de la muerte   b. del nacimiento   c. del cumpleaños

5. ¿Cuántos meses hay en un "año" *Haab*?

   a. 13   b. 18   c. 12

6. ¿Cuántos días hay en un "año" *Haab*?

   a. 18,980   b. 260   c. 365

7. ¿De cuántos días constaba el *Wayeb*?

   a. 5   b. 10   c. 6

8. ¿Qué comprenden los cuatro elementos del ciclo de 18,980 días de la Rueda Calendárica?

   a. el número + glifo *Kin*   b. el número + glifo *Winal*   c. el decimocuarto día

¿Cierto o falso? *Indicate whether each statement is true or false, using* **C** *for* **cierto** *(true) or* **F** *for* **falso** *(false). If a statement is false, provide a corrected statement in Spanish.*

1. C F   Hoy en día nadie utiliza el calendario Tzolkin.

   _____

2. C F   El calendario Tzolkin regía la vida cotidiana maya y todas las actividades religiosas.

   _____

   _____

3. C F   Todo el pueblo maya estudiaba las estrellas y controlaba el calendario.

   _____

4. C F Cada súbdito (*subject*) maya vivía bajo la influencia de su propio día.

   _____

5. C F Los mayas establecieron un calendario único.

   _____

6. C F El calendario solar *Haab* guarda cierta semejanza con el nuestro.

   _____

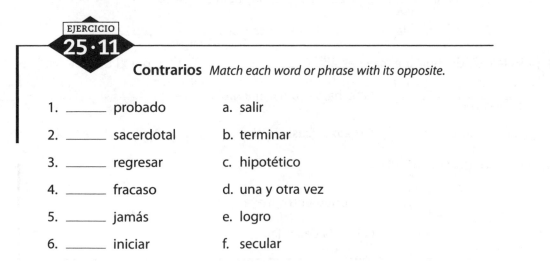

EJERCICIO
25·10

Mi vocabulario *Select the word that does not belong in each group.*

1. a. regir   b. dirigir   c. guiar   d. reaccionar
2. a. divino   b. sagrado   c. sagaz   d. sacrosanto
3. a. sueldo   b. suerte   c. destino   d. fortuna
4. a. tareas   b. quehaceres   c. trabajos   d. tarjetas
5. a. elaborar   b. alquilar   c. desarrollar   d. iniciar
6. a. números   b. cifras   c. nombres   d. símbolos
7. a. restante   b. sobrante   c. sobrino   d. extra
8. a. dividir   b. constar   c. componerse   d. consistir

EJERCICIO
25·11

Contrarios *Match each word or phrase with its opposite.*

1. _____ probado   a. salir
2. _____ sacerdotal   b. terminar
3. _____ regresar   c. hipotético
4. _____ fracaso   d. una y otra vez
5. _____ jamás   e. logro
6. _____ iniciar   f. secular

Equivalentes *Complete each sentence by substituting words or phrases from the following list for the words or phrases in small type.*

a través de	dirigir	posible	acaso
empezar	prácticas	se apoya	éxito
se refiere a	los clérigos	inscriben	tomado
coincidía con	invariable	trabajo	decidida
muchos	trayecto	denominado	objetivo
utilizado			

1. Mucho de lo que oímos acerca de los mayas _____ su calendario.
   <small>tiene que ver con</small>

   Fue el centro de su vida social y religiosa y _____ su
   <small>quizás</small>

   _____ cultural más importante.
   <small>logro</small>

2. _____ de los conocimientos matemáticos y astronómicos de
   <small>Derivado</small>

   _____, _____ en una cuenta continua de los días.
   <small>la casta sacerdotal</small>   <small>se basa</small>

3. _____ la historia los pueblos han sentido la necesidad de contar con
   <small>A lo largo de</small>

   un punto _____ donde _____ sus cálculos del
   <small>fijo</small>   <small>iniciar</small>

   tiempo. Con este _____, generalmente se ha determinado el punto
   <small>fin</small>

   inicial o bien usando un evento histórico [...] o por un evento _____.
   <small>hipotético</small>

4. El calendario *Tzolkin* de 260 días es el más _____ por los pueblos del
   <small>usado</small>

   mundo maya. Lo usaban para _____ los tiempos de su
   <small>regir</small>

   _____ agrícola, su ceremonial religioso y sus _____
   <small>quehacer</small>   <small>costumbres</small>

   familiares, pues la vida del hombre maya estaba _____ por el día del
   <small>predestinada</small>

   Tzolkin que _____ la fecha de su nacimiento.
   <small>correspondía a</small>

5. El calendario _____ *Haab* se basa en el _____ anual
   <small>llamado</small>   <small>recorrido</small>

   de la Tierra alrededor del Sol en 365 días.

6. Sin embargo, _____ monumentos mayas solamente
   <small>una gran cantidad de</small>

   _____ la fecha de la Rueda Calendárica.
   <small>registran</small>

Reflexiones *Consider the following themes and questions, and discuss them in Spanish.*

1. ¿Ya ha oído leyendas o fábulas sobre los mayas, como la de los extraterrestres? En su opinión, ¿por qué esta civilización lleva consigo tantas leyendas?

2. En su opinión, ¿por qué se cubrieron con tanto cuidado el friso de Tikal y su edificio?

3. ¿Conoce culturas que practican el culto de los ancestros? ¿Se practica también, en cierto sentido, entre nosotros en la cultura "occidental"?

4. Hoy en día, ¿es útil para una comunidad tener un calendario distinto? ¿Por qué? ¿Por qué no? ¿Conoce culturas que lo mantienen? ¿Cómo lo mantienen?

5. ¿Son universales las supersticiones? ¿Por qué? ¿Es usted supersticioso/a? ¿y los miembros de su familia? ¿sus amigos? ¿Sus supersticiones se basan en la astrología?

¡No se olvide! Los números ordinales

Review the Spanish ordinal numbers from 1 (*first*) to 20 (*twentieth*). Like **bueno** > **buen**, **primero** and **tercero** drop the **-o** before a masculine singular noun (**el primer ejercicio del libro** *the first exercise of the book*). Before feminine singular nouns, use **primera** and **tercera** (**la tercera lección** *the third lesson*).

primer, primero/a	*first*	undécimo/a	*eleventh*
segundo/a	*second*	duodécimo/a	*twelfth*
tercer, tercero/a	*third*	decimotercero/a	*thirteenth*
cuarto/a	*fourth*	decimocuarto/a	*fourteenth*
quinto/a	*fifth*	decimoquinto/a	*fifteenth*
sexto/a	*sixth*	decimosexto/a	*sixteenth*
séptimo/a	*seventh*	decimoséptimo/a	*seventeenth*
octavo/a	*eighth*	decimoctavo/a	*eighteenth*
noveno/a	*ninth*	decimonoveno/a	*nineteenth*
décimo/a	*tenth*	vigésimo/a	*twentieth*

EJERCICIO
25·14

Give a Spanish equivalent for each of the following phrases.

1. *the third man* _____

2. *her first birthday* _____

3. *the eighteenth day* _____

4. *our twentieth anniversary* _____

5. *the fourth hour* _____

6. *the fifteenth chapter* _____

¡No se olvide! El participio pasado (II)

Past participles in Spanish (for example, **decorado**, **entendido**, **abierto**) are often used with a conjugated form of **estar** or **ser**. In both cases, the past participle functions as an adjective and agrees in gender and number with the subject of **estar** or **ser**. (See Chapter 8.)

Estar + past participle describes the subject and usually expresses the result of an action.

La ventana **está cerrada**.	*The window is closed.*
Otros reinos **estaban ubicados** alrededor de Tikal.	*Other kingdoms were located around Tikal.*
Las tareas **estuvieron terminadas** a las cinco.	*The assignments were finished at five o'clock.*

Ser + past participle expresses the passive voice. The subject of the sentence is or has been affected (acted upon) by a specific agent. **Ser** + past participle can be followed by **por** + the agent of the action.

Cada noche la ventana **es cerrada por** el portero.	*Every night the window is shut by the custodian.*
Su pueblo **había sido** casi **conquistado por** los otros reyes.	*Its people had been almost entirely conquered by the other kings.*
Las tareas **fueron completadas por** esos estudiantes.	*The assignments were finished by those students.*

Spanish speakers tend to avoid the passive voice with **ser**, although it does appear in writing. The spoken language tends to use verbs with an active subject or, alternatively, the pronoun **se** + third-person conjugated verb. In sentences with **se**, the agent is generally not mentioned.

El portero cierra la ventana cada noche.	*The custodian shuts the window every night.*
Los otros reyes habían conquistado su pueblo.	*The other kings had conquered its people.*
Se completaron las tareas.	*The assignments were finished.*
Se hace la ensalada con verduras y aguacates.	*The salad is made with greens and avocados.*

EJERCICIO
25·15

*First (a) give the construction with **estar** + past participle or **ser** + past participle found in each of the following sentences. Then (b) re-create the sentence in the same tense without **estar** or **ser**, using either an active verb or **se** + third-person verb.*

MODELO   El friso está ricamente decorado con imágenes de dioses y gobernantes.

a. *está decorado*

b. *Los mayas decoran el friso con imágenes de dioses y gobernantes.*

OR

b. *El friso se decora con imágenes de dioses y gobernantes.*

1. Los reyes estaban ubicados alrededor de Tikal, junto a otros que eran enemigos del reino.

a. _____

b. _____

_____

2. Una de las cosas que llamó la atención [...] fue la forma en la que estaba preservado el friso.

a. _____

b. _____

_____

3. El lugar está cerrado al tráfico del público.

   a. _____

   b. _____

   _____

4. Pues está en un área de reserva natural que por ley está protegida.

   a. _____

   b. _____

   _____

5. Entonces estos dejaron de erigir estelas […] porque habían sido derrotados.

   a. _____

   b. _____

   _____

6. Y su pueblo había sido casi conquistado.

   a. _____

   b. _____

   _____

7. El calendario sagrado de 260 días era el más usado por los pueblos del mundo maya.

   a. _____

   b. _____

   _____

8. Así, días y cifras eran vistos por los mayas bajo un aspecto divino.

   a. _____

   b. _____

   _____

¡Vaya más lejos!

- Consulte un mapa para situar países, sitios, ciudades, edificios y templos mayas mencionados en este capítulo.

- Para más información, fotos y diseños gráficos sobre el descubrimiento en Holmul, busque los términos siguientes: **friso maya**, **Holmul**, **Petén**, **reinado de Tikal** o **Templo de Tikal**.

- Busque **la escritura maya** para ver ejemplos de jeroglíficos mayas.

- Busque **el calendario maya** para ver gráficas, glifos, números y diagramas sobre los calendarios.

- Busque **el juego de pelota** para descripciones y dibujos de ese juego antiguo.

Answer key

I ♦ FÁBULAS Y LEYENDAS

1 La Yusca, leyenda del Cedral

1·1   1. f   2. g   3. d   4. h   5. e   6. a   7. c   8. b

1·2   1. a, b, c   2. b   3. c   4. c   5. c   6. b   7. a, b

1·3   1. C   2. F, Su marido no era brujo.   3. C   4. F, La Yusca caminaba de prisa cuando iba a los velorios.   5. F, No la acusaron de matar a ningún vecino.   6. F, No decían que la Yusca podía prevenir la Muerte.

1·4   *Answers will vary.*

1·5   1. c   2. c   3. a   4. a   5. a   6. d   7. a   8. b

1·6   1. b   2. e   3. a   4. g   5. h   6. f   7. c   8. d

1·7   1. estaba ciega   2. solicitaba   3. se transformaba, su magia   4. saber, ignoraba, aventuras, desplazó   5. permaneció   6. erraba, sabía, muerto

1·8   1. tenía, description of characteristics in the past; era, description of characteristics in the past   2. pedía, habitual actions in the past; mendigaba, habitual actions in the past   3. estaba, description in the past; era, habitual action in the past   4. desconocía, habitual actions in the past; estaba, a place or location in the past   5. estaba, description in the past; caminaba, habitual action in the past   6. llegaba, habitual action in the past; moría, past situation in progress; estaba, a place or location in the past

2 La leyenda del Sajama

2·1   1. e   2. c   3. b   4. a   5. g   6. f   7. d

2·2   1. a   2. b, c   3. b   4. c   5. a, b, c   6. c

2·3   1. F, Dios está lejos y tenemos que negociar con sus intermediarios, las montañas.   2. F, Pacha perdió la paciencia después de la guerra cuando un imprudente discutió la victoria.   3. C   4. F, Ellas se hicieron pequeñitas.   5. F, Pacha empleó una honda para atacar al imprudente.   6. C   7. F, El imprudente quedó sin cabeza, con una planicie basta.

2·4   *Answers will vary.*

2·5   1. c   2. b   3. d   4. a   5. b   6. c   7. a   8. d

2·6   1. e   2. a   3. f   4. g   5. h   6. b   7. c   8. d

2·7   1. alturas, papel   2. hubo, bárbara   3. cesación de hostilidades, ganador   4. se opuso a   5. picaba, curadas, causado   6. ya no estaba, temerario

2·8   1. a. se creó b. was created c. crearse   2. a. tuvo lugar b. (there) took place c. tener lugar   3. a. ordenó
b. ordered c. ordenar   4. a. discutió b. objected to c. discutir   5. a. decidió b. decided c. decidir
6. a. hizo girar b. spun c. hacer girar   7. a. se hicieron b. became c. hacerse   8. a. escucharon
b. they heard c. escuchar   9. a. desapareció b. disappeared c. desaparecer

3   El nacimiento del arco iris

3·1   1. d   2. f   3. a   4. b   5. e   6. c

3·2   1. a, b   2. a   3. b   4. b, c   5. a, b, c   6. a, c

3·3   1. F, Las mariposas revoloteaban alrededor de las flores.   2. F, Al lado de las mariposas, las flores se sentían
opacadas.   3. F, Las mariposas se querían mucho.   4. C   5. F, Las mariposas permanecieron juntas.   6. C
7. C

3·4   *Answers will vary.*

3·5   1. colores   2. biológico   3. receptores de color   4. ojo   5. conos   6. primarios   7. sensible   8. longitud
de onda   9. arco iris   10. tres   11. secundarios   12. combinación   13. seis

3·6   1. e   2. d   3. a   4. c   5. b

3·7   1. a   2. d   3. a   4. c   5. c   6. d   7. c   8. c

3·8   1. c   2. a   3. g   4. i   5. h   6. e   7. d   8. b   9. f

3·9   1. lindeza, eclipsadas, mariposeaban, cerca de ellas   2. cercó, en seguida, lesión, fatal   3. poderosos,
recorrieron, se pusieron, relámpagos, borrasca, jamás vista

3·10   1. ser, imperfect, continuous   2. recorrer, imperfect, repeated   3. parecer, imperfect, descriptive   4. herirse,
preterit, single action   5. poder, preterit, single action   6. rodear, preterit, single action   7. comprender,
preterit, single action   8. ser, imperfect, descriptive   9. volar, preterit, single action   10. ofrecer, preterit,
single action   11. quebrar, preterit, single action   12. preguntar, preterit, single action   13. estar, imperfect,
state or condition   14. contestar, preterit, single action

3·11   1. cruzaron   2. se volvieron   3. formaron   4. envolvió   5. elevó   6. se calmó   7. se disponía   8. cruzó
9. estaba   10. brillaba   11. temieron

 II BIENESTAR Y COMIDA

4   ¿Qué comemos? La alimentación y la salud

4·1   1. No   2. No   3. No   4. Sí   5. Sí   6. No   7. Sí   8. Sí

4·2   1. b, c   2. a, b, c   3. b, c   4. b   5. a, c   6. b, c

4·3   1. F, En el supermercado, es mejor comprar las ofertas de la semana.   2. C   3. F, Un plátano se constituye
principalmente por glúcidos.   4. F, El pan, las papas y las pastas son fuentes importantes de vitaminas y
minerales.   5. C   6. F, Las gelatinas no endurecen especialmente las uñas.   7. C

4·4   *Answers will vary.*

4·5   *Answers will vary.*

4·6   1. c   2. a   3. a   4. b   5. c   6. d   7. c   8. b

4·7   1. c   2. e   3. h   4. g   5. a   6. d   7. f   8. b

4·8   1. Proyecte, según   2. Sígala, el almacén   3. Es importante, darse cuenta   4. ascienden, se retiran
5. al contrario de, opinión   6. se emplea   7. derrite

4·9   1. a. hacer   2. a. ir   3. a. mantener   4. a. leer   5. a. escoger   6. a. utilizar   7. a. consumir   *For new
sentences using the imperative, answers will vary.*

5 Para tener hijos sanos...

5·1 1. a, e 2. b, h 3. a 4. b 5. g 6. d 7. c 8. f

5·2 1. a, b 2. c 3. b, c 4. b, c 5. a 6. a, b 7. a, c 8. a, b, c

5·3 1. F, Las mamás se olvidan a menudo de su propia salud y necesidades. 2. C 3. F, Es lógico/normal tratar de cumplir con las labores profesionales así como con los asuntos del hogar. 4. C 5. C 6. F, Son los padres, no los amigos de sus hijos. 7. F, Los niños siempre observan e imitan a sus padres. 8. C

5·4 *Answers will vary.*

5·5 1. d 2. b 3. a 4. c 5. a 6. d 7. c 8. c 9. b 10. d

5·6 1. d 2. f 3. e 4. a 5. h 6. b 7. c 8. g 9. i

5·7 1. De vez en cuando, no recuerdan, exigencias, prefiriendo 2. empiezan, vitales 3. Evidentemente, se te agota 4. Hay, fatigarse 5. apreciar, exigen 6. adivinan, reciben 7. otra vez, deja bien claro, equilibrio, conocimiento de sí mismo, destino

5·8 1. a. Pregúntate b. preguntarse 2. a. Recuerda b. recordar 3. a. Tómate b. tomarse 4. a. tómate b. tomarse 5. a. llena b. llenar 6. a. sé b. ser 7. a. supera b. superar 8. a. Tómate b. tomarse 9. a. Sé b. ser 10. a. apaga b. apagar 11. a. realiza b. realizar *For new sentences using the imperative, answers will vary.*

6 La chía, un súper alimento con pasado y mucho futuro

6·1 1. A 2. AA 3. A 4. N 5. N 6. AA 7. A

6·2 1. b 2. a, b, c 3. a, b, c 4. b, c 5. c 6. a, b

6·3 1. C 2. F, La *Salvia hispanica* es muy fácil de cultivar. 3. C 4. F, Los españoles de la Nueva España prohibían y castigaban el cultivo de la chía. 5. F, Las semillas de chía se pueden añadir al pan. 6. F, Un guerrero azteca necesitaba solamente pequeñas cantidades de chía durante cada marcha.

6·4 *Answers will vary.*

6·5 1. d 2. c 3. b 4. a 5. b 6. a 7. c 8. d

6·6 1. a 2. f 3. b 4. e 5. c 6. d 7. h 8. g

6·7 1. es basada en, tiene, consumo, enfermedades, aumenta/ayuda, ayuda/aumenta 2. Además, prohibiciones 3. por consiguiente, la posibilidad, sufrir de 4. cotidiana, recomendada

6·8 1. Los trabajos científicos están creciendo rápidamente. 2. Su dieta equilibrada está mejorando su salud. 3. ¿Estás comiendo menos alimentos salados? 4. ¿La cena? La estoy preparando ahora. / Estoy preparándola ahora. 5. Se están añadiendo a los productos horneados.

7 Consejos para mejorar nuestra memoria

7·1 1. b, e 2. c 3. a 4. b, h 5. b 6. b, d 7. f 8. g

7·2 1. a, b 2. a, c 3. a, b 4. b, c 5. a, b, c 6. a 7. b 8. a, b

7·3 1. F, Eliminar el estrés podría servir para fortalecer una memoria defectuosa. 2. C 3. C 4. F, Enseñar a otra persona podría ayudarse a sí mismo a recordar el material. 5. F, Los huevos son ricos en vitaminas B. 6. F, Se recomienda que los niños tomen leche entera. 7. C 8. C

7·4 *Answers will vary.*

7·5 1. d 2. b 3. a 4. c 5. a 6. b 7. a 8. d 9. c 10. b

7·6 1. c 2. a 3. e 4. h 5. b 6. d 7. f 8. g 9. i

7·7 1. Disminuir, ruinoso 2. Luego, incluyan, combinación, beneficiosa, a la larga 3. objetivo, acordarse de, tienen que, aprendiendo 4. Enfocarse en, encontrarse, manual, tratamos de 5. Aprender, se ha probado, aumenta, competencia

7·8 1. hacer, impersonal command; mantener, impersonal command   2. ejercitar, following a verb that requires a preposition   3. engullir, following a verb that requires a preposition   4. disfrutar, subject of a sentence 5. recordar, following a verb of desire; escribir, subject of a sentence; ayudar, following a verb of ability 6. evocar, object of a preposition   7. enviar, following a verb of ability   8. escatimar, subject of a sentence; ser, following a verb of ability   9. visualizar, impersonal command; recordar, object of a preposition 10. visualizar, following a verb of obligation   11. tratar, impersonal command; hacer, following a verb that requires a preposition; recordar, following a verb of intentionality   12. agregar, following a verb of obligation

8 La granada

8·1   1. e   2. g   3. f   4. a   5. b   6. d   7. c

8·2   1. b   2. a, b, c   3. c   4. a, b   5. a, b, c   6. a, c   7. a, b, c

8·3   1. C   2. F, El narrador tiene buenos recuerdos de esos sentimientos y sensaciones.   3. F, El autor ya no tiene un huerto de granados.   4. F, No afirma que el calidoscopio era su juguete preferido.   5. C   6. C   7. C

8·4   *Answers will vary.*

8·5   *Answers will vary.*

8·6   1. a   2. d   3. b   4. c   5. d   6. b   7. d

8·7   1. c   2. f   3. h   4. e   5. a   6. b   7. d   8. g

8·8   1. g   2. b   3. g   4. e   5. a   6. c   7. d   8. f

8·9   1. a. escogida b. escoger c. to choose   2. a. agarrada b. agarrar c. to grasp/grab   3. a. hecha b. hacer c. to do/make   4. a. pegados b. pegar c. to attach/glue   5. a. apretado b. apretar c. to squeeze/press 6. a. perdido b. perder c. to lose   7. a. caídas b. caer c. to fall down   8. a. abiertas b. abrir c. to open 9. a. reposados b. reposar c. to rest   10. a. entrada b. entrar c. to enter

III ◆ VIDA COTIDIANA

9 Cómo conducir de forma eficiente, en diez consejos

9·1   1. f   2. h   3. h, i   4. a   5. b   6. c   7. g   8. j   9. e   10. d

9·2   1. a, b, c   2. a, b, c   3. b, c   4. c   5. a, b, c   6. a, c   7. a   8. c

9·3   1. F, Se necesita leer el libro de mantenimiento de su coche.   2. F, Los neumáticos con una presión inferior a la marcada por el fabricante pueden aumentar el consumo de carburante.   3. C   4. C   5. F, Gastar carburante con el coche parado es de tontos.   6. C   7. F, Las marchas largas (4ª, 5ª y 6ª) son las que menos carburante consumen.   8. C

9·4   *Answers will vary.*

9·5   1. a   2. d   3. b   4. d   5. c   6. b   7. b   8. a   9. c   10. d   11. c   12. b

9·6   1. e   2. f   3. a   4. g   5. c   6. d   7. h   8. b   9. i

9·7   1. mantenido, gasta, poluciona   2. no tienen sentido, llevar, un contenedor, fugas   3. carburante, ocurre, muchas reglas generales   4. consumir, detenido, estúpido   5. Se desconecta, se conecta   6. cambiemos, calmar, rotaciones

9·8   1. vaya   2. circule, lleve   3. sea   4. encienda, esté   5. se vaya   6. pillen   7. pasemos   8. sea

10 Zapatos

10·1   1. c   2. f   3. a   4. g   5. e   6. b   7. d

10·2   1. a, c   2. c   3. b   4. b, c   5. a   6. a, b, c   7. a, b

10·3 1. F, El narrador desmontó su lavadora.   2. F, La vecina de abajo no robaba nada.   3. F, Los calcetines nunca se caían sobre el tendedero.   4. F, Cuando dejó los calcetines fuera de los zapatos, cesaron las desapariciones.   5. C   6. C   7. F, Continuará poniéndose calcetines que continuarán desapareciéndose.

10·4 *Answers will vary.*

10·5 1. b   2. b   3. d   4. c   5. a   6. c   7. d   8. a

10·6 1. i   2. e   3. h   4. c   5. a   6. b   7. f   8. g   9. d

10·7 1. Desarmé, enredados, busqué por   2. habían desaparecido otra vez   3. entendí   4. cincuenta por ciento, se quedaba, se resbalaba, zapato   5. golosa, se acabó   6. cuando iba a la cama   7. súbitamente   8. se parecen a un

10·8 1. a. le pregunté   b. The neighbor might have seen the deluge of socks before he asked her the question.   2. a. a los quince días   b. The socks disappeared before the two weeks were over.   3. a. al día siguiente   b. That sock vanished before the beginning of the next day.

10·9 1. se había ido   2. habían cumplido   3. se había cambiado   4. había sido vendido   5. se habían casado

10·10 1. a. Esperaba   b. an expression of hoping   2. a. Queríamos   b. an expression of wishing   3. a. Era triste   b. an expression of emotion   4. a. Fue importante   b. an impersonal expression of suggestion, demand, or opinion   5. a. Ojalá   b. an expression of wishing or hoping

11   ¿Diferencias culturales?

11·1 1. N   2. A, V   3. A   4. A, V   5. V   6. N

11·2 1. a, c   2. a, b   3. b   4. a, b   5. a   6. b, c   7, a, c

11·3 1. F, Angélica no hacía jogging.   2. C   3. C   4. F, A Ariel no le gustan los perros; no tenía perros.   5. C

11·4 *Answers will vary.*

11·5 1. b   2. d   3. a   4. c   5. b   6. d   7. d   8. a

11·6 1. g   2. e   3. h   4. c   5. a   6. f   7. d   8. b

11·7 1. debí enfrentar, ocurrió   2. señalar, eran, de los habitantes   3. semejante   4. indigentes, necesitaban, domicilio   5. recorriera, barrio, indecente

11·8 1. a. atravesara   b. atravesar   c. person does not yet exist   2. a. me pusiera   b. ponerse   c. worry and anticipation   3. a. ocurriera   b. ocurrir   c. after sin que, conjunction of anticipation   4. a. si se hubiera puesto   b. ponerse   c. conditional sentence with si-clause   5. a. pasara   b. pasar   c. after cuando used as a conjunction of anticipation   6. a. dejara   b. dejar   c. after verb of volition (command)

IV   NIÑEZ Y JUVENTUD

12   El canario vuela • El canario se muere

12·1 1. e   2. a   3. g   4. d   5. b   6. c   7. f

12·2 1. a   2. b   3. c   4. a   5. a, c   6. a, b   7. a, b, c

12·3 1. C   2. C   3. F, Nadie abrió la jaula.   4. F, Diana es un perro.   5. F, El canario regresó a la jaula.   6. C

12·4 1. d   2. c   3. a   4. a   5. c   6. c

12·5 1. d   2. e   3. f   4. a   5. c   6. b

12·6 1. se escapó   2. Voló   3. veranda   4. descansaba   5. danzaban, aplaudiendo, enrojecidos, alegres

12·7 1. N, C   2. C   3. M   4. N   5. B   6. N, M, C, B, P

12·8 1. b   2. b   3. c   4. a, c   5. a, b   6. a   7. b, c

12·9 1. F, El canario estaba muerto.   2. C   3. C   4. F, El mayor de los niños cuidaba al canario.   5. C   6. F, Creen que han de ver al pájaro salir de una rosa blanca.

12·10   1. b   2. c   3. a   4. d   5. d

12·11   1. b   2. f   3. d   4. e   5. a   6. c

12·12   1. se ha aparecido   2. recuerdas   3. débil   4. tumbado, se ha precipitado   5. y no hay motivo   6. azules
7. trazo

12·13   *Answers will vary.*

12·14   1. a. alegres y con mejillas rojas   b. se parecía a un pájaro activo   2. movimiento del pelo gris.

12·15   *Answers will vary.*

13   Jíbara

13·1   1. d   2. g   3. a   4. b   5. h   6. c   7. e   8. f

13·2   1. a   2. a, b, c   3. b   4. b, c   5. a, c   6. a, b   7. a, b, c   8. c

13·3   1. F, La familia acababa de mudar de casa.   2. C   3. C   4. F, Papi ya está arreglando el piso.   5. F, Papi no quiere que Negi le ayude a hacerlo; Papi rechaza la ayuda.   6. C   7. F, Ellas no ayudan a sus padres; juegan en el columpio.   8. C

13·4   *Answers will vary.*

13·5   1. a   2. d   3. d   4. c   5. d   6. b   7. a   8. b   9. a   10. d

13·6   1. j   2. i   3. g   4. k   5. e   6. d   7. a   8. b   9. c   10. f   11. h

13·7   1. entró en, bosque, del retrete   2. crujían, sin zapatos, picándome   3. tarareaba   4. aproximó, aleteó
5. atemorizó, cocotazo, envió, la tierra   6. se me entraba, susurró, temerosa

13·8   1. preterit, quemarse   2. preterit, poder chuparse   3. imperfect, empinarse   4. preterit, frotarse   5. present, salirse; present, meterse   6. infinitive, sobarse   7. present participle, rascarse   8. familiar command, venirse   9. plural command, acercarse   10. preterit, meterse   11. preterit, asustarse   12. imperfect, meterse   13. present (passive voice), tocar   14. imperfect (passive voice), decir   15. imperfect (passive voice), poder utilizar

V   MEDIO AMBIENTE

14   El hogar natural: Plantar una huerta

14·1   *Answers will vary.*

14·2   1. a, b, c   2. a, b   3. b, c   4. b   5. a, b   6. c   7. a, b   8. a, b

14·3   1. F, Las verduras de raíces son las que más agotan el suelo.   2. C   3. C   4. F, Los herbicidas pueden atacar las plantas.   5. C   6. F, Una buena orientación de la huerta sería al sur.   7. F, Las verduras de raíz se conservan muy bien.   8. C

14·4   *Answers will vary.*

14·5   1. b   2. a   3. d   4. c   5. b   6. b   7. c   8. a   9. c   10. b

14·6   1. d   2. f   3. h   4. g   5. b   6. e   7. a   8. c   9. i

14·7   1. tendrá a su disposición, terreno, considerar, queremos, cubre, dará   2. Por suerte, variedades, sabrosas
3. encerrar, la parcela, las mascotas, entraran, dañaran, el trabajo acabado, disposición   4. Recuerde bien, consagrarle, en buen estado, cogidas   5. progresar, propagación, vivero, los brotes   6. Necesita, protegida, irrigación

14·8   1. a. First we should/would carry out   2. a. Then you should enclose/fence in   3. a. a good orientation would be to/facing (the) south   4. a. we could not / would not be able to pull them out   *For new sentences using the conditional, answers will vary.*

14·9   1. ¿Podría decirme dónde está la farmacia?   2. Esta noche me gustaría ver una película clásica.   3. Deberías plantar una huerta este año.   4. Sabía que no podríamos hacerlo.   5. Marina y Gloria dijeron que comprarían las semillas.   6. ¿Si llamara a Jorge, nos ayudaría?   7. ¿Comerían las espinacas si las recogiera?   8. Llegó tarde; nevaría.   9. Veo un mensaje; Silvia llamaría.

15   Jornada especial de reciclaje este domingo

15·1   1. periódicos   2. artefactos electrónicos   3. cajas, cartón, embalaje, sobres, papel blanco   4. papel blanco, papel de color   5. botellas de plástico, botellas de vidrio   6. folletos, papel blanco, papel de color, periódicos, revistas, sobres   7. cartuchos de impresión

15·2   1. a, b   2. b, c   3. b, c   4. a   5. b   6. a, b   7. b, c   8. a, c

15·3   1. F, La ONG EcoClick se compone de ciudadanos conscientes.   2. F, El Día Mundial de la Tierra se celebra en el mes de abril.   3. C   4. C   5. F, En este evento habrá música/entretenimiento.   6. F, Para esta recolección debe separar el papel en tres grupos.   7. F, Vitaambiente se compone de empresarios.   8. F, Durante el año EcoClick organiza varios días de reciclaje.

15·4   *Answers will vary.*

15·5   1. d   2. c   3. d   4. a   5. a   6. c   7. b   8. c   9. a   10. c

15·6   1. f   2. c   3. j   4. h   5. g   6. b   7. i   8. a   9. e   10. d

15·7   1. preocupación, hombres de negocios, aceptar, iniciar   2. Ofreciéndole, camino, residuo, nocivo
3. se transforma, sabemos, gozar   4. comprender, carga, perturbar   5. deber, pequeño esfuerzo, ambiente, futuras

15·8   1. Se estarán recibiendo / Se recibirán residuos de papel y cartón. / Serán aceptados residuos de papel y cartón.   2. Organizaron una jornada especial de reciclaje.   3. También recibirán bombillos y pilas. / También se estarán recibiendo / se recibirán bombillos y pilas.   4. Se está solicitando/pidiendo a los donantes separar sus residuos de papel en tres grupos.   5. Es importante asumir la responsabilidad de conservar el entorno / el medio ambiente.

16   El olinguito, nuevo carnívoro descubierto

16·1   1. N   2. Z   3. O   4. Z   5. O   6. N   7. Z   8. O

16·2   1. b, c   2. a, c   3. a, c   4. a, b, c   5. a, b, c   6. b   7. c   8. b

16·3   1. F, El olinguito existía, pero no había sido clasificado.   2. F, Muchas pieles de olinguito se encuentran en los museos; se exhiben también en los zoológicos, pero con otro nombre.   3. F, Son en realidad omnívoros; comen principalmente frutas.   4. C   5. F, Los científicos realizaron también análisis de ADN.   6. F, Los olinguitos tienen una cría por vez.   7. C

16·4   *Answers will vary.*

16·5   1. d   2. a   3. d   4. c   5. a   6. b   7. a   8. b   9. c   10. d

16·6   1. f   2. c   3. g   4. h   5. a   6. e   7. d   8. b

16·7   1. nos recuerda a, combinación, colocarse   2. Estas evidencias, derivan, recogidos, a principios del
3. suscitó, pendientes, principalmente, registró, casi nunca, un cachorro

16·8   1. abrir   2. cubrir   3. decir   4. escribir   5. hacer   6. ir   7. morir   8. poner   9. romper   10. ser
11. ver   12. volver

16·9   1. a. have identified   b. identificar   c. identificaron   2. a. has been observed   b. observar(se)   c. se observó
3. a. it has been exhibited   b. exhibir(se)   c. se le exhibió   4. a. has been   b. ser   c. fue   5. a. has not been explored   b. explorar(se)   c. se exploró   6. a. have not been revealed   b. revelar(se)   c. no se revelaron
7. a. has been converted   b. convertir(se)   c. se convirtió

FRAGMENTOS LITERARIOS

17 Diálogo entre Babieca y Rocinante

17·1 1. B   2. B   3. R   4. R   5. R   6. B

17·2 1. b   2. b, c   3. a, b, c   4. a, b   5. b, c   6. a, c

17·3 1. F, Pertenecen a dos siglos diferentes.   2. C   3. F, Rocinante le llama asno a su amo don Quijote.
4. F, Rocinante no cree en el amor.   5. C   6. C

17·4 *Answers will vary.*

17·5 1. b   2. a   3. b   4. d   5. c   6. a   7. d

17·6 1. c   2. f   3. e   4. a   5. d   6. g   7. b

17·7 1. flaco   2. patrón   3. educado   4. insulta   5. del nacimiento a la muerte   6. tontería, juicioso
7. Filósofo   8. suficientemente   9. lamentar, sufrimiento   10. ignorantes

17·8 1. estás, está   2. dices, dice   3. ¿Quieres (tú) verlo?, ¿Quiere (usted) verlo?   4. pareces, parece   5. Míralo
(tú), Mírelo (usted)   6. Quéjate (tú), Quéjese (usted)

18 Llegada a Barcelona

18·1 1. N   2. N   3. P   4. C   5. P   6. N

18·2 1. b   2. a, b   3. a, c   4. a   5. a, c   6. a, b   7. b

18·3 1. C   2. F, Ella no iba a tomar el expreso; ella tomó un coche de caballos.   3. C   4. F, A Andrea le gusta
mucho la ciudad.   5. C

18·4 *Answers will vary.*

18·5 1. a   2. c   3. c   4. d   5. b   6. b   7. c   8. d

18·6 1. c   2. e   3. d   4. b   5. f   6. g   7. h   8. a

18·7 1. problemas, obtener   2. Comencé, la dirección, equipaje, puerta   3. carruajes, han reaparecido, paró, dudar,
el resentimiento, se tiraba

18·8 1. por: due to (because); para: in (order to)   2. por el contrario: on the contrary   3. para mí: in my opinion
4. por fin: finally; por: due to (because)   5. por: through, around

19 Yo soy un hombre sincero • Guajira Guantanamera

19·1 1. d   2. a   3. h   4. b   5. c   6. g   7. e   8. f

19·2 1. a, b, c   2. b, c   3. a, c   4. a, b   5. c   6. b   7. c   8. b, c

19·3 1. F, El poeta viene de un lugar tropical, de donde crece la palma.   2. C   3. F, El poeta tiene al menos un
hijo.   4. C   5. C   6. C   7. F, El poeta dice que únicamente los necios se entierran con lujo y con llanto.
8. F, Al final del poema se quita la pompa del rimador; es poeta de otro tipo.

19·4 *Answers will vary.*

19·5 1. b   2. c   3. a   4. c   5. a   6. a   7. d   8. b   9. c   10. b

19·6 1. e   2. g   3. i   4. b   5. h   6. c   7. j   8. a   9. f   10. d

19·7 1. entiendo, la tierra, se abandona, pálido, reposo, río, tranquilo   2. audaz, felicidad, rígida, extinguida, bajó,
enfrente de   3. brillante, rojo, tocado, refugio   4. destino, unir, las montañas, contenta

19·8 1. ¿Sabe (usted) preparar el almuerzo?   2. Pensamos ir de vacaciones en verano.   3. Bárbara se olvida de
llevar su paraguas.   4. (Ellos) no pueden llegar a tiempo.   5. Me contento con ir a la playa.   6. (Ustedes)
dejan de comer carnes rojas.   7. Acabas de plantar los bulbos.   8. (Él) insiste en adoptar a este perro.
9. Estamos por salir a cenar esta noche.   10. (Ellas) se preparan a presentarse al examen.   11. (Usted) ayuda
a transportar al enfermo.   12. ¿Aprendes a hablar portugués?

19·9   1. a. I want to release/pour b. querer   2. a. I saw raining down b. ver   3. a. I saw . . . being born b. ver   4. a. I saw . . . live/living b. ver   5. a. I saw . . . fly/flying b. ver   6. a. I want to throw in b. querer

20   El alma de la máquina

20·1   1. O 2. M 3. O 4. O 5. M 6. O 7. M

20·2   1. b 2. a, b, c 3. c 4. a, b 5. a, c 6. a, c 7. a, b

20·3   1. C 2. F, El maquinista tiene una relación hostil y adversa con la máquina.   3. C 4. F, El maquinista no les dice nada a los obreros.   5. C 6. C 7. F, El aparato se para sin ruido y sin sacudidas.

20·4   1. c 2. a 3. b 4. c 5. d 6. c 7. b 8. b 9. c

20·5   1. e 2. g 3. f 4. d 5. a 6. h 7. c 8. b

20·6   1. se distingue, alba 2. horario, sin interrupción 3. arrancan, observan, celos 4. quemados, mojados, luchan, descanso, moviendo, carretillas

20·7   1. e 2. a 3. b 4. g 5. d 6. c 7. i 8. h 9. f

20·8   1. b, c 2. a 3. a, b, c 4. c 5. a, b 6. b 7. a

20·9   1. F, El maquinista trabaja de manera automática.   2. C 3. C 4. F, El turno de doce horas empieza al amanecer / al alba.   5. F, El maquinista primero debe recobrar sus facultades.   6. C 7. C

20·10   1. d 2. a 3. b 4. c 5. a 6. d 7. c 8. d 9. b

20·11   1. e 2. d 3. h 4. i 5. b 6. g 7. c 8. a 9. f

20·12   1. A las órdenes, aparato, extiende 2. siguen, asciende, baja, anochecer, sube, rápidamente, oscuridad 3. Súbitamente, muy fuerte, dejan caer, se levantan, enérgicos 4. Recupera, con dificultad, tullidas

20·13   *Answers will vary.*

20·14   1. a. el maquinista b. Los obreros… miran al maquinista con envidia.   2. a. los tumbadores b. viendo cómo el ascensor aguarda los tumbadores con una nueva carga 3. a. eso (neuter singular, that) b. y una revolución más, demasiado lo sabe eso el maquinista, es: el ascensor estrellándose 4. a. la flecha de parada b. Antes que cruce a la flecha de parada, atrae hacia sí la manivela. 5. a. la placa metálica b. el martillo hiere de nuevo la placa metálica con un golpe seco 6. a. el maquinista b. Permanece inmóvil en la semioscuridad que rodea al maquinista.

20·15   1. a. a los tumbadores b. mientras el maquinista parece decirles a los tumbadores con su severa mirada... —¡Más a prisa, holgazanes...! 2. a. a los tumbadores b. para abrumarles a los tumbadores la fatiga no necesita sino alargar y encoger el brazo 3. a. a los tumbadores b. Jamás podrán comprender que esa labor que les parece a los tumbadores tan insignificante 4. a. al maquinista b. un doble campanillazo le avisa al maquinista que, abajo, el otro espera ya con su carga completa

VII   BELLAS ARTES Y CINE

21   La música salva vidas en mi país: Entrevista a Gustavo Dudamel

21·1   1. b 2. e 3. f 4. g 5. d 6. a 7. c

21·2   1. b 2. b 3. a, b, c 4. b, c 5. c

21·3   1. F, De pequeño Gustavo dirigía las orquestas de los discos de su papá.   2. C 3. F, Su fama personal no le importa mucho a Gustavo. Dice que no es cuestión de uno, sino de muchos.   4. C 5. F, Los niños vienen casi todos de familias pobres.

21·4   *Answers will vary.*

21·5   1. c 2. b 3. c 4. d 5. c

21·6   1. e 2. f 3. a 4. g 5. d 6. b 7. c

21·7 1. niño 2. interrumpía 3. presionar el botón 4. prestar atención 5. nuevo, del Caribe 6. se realizan 7. dirige

21·8 1. la universidad más vieja del país 2. el peor restaurant del barrio 3. la profesora más inteligente que conocemos 4. la película menos interesante que he visto 5. los mejores músicos de la orquesta 6. el trabajo más importante que haces

21·9 1. bellísimo 2. buenísimo 3. dificilísimo 4. muchísimo 5. grandísimo 6. facilísimo

21·10 1. a. imperfect subjunctive b. indicar 2. a. imperfect subjunctive b. ser 3. a. present subjunctive b. ver 4. a. imperfect subjunctive b. ser 5. a. present subjunctive b. acabarse

22 Les dejo de herencia mi libertad: Entrevista a Chavela Vargas

22·1 1. d 2. a 3. g 4. f 5. h 6. b 7. i 8. c 9. e

22·2 1. c 2. a, b, d 3. a, b 4. c 5. b, c, d 6. a 7. a, b, c, d 8. b, c

22·3 1. C 2. C 3. C 4. C 5. F, Frida Kahlo no afirmó que… eran comunistas. 6. F, Según Chavela, Frida no expresó su propia genialidad; se la negó. 7. F, Diego Rivera no admiraba su arte; dijo que de ahí no pasarían. 8. C

22·4 1. c 2. a, b, c 3. a, c 4. b, c 5. a, b, c

22·5 1. If because I love you, you love me, Llorona 2. You want me to love you (even) more 3. If I have given you my life, Llorona 4. What more do you want? 5. Do you want (even) more?

22·6 *Answers will vary.*

22·7 1. c 2. d 3. c 4. b 5. a 6. b

22·8 1. e 2. g 3. b 4. a 5. c 6. f 7. d

22·9 1. llaman 2. rico 3. Cúbreme 4. ame 5. ofrecido 6. encontrar, encontramos

22·10 1. ¿Usted cómo se ve? 2. Cuando hable de México lo hace con orgullo. 3. ¿Qué fue para usted participar en la película *Frida*?

23 Diego Rivera: Arte y revolución

23·1 1. e 2. d 3. f 4. g 5. a 6. c 7. b 8. h

23·2 1. c 2. a 3. b 4. a, b, c 5. c 6. a, b, c 7. a, b, c

23·3 1. C 2. F, La exposición incluye también óleos, bocetos y otras obras. 3. F, *Electric Welding* fue pintado para el Museo de Arte Moderno de Nueva York en 1931. 4. F, El movimiento muralista mexicano se dirigía a las masas así como al público burgués. 5. F, La Revolución Mexicana inició la reorganización, no el cambio total, en México. 6. C 7. F, Rivera admiraba al progreso industrial; lo entendía muy bien.

23·4 *Answers will vary.*

23·5 1. b 2. d 3. c 4. c 5. a 6. d 7. b 8. a

23·6 1. e 2. b 3. i 4. a 5. d 6. h 7. g 8. c 9. f

23·7 1. artista, supera, las predilecciones 2. se demuestra, alterna, aspectos 3. pinturas, inolvidables, fase 4. astuto, elaboración, abraza

23·8 1. sus modelos 2. muchos artistas famosos 3. madres e hijos 4. un Diego joven 5. Notre Dame 6. el sector social oprimido 7. el nutrido despliegue

23·9 1. Busco a mi hija. 2. Ven a muchos amigos el fin de semana. 3. Frida quiere a Diego. 4. ¿Conoces bien a tus vecinos? 5. Amamos a la humanidad.

24 El primer cine

24·1 1. d 2. e 3. g 4. c 5. h 6. a 7. f 8. b

24·2 1. b 2. a, c 3. c 4. b 5. a, c 6. b, c 7. a, c 8. b

24·3 1. F, El primer cine se dirige a las masas. 2. C 3. F, Las primeras imágenes que vio eran pintadas imagen a imagen. 4. F, Desde la cocina Buñuel y su prima podían ver películas mudas. 5. C 6. F, A la madre de Buñuel, no le interesaba mucho la carrera artística de su hijo. 7. C 8. F, Buñuel y Dalí sabían que su película no tendría éxito entre el gran público.

24·4 *Answers will vary.*

24·5 1. a 2. c 3. d 4. c 5. b 6. d 7. c 8. a 9. b 10. c

24·6 1. g 2. a 3. e 4. h 5. b 6. j 7. c 8. i 9. f 10. d

24·7 1. típico, masa, futuro 2. periodista 3. crear, se enojó, saltimbanqui 4. mediara, formalmente, suficiente, realizar, filmadas 5. persuadir, pagado

24·8 1. still, yet 2. outside 3. always 4. of course, naturally 5. everywhere 6. even, including 7. hardly 8. then, later 9. taking turns 10. standing, on foot 11. then, later 12. now 13. thus, hence 14. never 15. certainly 16. progressively 17. on top of 18. just like 19. rather 20. almost

24·9 1. serio, seriously 2. también, also 3. poco antes, a short time before 4. a su vez, in turn 5. en un principio, at first 6. pronto, soon 7. en menos de, in less than 8. de común acuerdo, by mutual agreement 9. en ningún momento, never 10. de inmediato, immediately 11. al momento, at the same time 12. en seguida, immediately

24·10 1. a. único 2. a. definitivo 3. a. bullicioso 4. a. perfecto 5. a. total 6. a. insensible 7. a. desmesurado 8. a. inmediato *For new sentences using adverbs, answers will vary.*

VIII ARQUEOLOGÍA Y ANTROPOLOGÍA

25 El mundo maya

25·1 1. f 2. b 3. e 4. h 5. g 6. a 7. c 8. d

25·2 1. a, b, c 2. a 3. a, b 4. a, b, c 5. c 6. a, c 7. a, c 8. a, b, c 9. b, c 10. a, c

25·3 1. F, A los mayas no se los llevaron los extraterrestres. 2. C 3. F, Las inscripciones son tan significativas como las esculturas. 4. C 5. F, Hay pocos lugares que mencionan el reino de Tikal. 6. F, Los científicos todavía tienen que descubrir el edificio. 7. F, El arqueólogo tiene miedo que el sitio no sea seguro. 8. C

25·4 1. b 2. a 3. d 4. c 5. d 6. b 7. a 8. d 9. c 10. b 11. a

25·5 1. d 2. e 3. h 4. f 5. g 6. a 7. c 8. b

25·6 1. explique, misteriosos, portaron, marcianos 2. monarcas, fuertes, quisieron, someter, se convirtieron en 3. La construcción, taparon, colocaron, esmero, conservadas, barro

25·7 1. e 2. a 3. f 4. c 5. b 6. d

25·8 1. b 2. c 3. b, c 4. b, c 5. b 6. c 7. a 8. b

25·9 1. F, Hoy en día ciertas comunidades indígenas utilizan el calendario Tzolkin. 2. C 3. F, Los sacerdotes estudiaban las estrellas y controlaban el calendario. 4. C 5. F, Los mayas establecieron varios calendarios. 6. C

25·10 1. d 2. c 3. a 4. d 5. b 6. c 7. c 8. a

25·11 1. c 2. f 3. a 4. e 5. d 6. b

25·12 1. se refiere a, acaso, éxito 2. Tomado, los clérigos, se apoya 3. A través de, invariable, empezar, objetivo, posible 4. utilizado, dirigir, trabajo, prácticas, decidida, coincidía con 5. denominado, trayecto 6. muchos, inscriben

25·13 *Answers will vary.*

25·14 1. el tercer hombre   2. su primer cumpleaños   3. el decimoctavo día   4. nuestro vigésimo aniversario   5. la cuarta hora   6. el decimoquinto capítulo

25·15 1. a. estaban ubicados   b. Los reyes se ubicaban alrededor de Tikal, juntos a otros que eran enemigos del reino. 2. a. estaba preservado   b. Una de las cosas que llamó la atención [...] fue la forma en la que se preservaba el friso.   3. a. está cerrado   b. Se cierra el lugar al tráfico del público.   4. a. está protegida   b. Pues está en un área natural que se protege por ley.   5. a. habían sido derrotados   b. Entonces estos dejaron de erigir estelas porque (los reyes enemigos) los habían derrotado.   6. a. había sido... conquistado   b. Y (los reyes enemigos) habían casi conquistado a su pueblo.   7. a. era (el más) usado   b. Los pueblos del mundo maya usaban mayormente el calendario sagrado de 260 días.   8. a. eran vistos   b. Así, los mayas veían días y cifras bajo un aspecto divino.